BARRON'S

HOW TO PREPARE FOR THE

CLAST

2ND EDITION

Dr. Robert Postman
Professor, Mercy College

BARRON'S

To my wife Liz,
A job to behold

Some sections of this text were extracted from Barron's *How to Prepare for the
Praxis* by Robert D. Postman.

All inquiries should be addressed to:
Barron's Educational Series, Inc.
250 Wireless Boulevard
Hauppauge, NY 11788
http://www.barronseduc.com

Library of Congress Catalog Card No. 2002033229

ISBN-13: 978-0-7641-2033-6
ISBN-10: 0-7641-2033-6

Library of Congress Cataloging-in-Publication Data
Postman, Robert D.
    How to prepare for the CLAST / by Robert Postman.—2nd ed.
        p. cm.
    ISBN 0-7641-2033-6 (alk. paper)
        1. College Level Academic Skills Test–Study guides.   I. Title: CLAST.
II. Title.

LB2353.7.C64 P67 2003
378.166'2–dc21

2002033229

PRINTED IN THE UNITED STATES OF AMERICA
9 8 7 6

CONTENTS

(CLAST objectives are presented in the order taught, not in alphabetical or numerical order.)

PREFACE

This book shows you how to pass the CLAST. It shows you how to answer every type of question and includes proven strategies for taking the CLAST. The book has been tried out by students and reviewed by subject-matter and CLAST experts. The practice tests in this book have the same question types and question-and-answer formats as the real tests.

This book also shows you how to take and pass the computer adaptive CLAST. I have worked closely with the Florida Department of Education to ensure that this book correctly reflects the new 1997 CLAST regulations.

My wife Liz was a constant source of support and she contributed significantly to this book. My children Chad, Blaire, and Ryan have also been a source of inspiration as I worked on this and other books during the past several years.

Barron's is simply the best publisher of test preparation books. The editorial department, under the leadership of Mark Miele, spared no effort to assure that this book is of the highest quality and most helpful to you, the test-taker.

David Rodman, editor at Barron's, did a wonderful job with this manuscript. Credit is also due to Frank Pasquale.

Special thanks are due to Dr. Maria Pitner of the Florida Department of Education, who provided expert guidance. I can't name all the others who contributed to this book, but I am especially grateful to Ryan Postman, who made significant contributions to the mathematics section. Thanks also to those who field-tested and read drafts of the book and to those at Florida colleges who talked to me about their experience with the computer CLAST.

Robert D. Postman
August, 2002

# INTRODUCTION TO THE CLAST

This book is your key to success on the College-Level Academic Skills Test (CLAST). It includes the kinds of review you need to pass the CLAST. The review sections are clear and easy to follow. You'll learn strategies for each test and ways of answering each type of question.

There are two full-length practice tests. Each practice test is like a real CLAST. They have the number and types of questions you'll find on the real thing. The answer to every test question is explained, with hints for avoiding incorrect answers.

Most students have difficulty with the mathematics test. This book has a specially designed, extensive mathematics review section. It includes practice exercises, all with answers and explanations.

There are paper-and-pencil CLASTs and computer-adaptive CLASTs. This book shows you how to prepare for both types.

There have been significant changes in how you can be exempt from taking the CLAST. The changes are explained below.

THE CLAST

Do I Have to Take the CLAST? If So, Can I Get an Exemption?

Read below to find out if you must take the CLAST. Then read on to find out if there is a way you can be exempt from the CLAST.

You Must Take the CLAST if You Are in One of These Groups:

1. You are in an A. A. (Associate of Arts) program at a public community college.

2. You are in a bachelor's degree program at a four-year public college.

3. You are enrolled in a private college and receive state financial aid.

You Can be Exempted from the CLAST in the Following Ways:

College Students. You may be exempt from the CLAST as a college graduation requirement if you pass the Florida College Entry Level Placement Test and have a 2.5 average in certain college courses. Check with your advisor or counselor.

High School Students. High school students may now take the Florida College Entry Placement Test starting in tenth grade. You can be exempt from the CLAST as a college graduation requirement if you pass the Placement Test and have a 3.0 average in certain high school courses. Check with your guidance counselor or advisor.

What Is the CLAST?

The CLAST consists of four subtests: Essay, English Language Skills, Reading, and Mathematics. These subtests are organized into three testing sections. A brief overview is given below.

CLAST OVERVIEW

Section	Questions	Time
Essay	Write an essay on one of two topics.	60 minutes
English Language Skills	40 multiple-choice items—35 are scored	80 minutes
Reading	41 multiple-choice items—36 are scored	
Mathematics	55 multiple-choice items—50 are scored	90 minutes

Where Is the CLAST Given?

The paper-and-pencil CLAST is given at every public college and many private colleges in Florida.

Must I Register for the CLAST?

Yes. Register early through your college. Space is often limited and registration closes four weeks before the test administration dates.

On Which Dates Is the CLAST Given?

Regular paper-and-pencil CLAST administrations for undergraduate students are given according to this schedule:

	2002–2003	2003–2004
First Saturday in October	October 5, 2002	October 4, 2003
Third Saturday in February	February 19, 2003	February 21, 2004
First Saturday in June	June 7, 2003	June 5, 2004

If your religious beliefs prevent you from taking the test on Saturday, an alternate administration is given the Monday following the regular test date.

What's the Schedule on Test Day?

The entire CLAST lasts about 5 hours from check-in, including instructions and breaks. The approximate test schedule is shown below.

7:30 – 8:00 AM	Arrive and check in
8:00 – 8:30	Seating and test overview
8:30 – 9:30	Essay subtest
9:40 – 11:00	English Language Skills and Reading subtests
11:20 – 12:50 PM	Mathematics subtest

What if I Have a Disability?

Special arrangements, including test aids and extra time, are available for those with disabilities. Contact your college counselor several months before the test to find out how to request special test arrangements.

What Scores Do I Need to Pass?

Essay

Your essay is read by two raters. They each assign your essay a score of 1 through 6 for a *possible total score of 12.* If the scores differ by more than one point, the essay is read by a third person. To pass *you need a total score of 6.*

Raters classify essays as top third (5–6), middle third (3–4) and lower third (1–2). Then the raters assign one of the two scores in that third. Your goal is to write an essay that falls in the middle third, for a potential score of 6, 7, or 8.

Multiple Choice

Every multiple-choice subtest includes five experimental items. Experimental items don't count. You never know which items are experimental, so do your best on each item on the test.

The required passing score for each test is a scaled score of 295. Scaled scores being what they are, the number correct needed to pass can vary somewhat from test to test. Our analysis of previous passing scores reveals the following.

English Language Skills (40 items, 35 scored):
You must usually get from 74 percent (26) correct to 80 percent (28) correct to pass the English Language Skills test. Experts report that this section is tightly scored, so work carefully.

Reading (41 items, 36 scored):
You must usually get from 67 percent (24) correct to 72 percent (26) correct to pass the Reading test.

Mathematics (55 items, 50 items scored):
You must usually get from 66 percent (33) correct to 70 percent (35) correct to pass the Mathematics test.

OK. What if I Don't Pass One or More of the Subtests?

You take it again. There is no limit on the number of times you can retake the test. Here are your options.

If you don't pass a multiple-choice subtest, you may take it again as a paper-and-pencil test or as the computer-adaptive CLAST (CAT-CLAST). No matter which version you take, you will have twice the time to complete each subtest as you did on the original administration.

Our recommendation is that you should take the CAT-CLAST. The last chapter of this book tells you about the CAT-CLAST and gives you strategies for passing the test.

If you don't pass the essay test, you should retake it at the next scheduled CLAST administration. You will have two hours to write your essay the second time.

PREPARING FOR THE CLAST

OK. How Do I Get Ready for the CLAST?

Follow this carefully devised study plan to do your absolute best on the CLAST. Use the Review Checklist on the next page. Complete the steps in the order shown. If you have already passed one or more of the subtests, skip that part of the review.

BY MONDAY

Make sure you have your admission ticket.

Make sure you know where the test is given.

Make sure you know how you're getting there.

BY TUESDAY

Write on 3 × 5 index cards any special terms or formulas you must remember for the test.

Visit the test site, if you haven't done it already. You don't want any surprises this Saturday.

BY WEDNESDAY

Get some sharpened No. 2 pencils, a digital watch or pocket clock, and a good big eraser and put them aside.

ON FRIDAY

Review your index cards one last time.

Complete any forms you have to bring to the test.

Prepare any snacks or food you want to bring with you to eat during breaks.

Talk to someone who makes you feel good or do something enjoyable and relaxing.

Have a good night's sleep.

CLAST Review Checklist

Complete the steps in the order shown.

☐ **Strategies**

    ☐ Review the test strategies beginning on the next page.

☐ **Reading**

    ☐ Complete the Reading chapter that begins on page 9.
    ☐ Take the Reading subtest of Practice Test 1 on page 242.
    ☐ Check your answers and go over the explanations on page 261.
      Note the kinds of questions you got wrong.

☐ **English**

    ☐ Complete the English Language Skills chapter that begins on page 49.
    ☐ Take the English Language Skills subtest in Practice Test 1 on page 232.
    ☐ Check your answers and go over the explanations on page 260.
      Note the kinds of questions you got wrong.

☐ **Essay**

    ☐ Complete the Essay chapter that begins on page 92.
    ☐ Take the Essay subtest of Practice Test 1 on page 229.
    ☐ Review your essay evaluations.
      Note the areas in which improvement is indicated.

☐ **Math**

    ☐ Complete the Math chapter that begins on page 102.
    ☐ Take the Math subtest of Practice Test 1 on page 249.
    ☐ Check your answers and go over the explanations on page 262.
      Note the kinds of questions you got wrong.

☐ **Three weeks to go**

    ☐ Use the review chapters and go over the areas with which you
      had problems.
    ☐ Review the test preparation and test-taking strategies on pages 4–8.
    ☐ Review the special test-taking tips and steps.
    ☐ Essay (page 93), ☐ English (page 81), ☐ Reading (page 35) and
      ☐ Math (page 224)

☐ **Two weeks before**

    ☐ Take Practice Test 2 on page 266 under exact test conditions.
    ☐ Check your answers on page 298 and review any problem areas.

☐ **One week to go**

    ☐ Follow the steps on pages 4 and 6.

SATURDAY—TEST DAY

Don't forget to get up!

Dress comfortably. Be prepared for air conditioning that may be freezing, or that may be off.

Eat that same kind of breakfast you've been eating each morning.

Don't stuff yourself. You want your blood racing through your brain, not your stomach.

Get together things to bring to the test including: registration ticket, identification forms, pencils, eraser, tissues, mints, snacks, or food.

Get to the test room, not the parking lot, about 10 to 15 minutes before the start time.

Remember to leave time for parking and walking to the test site.

Use the restroom before the test; there is no break after the first test.

Hand in your forms—you're in the door. You're ready. This is the easy part.

Follow the test-taking strategies in the next section.

SOME PROVEN TEST-TAKING STRATEGIES

Test designers like to pretend that test-taking strategies don't help that much. They act like that because they want everyone to think that their tests only measure your knowledge of the subject. Of course, they are just pretending; knowing test-taking strategies can make a big difference.

However, there is nothing better than being prepared for the subject matter on this test. These strategies will do you little good if you lack this fundamental knowledge. If you are prepared, then these strategies can make a difference. Use them. Other people will be. Not using them may very well lower your score.

Be Comfortable.

Get a good seat. Don't sit near anyone or anything that will distract you. Stay away from your friends. You see them all the time anyhow. If you don't like where you are sitting, move or ask for another seat.

You Will Make Mistakes.

You are going to make mistakes on this test. The people who wrote the test expect you to make them. The average passing score is about 70 percent correct.

You Are Not Competing with Anyone.

Don't worry about how anyone else is doing. Your score does not depend on theirs. When the score report comes out it doesn't say, "Nancy got 61 percent, but Blaire got 70 percent." You just want to get a passing score. If you can do better, that's great. Stay focused. Remember your goal.

MULTIPLE-CHOICE TESTING STRATEGIES

It's Not What You Know That Matters, It's Just Which Circle You Fill In.

No one you know or care about will see your test. An impersonal machine scores all multiple-choice questions. The machine just senses whether the correct circle on the answer sheet is filled in. That is the way the test makers want it. If that's good enough for them, it should be good enough for you. Concentrate on filling in the correct circle.

You Can Be Right but Be Marked Wrong.

If you get the right answer but fill in the wrong circle, the machine will mark it wrong. We told you that filling in the right circle was what mattered. We strongly recommend that you follow this strategy.

Write the letter for your answer big in the test booklet next to the number for the problem. If you change your mind about an answer, cross off the "old" letter and write the "new" one. At the end of each section, transfer all the answers together from the test booklet to the answer sheet.

Do Your Work in the Test Booklet.

You can write anything you want in your test booklet. The test booklet is not used for scoring and no one will look at it. You can't bring scratch paper to the test so use your booklet instead. When the test is over, someone will throw the booklet away. It may even be incinerated!

Some of the strategies we recommend involve writing in and marking up the booklet. These strategies work and we strongly recommend that you use them.

Do your work for a question near that question in the test booklet. You can also do work on the cover or wherever else suits you. You may want to do calculations, underline important words, mark up a picture, or draw a diagram.

Watch That Answer Sheet.

Remember that a machine is doing the marking. Fill in the correct answer circle completely. Don't put extra pencil marks on the answer section of the answer sheet. Stray marks could be mistaken for answers.

Some Questions Are Traps.

Some questions include the words *not*, *least*, or *except*. You are being asked for the answer that doesn't fit with the rest. Be alert for these types of questions.

Save the Hard Questions for Last.

You're not supposed to get all the questions correct, and some of them will be too difficult for you. Work through the questions and skip the hardest ones; draw a circle around these question numbers in the test booklet. Save these questions until the very end.

They Show You the Answer.

Every multiple-choice test shows you the correct answer for each question. The answer is staring right at you. You just have to figure out which one it is. There is a 20 or 25 percent chance you'll get it right by just closing your eyes and pointing.

Some Answers Are Traps.

When someone writes a test question, they often include distracters. Distracters are traps—incorrect answers that look like correct answers. It might be an answer to an addition problem when you should be multiplying. It might be a correct answer to a different question. It might just be an answer that catches your eye. Watch out for this type of incorrect answer.

Eliminate the Incorrect Answers.

If you can't figure out which answer is correct, then decide which answers can't be correct. Determine the answers you're sure are incorrect. Cross them off in the test booklet. Only one left? That's the correct answer.

Guess, Guess, Guess.

If there are still two or more answers left, then guess. Guess the answer from those remaining. *Never* leave any item blank. There is no penalty for guessing.

2 READING

Recommended Time: 55 minutes

The CLAST reading test has 36 scored multiple-choice questions. There are 12 question types based on the following 12 objectives. This chapter covers the objectives in the order shown below. You can expect each question type to appear 3 or 4 times on the CLAST. Occasionally, a question type may appear as few as 2, or as many as 5 times.

Literal Comprehension
A1 - Recognize the Main Idea
A2 - Identify Supporting Details
A3 - Determine the Meaning of Words in Context

Critical Comprehension
B1 - Recognize the Author's Purpose
B3 - Distinguish Between Fact and Opinion
B4 - Detect Bias
B5 - Recognize the Author's Tone
B2 - Identity the Author's Overall Organizational Pattern
B6 - Recognize Relationships Within Sentences
B7 - Recognize Relationships Between Sentences
B8 - Recognize Valid Arguments
B9 - Draw Logical Inferences and Conclusions

PASSING THE READING TEST

You usually need to get from 67 percent (24) correct to 74 percent (26) correct to pass the Reading Test. The passing scores vary slightly depending on how all students did on a particular test administration. Approximately 64 percent of all students pass this test the first time they take it.

Using This Section

First you will find out about the twelve different types of questions on the reading test. After each explanation are examples of the types of test questions associated with that objective.

Then you will learn The Five Step Approach to taking the test and work through a series of examples that show you how to apply that approach.

There are two complete practice reading tests in this book beginning on page 242 and on page 280.

Reading About Reading

Reading seems to be a natural process. Reading about reading and about steps to taking reading tests can seem contrived and confusing. However, we know that these techniques work. Once you apply them to the practice exercises, your reading ability and scores will improve.

Reading Diagnosis

The CLAST reading test is unlike any other reading test. There are a few reading comprehension questions. But most of the other questions, though, ask for responses that would only be found on the CLAST. For that reason, there is no diagnostic test.

The reading review section is in two parts. The first part reviews each reading objective and provides a sample question. The second part presents steps for taking the reading test along with additional practice questions.

Review the individual reading objectives and sample questions. If you can correctly answer all but two or three of the sample questions, skip the second part of this chapter.

LITERAL COMPREHENSION

RECOGNIZE THE MAIN IDEA (A1)

TEST TIP:

You will read a passage. A multiple-choice question will ask you to identify the main idea or central idea of a passage.

Each of these multiple-choice questions has four answer choices.

Topic and Main Idea

The *topic* is what the paragraph or passage is all about. The topic is often found in the first or last sentences. Skim these sentences to find the topic.

The *main idea* describes the topic. The main idea is what the writer has to say about the topic. The main idea answers who, what, where, when, why, or how questions about the topic. A main idea may be stated or unstated.

Identifying the Main Idea

Stated Topic and Main Idea

Look at this paragraph.

There are many types of boats. Some are very fast while others could sleep a whole platoon of soldiers. I prefer the old putt-putt fishing boat with a ten horsepower motor. That was a boat with a purpose. You didn't scare many people, but the fish were sure worried.

The topic of this paragraph is boats. The main idea is that the writer prefers small fishing boats to other boats.

Unstated Topic and Main Idea

Sometimes the topic and main idea are not stated. Consider this passage.

The Chinese were the first to use sails thousands of years ago, hundreds of years before sails were used in Europe. The Chinese also used the wheel and the kite long before they were used on the European continent. Experts believe that many other Chinese inventions were used from three hundred to one thousand three hundred years before they were used in Europe.

The topic of this paragraph is inventions. The main idea of the paragraph is that the Chinese invented and used many things hundreds and thousands of years before they appeared in Europe.

Practice Question

I grew up in Kearny, New Jersey, now known as Soccer Town, USA. I played football in high school and barely knew that the soccer team existed. However, a look back at my high school yearbook revealed that the soccer team won the state championship and we had a .500 season.

1. What is the main idea of this passage?
   (A) Soccer builds character and football does not.
   (B) Football players are not intelligent.
   (C) High school yearbooks are important records of the past.
   (D) People can sometimes be unaware of the obvious.

Answer on page 33.

IDENTIFY SUPPORTING DETAILS (A2)

TEST TIP:

You will read a passage. The multiple-choice question may ask you to identify details in the passage. You may also be asked to identify which detail does not occur in the passage, or which detail was used to support, illustrate, or describe, a particular idea or concept.

Each of these multiple-choice questions has four answer choices.

Reading Sentences

Every sentence has a subject that tells what the sentence is about. The sentence also has a verb that tells what the subject is doing or links the subject to the complement. The sentence may also contain a complement that receives the action or describes what is being said about the subject. The words underlined in the following examples are the ones you would focus on as you read the details.

1. The famous educator <u>John Dewey founded</u> an educational movement called <u>progressive education.</u>

2. Sad to say, we have learned <u>American school children</u> of all ages <u>are poorly nourished.</u>

Fact, Opinion, or Fiction

If it is a factual passage, the author will present the fact and support it with details and examples. If the passage presents an opinion, the author will give the opinion and support it with arguments, examples, and other details. Many passages combine fact and opinion. If it is a fiction passage, the author will tell a story with details, descriptions, and examples about people, places, or things.

Practice Question

The American alligator is found in Florida and Georgia, and has also been reported in other states, including North and South Carolina. Weighing in at more than 400 pounds, the length of an adult alligator is twice that of its tail. Adult alligators eat fish and small mammals while young alligators prefer insects, shrimp, and frogs.

An untrained person may mistake a crocodile for an alligator. Crocodiles are found in the same areas as alligators and both have prominent snouts with many teeth. The crocodile has a long thin snout with teeth in both jaws. The alligator's snout is wider with teeth only in the upper jaw.

1. Which of the following describes a characteristic that distinguishes an alligator from a crocodile?
   (A) the number of teeth
   (B) shape of the snout
   (C) habitat
   (D) diet

Answer on page 33.

DETERMINE THE MEANING OF WORDS IN CONTEXT (A3)

TEST TIP:

You will read a passage. A multiple-choice question will ask you to identify the meaning of a word from the context of the passage. The word may be difficult or have several meanings, one of which must be determined from the context. You may also be asked to choose a synonym or antonym for a word in the passage.

Each of these multiple-choice questions has four answer choices.

Context Clues

Many times you can figure out a word from its context. Look at these examples. Synonyms, antonyms, examples, or descriptions may help you figure out the word.

1. The woman's mind wandered as her two friends **prated** on. It really did not bother her though. In all the years she had known them, they had always *babbled* about their lives. It was almost comforting.

2. The wind **abated** in the late afternoon. Things were different yesterday when the wind had *picked up* toward the end of the day.

3. The argument with her boss had been her **Waterloo.** She wondered if the *defeat* suffered by Napoleon *at this famous place* had felt the same.

4. The events swept the politician into a **vortex** of controversy. The politician knew what it meant to be spun around like a toy boat in the *swirl of water* that swept down the bathtub drain.

> Passage 1 gives a synonym for the unknown word. We can tell that *prated* means babbled. *Babbled* is used as a synonym of *prated* in the passage.
>
> Passage 2 gives an antonym for the unknown word. We can tell that *abated* means slowed down or diminished because *picked up* is used as an antonym of *abated*.
>
> Passage 3 gives a description of the unknown word. The description of *Waterloo* tells us that the word means *defeat*.
>
> Passage 4 gives an example of the unknown word. The example of a *swirl of water* going down the bathtub drain gives us a good idea of what a *vortex* is.

There are other ways to identify words.

Roots

A root is the basic element of a word. The root is usually related to the word's origin. Roots can often help you figure out the word's meaning. Here are some roots that may help you.

Root	Meaning	Examples
bio	life	biography, biology
circu	around	circumference, circular
frac	break	fraction, refract
geo	earth	geology, geography
mal	bad	malicious, malcontent
matr, mater	mother	maternal, matron
neo	new	neonate, neoclassic
patr, pater	father	paternal, patron
spec	look	spectacles, specimen
tele	distant	telephone, television

Prefixes

Prefixes are syllables that come at the beginning of a word. Prefixes usually have a standard meaning. They can often help you figure out the word's meaning. Here is a list of prefixes that may help you figure out a word.

Prefix	Meaning	Examples
a-	not	amoral, apolitical
il-, im-, ir-	not	illegitimate, immoral, incorrect
un-	not	unbearable, unknown
non-	not	nonbeliever, nonsense
ant-, anti-	against	antiwar, antidote
de-	opposite	defoliate, declaw
mis-	wrong	misstep, misdeed
ante-	before	antedate, antecedent
fore-	before	foretell, forecast
post-	after	postflight, postoperative
re-	again	refurbish, redo
super-	above	superior, superstar
sub-	below	subsonic, subpar

Practice Question

The college sororities are "interviewed" by students during rush week. Rush week is a time when students get to know about the different sororities and decide which ones they want to join. Each student can *pledge* only one sorority. Once students have
Line chosen the three they are most interested in, the intrigue begins. The sororities then
(5) choose from among the students who have chosen them.

1. In this context the word *pledge*
   (line 3) means
   (A) donation.
   (B) young bird.
   (C) attempt to join.
   (D) promise.

Answer on page 33.

THE VOCABULARY LIST

Knowing the definition of a word helps. Here is a list of a few hundred vocabulary words. Read through the list and visualize the words and their definitions. After a while you will become very familiar with them.

Of course, this is not anywhere near all the words you need to know for the CLAST. But they will give you a start. These words also will give you some idea of the kinds of words you may encounter.

Another great way to develop a vocabulary is to read a paper every day and a news magazine every week, in addition to the other reading you are doing. There are also several inexpensive books, including *1100 Words You Need to Know* and *Pocket Guide to Vocabulary* from Barron's, which may help you develop your vocabulary further.

abhor To regard with horror
I abhor violence.

abstain To refrain by choice
Ray decided to abstain from fattening foods.

abstract Not related to any object, theoretical
Mathematics can be very abstract.

acquisition An addition to an established group or collection
The museum's most recent acquisition was an early Roman vase.

admonish To correct firmly but kindly
The teacher admonished the student not to chew gum in class.

adroit Skillful or nimble in difficult circumstances
The nine year old was already an adroit gymnast.

adversary A foe or enemy
The wildebeast was ever-alert for its ancient adversary, the lion.

advocate To speak for an idea; a person who speaks for an idea
Lou was an advocate of gun control.

aesthetic Pertaining to beauty
Ron found the painting a moving aesthetic experience.

alias An assumed name
The check forger had used an alias.

alleviate To reduce or make more bearable
The hot shower helped alleviate the pain in her back.

allude To make an indirect reference to, hint at
Elaine only alluded to her previous trips through the state.

ambiguous Open to many interpretations
That is an ambiguous statement.

apathy Absence of passion or emotion
The teacher tried to overcome their apathy toward the subject.

apprehensive Fear or unease about possible outcomes
Bob was apprehensive about visiting the dentist.

aptitude The ability to gain from a particular type of instruction
The professor pointed out that aptitude, alone, was not enough for success in school.

articulate To speak clearly and distinctly, present a point of view
Chris was chosen to articulate the group's point of view.

assess To measure or determine an outcome or value
There are many informal ways to assess learning.

attest To affirm or certify
I can attest to Cathy's ability as a softball pitcher.

augment To increase or add to
The new coins augmented the already large collection.

belated Past time or tardy
George sent a belated birthday card.

benevolent Expresses goodwill or kindly feelings
The club was devoted to performing benevolent acts.

biased A prejudiced view or action
The judge ruled that the decision was biased.

bolster To shore up, support
The explorer sang to bolster her courage.

candid Direct and outspoken
Lee was well known for her candid comments.

caricature Exaggerated, ludicrous picture, in words or a cartoon
The satirist presented world leaders as caricatures.

carnivorous Flesh eating or predatory
The lion is a carnivorous animal.

censor A person who judges the morality of others; act on that judgment
Please don't censor my views!

censure Expression of disapproval, reprimand
The senate acted to censure the congressman.

cessation The act of ceasing or halting
The eleventh hour marked the cessation of hostilities.

chronic Continuing and constant
Asthma can be a chronic condition.

clandestine Concealed or secret
The spy engaged in clandestine activities.

cogent Intellectually convincing
He presented a cogent argument.

cognitive Relates to the intellectual area of learning
Lou read the Taxonomy of Education Objectives: Cognitive Domain.

competency Demonstrated ability
Bert demonstrated the specified mathematics competency.

complacent Unaware self-satisfaction
The tennis player realized she had become complacent.

concept A generalization
The professor lectured on concept development.

congenital Existing at birth but non-hereditary
The baby had a small congenital defect.

contemporaries Belonging in the same time period, about the same age
Piaget and Bruner were contemporaries.

contempt Feeling or showing disdain or scorn
She feld nothing but contempt for their actions.

contentious Argumentative
Tim was in a contentious mood.

corroborate To make certain with other information, to confirm
The reporter would always corroborate a story before publication.

credence Claim to acceptance or trustworthiness
They did not want to lend credence to his views.

cursory Surface, not in depth
Ron gave his car a cursory inspection.

daunt To intimidate with fear
Harry did not let the difficulty of the task daunt him.

debacle Disastrous collapse or rout
The whole trip had been a debacle.

debilitate To make feeble
He was concerned that the flu would debilitate him.

decadent Condition of decline/decay
Joan said in a frustration, "We live in a decadent society."

deductive Learning that proceeds from general to specific
He proved his premise using deductive logic.

demographic Population data
The census gathers demographic information.

denounce To condemn a person or idea
The diplomat rose in the United Nations to denounce the plan.

deter To prevent or stop an action, usually by some threat
The president felt that the peace conference would help deter aggression.

diligent A persistent effort; a person who makes such an effort
The investigator was diligent in her pursuit of the truth.

discern To perceive or recognize, often by insight
The principal attempted to discern which student was telling the truth.

discord Disagreement or disharmony
Gail's early promotion led to discord in the office.

discriminate To distinguish among people or groups based on their characteristics
It is not appropriate to discriminate based on race or ethnicity.

disdain To show or act with contempt
The professional showed disdain for her amateurish efforts.

disseminate To send around, scatter
The health organization will disseminate any new information on the flu.

divergent Thinking that extends in many directions, is not focused
Les was an intelligent but divergent thinker.

diverse Not uniform, varied
Alan came from a diverse neighborhood.

duress Coercion
He claimed that he confessed under duress.

eccentric Behaves unusually, different from the norm
His long hair and midnight walks made Albert appear eccentric.

eclectic Drawing from several ideas or practices
Joe preferred an eclectic approach to the practice of psychology.

eloquent Vivid, articulate expression
The congregation was held spellbound by the eloquent sermon.

emanate To flow out, come forth
How could such wisdom emanate from one so young?

embellish To make things seem more than they are
Art loved to embellish on the truth.

empirical From observation or experiment
The scientist's conclusions were based on empirical evidence.

employment A job or professional position (paid)
You seek employment so you can make the big bucks.

enduring Lasting over the long term
Their frienship grew into an enduring relationship.

enhance To improve or build up
The mechanic used a fuel additive to enhance the car's performance.

enigma A mystery or puzzle
The communist bloc is an "enigma wrapped inside a mystery." (Churchill)

equity Equal attention or treatment
The workers were seeking pay equity with others in their industry.

equivocal Uncertain, capable of multiple interpretations
In an attempt to avoid conflict the negotiator took an equivocal stand.

expedite To speed up, facilitate
Hal's job at the shipping company was to expedite deliveries.

exploit Take maximum advantage of, perhaps unethically
Her adversary tried to exploit her grief to gain an advantage.

farce A mockery
The attorney objected, saying that the testimony made the trial a farce.

feign To pretend, make a false appearance of
Some people feign illness to get out of work.

fervent Marked by intense feeling
The spokesman presented a fervent defense of the company's actions.

fiasco Total failure
They had not prepared for the presentation, and it turned into a fiasco.

formidable Difficult to surmount
State certification requirements can present a formidable obstacle.

fracas A noisy quarrel or a scrap
The debat turned into a full-fledged fracas.

gamut Complete range or extent
Waiting to take the test, her mind ran the gamut of emotions.

glib Quickness suggesting insincerity
The glib response made Rita wonder about the speaker's sincerity.

grave Very serious or weighty
The supervisor had grave concerns about the worker's ability.

guile Cunning, crafty, duplicitous
When the truth failed, he tried to win his point with guile.

handicapped Having one or more disabilities
The child study team classified Loren as handicapped.

harass Both persistently
Some fans came to harass the players on the opposing team.

homogeneous A group with little variation in ability or performance
The school used test scores to place students in homogeneous groups.

hypocrite One who feigns a virtuous character or belief
Speaking against drinking and then driving drunk made him a hypocrite!

immune Protected or exempt from disease or harm
The vaccination made Ray immune to measles.

impartial Fair and objective
The contestants agreed on an objective, impartial referee.

impasse Situation with no workable solution
The talks had not stopped, but they had reached an impasse.

impede To retard or obstruct
Mason did not let adversity impede his progress.

implicit Understood but not directly stated
They never spoke about the matter, but they had an implicit understanding.

indifferent Uncaring or apathetic
The teacher was indifferent to the student's pleas for an extension.

indigenous Native to an area
The botanist recognized it as an indigenous plant.

inductive Learning that proceeds from specific to general
Science uses an inductive process, from examples to a generalization.

inevitable Certain and unavoidable
After the rains, the collapse of the dam was inevitable.

infer To reach a conclusion not explicitly stated
The advertisement sought to infer that the product was superior.

inhibit To hold back or restrain
The hormone was used to inhibit growth.

innovate To introduce something new or change established procedure
Mere change was not enough, they had to innovate the procedure.

inquiry Question-based Socratic learning
Much of science teaching uses inquiry-based learning.

inundate To overwhelm, flood
It was December, and mail began to inundate the Post Office.

jocular Characterized by joking or good nature
The smiling man seemed to be a jocular fellow

judicial Relating to the administration of justice
His goal was to have no dealings with the judicial system.

knack A talent for doing something
Ron had a real knack for mechanical work.

languid Weak, lacking energy
*The sunbather enjoyed a languid afternoon
at the shore.*

liaison An illicit relationship or a means of communication
*The governor appointed his chief aid liaison
to the senate.*

lucid Clear and easily understood
*The teacher answered the question in a
direct and lucid way.*

magnanimous Generous in forgiving
Loretta is magnanimous to a fault.

malignant Very injurious, evil
Crime is a malignant sore on our society.

malleable Open to being shaped or influenced
He had a malleable position on gun control.

meticulous Very careful and precise
Gina took meticulous care of the fine china.

miser A money hoarder
*The old miser had more money than he could
ever use.*

monotonous Repetitive and boring
*Circling the airport, waiting to land, became
dull and monotonous.*

mores Understood rules of society
*Linda made following social mores her goal
in life.*

motivation Something that creates interest or
action
*Most good lessons begin with a good
motivation.*

myriad Large indefinite number
*Look skyward and be amazed by the myriad
of stars.*

naive Lacking sophistication
*Laura is unaware, and a little naive, about
the impact she has on others.*

nemesis A formidable rival
Lex Luthor is Superman's nemesis.

novice A beginner
*Her unsteady legs revealed that Sue was a
novice skater.*

nullified Removed the importance of
*The penalty nullified the 20-yard gain made
by the running back.*

objective A goal
*The teacher wrote an objective for each les-
son.*

oblivious Unaware and unmindful
*Les was half asleep and oblivious to the
racket around him.*

obscure Vague, unclear, uncertain
The lawyer quoted an obscure reference.

ominous Threatening or menacing
*There were ominous black storm clouds on
the horizon.*

palatable Agreeable, acceptable
*Sandy's friends tried to make her
punishment more palatable.*

panorama A comprehensive view or picture
*The visitor's center offered a panorama of
the canyon below.*

pedagogy The science of teaching
Part of certification tests focus on pedagogy.

perpetuate To continue or cause to be remembered
*A plaque was put up to perpetuate the mem-
ory of the retiring teacher.*

pompous Exaggerated self-importance
*Rona acted pompous, but Lynne suspected
she was very empty inside.*

precarious Uncertain, beyond one's control
*A diver sat on a precarious perch on a cliff
above the water.*

precedent An act or instance that sets the
standard
*The judge's ruling set a precedent for later
cases.*

preclude To act to make impossible or impracti-
cable
Beau did not want to preclude any options.

precocious Very early developtment
*Chad was very precocious and ran at six
months.*

prolific Abundant producer
*Isaac Asimov was a prolific science fiction
writer.*

prognosis A forecast or prediction
*The stockbroker gave a guarded prognosis for
continued growth.*

provoke To stir up or anger
*Children banging on the cage would provoke
the circus lion to growl.*

quagmire Predicament or difficult situation
*The regulations were a quagmire of
conflicting rules and vague terms.*

qualm Feeling of doubt or misgiving
*The teacher had not a single qualm about
giving the student a low grade.*

quandary A dilemma
*The absence of the teacher aide left the
teacher in a quandary.*

quench To put out, satisfy
*The glass of water was not enough to quench
his thirst.*

rancor Bitter continuing resentment
A deep rancor had existed between the two friends since the accident.

rationale The basis or reason for something
The speeder tried to present a rationale to the officer who stopped her.

reciprocal Mutual interchange
Each person got something out of their reciprocal arrangement.

refute To prove false
The lawyer used new evidence to refute claims made by the prosecution.

remedial Designed to compensate for learning deficits
Jim spent one period a day in remedial instruction.

reprove Criticize gently
The teacher would reprove students for chewing gum in class.

repudiate To reject or disown
The senator repudiated membership in an all male club.

resolve To reach a definite conclusion
A mediator was called in to resolve the situation.

retrospect Contemplation of the past
Ryan noted, in retrospect, that leaving home was his best decision.

revere To hold in the highest regard
Citizens of the town revere their long time mayor.

sanction To issue authoritative approval or a penalty
The boxing comissioner had to sanction the match.

scrutinize To inspect with great care
You should scrutinize any document before signing it.

siblings Brothers or sisters
The holidays give me the chance to spend time with my siblings.

skeptical Doubting, questioning the validity
The principal was skeptical about the students' reason for being late.

solace Comfort in misfortune
Her friends provided solace in her time of grief.

solitude Being alone
Pat enjoyed her Sunday afternoon moments of solitude.

stagnant Inert, contaminated
In dry weather the lake shrank to a stagnant pool.

stereotype An oversimplified generalized view or belief
We are all guilty of fitting people into a stereotype.

subsidy Financial assistance
Chris received a subsidy from her company so she could attend school.

subtle Faint, not easy to find or understand
Subtle changes in the teller's actions alerted the police to the robbery.

subterfuge A deceptive strategy
The spy used a subterfuge to gain access to the secret materials.

superficial Surface, not profound
The inspector gave the car a quick superficial inspection.

tacit Not spoken, inferred
They had a tacit agreement.

tenacious Persistent and determined
The police officer was tenacious in pursuit of a criminal.

tentative Unsure, uncertain
The athletic director set up a tentative basketball schedule.

terminate To end, conclude
He wanted to terminate the relationship.

transition Passage from one activity to another
The transition from college student to teacher was not easy.

trepidation Apprehension, state of dread
Erin felt some trepidation about beginning her new job.

trivial Unimportant, ordinary
The seemingly trivial occurrence had taken on added importance.

ubiquitous Everywhere, omnipresent
A walk through the forest invited attacks from the ubiquitous mosquitoes.

ultimatum A final demand
After a trying day, the teacher issued an ultimatum to the class.

usurp To wrongfully and forcefully seize and hold, particularly power
The association vice president tried to usurp the president's power.

vacillate To swing indecisively
He had a tendency to vacillate in his stance on discipline.

valid Logically correct
The math teacher was explaining a valid mathematical proof.

vehement Forceful, passionate
The child had a vehement reaction to the teacher's criticism.

vestige A sign of something no longer there or existing
Old John was the last vestige of the first teachers to work at the school.

vicarious Experience through the activities or feelings of others
He had to experience sports in a vicarious way through his students.

virulent Very poisonous or noxious
The coral snake has a particularly virulent venom.

vital Important and essential
The school secretary was a vital part of the school.

waffle To write or speak in a misleading way
The spokesperson waffled as she tried to explain away the mistake.

wary Watchful, on guard
The soldiers were very wary of any movements across the DMZ.

Xanadu An idyllic, perfect place
All wished for some time in Xanadu.

yearned Longed or hoped for
Liz yearned for a small class.

zeal Diligent devotion to a cause
Ron approached his job with considerable zeal.

CRITICAL COMPREHENSION

RECOGNIZE THE AUTHOR'S PURPOSE (B1)

TEST TIP:

You will read a passage. A multiple-choice question will ask you to identify the author's purpose or reason for writing the passage. You may also be asked about the author's purpose in writing a particular paragraph in the passage.

This type of question has four answer choices.

The author's primary purpose explains why the author wrote the passage. The purpose is closely related to the main idea. You might think. "Fine, I know the main idea. But why did the author take the time to write about that main idea?" "What is the author trying to make me know or feel?"

The author's purpose will be in one of five categories. The categories and their descriptions are given below.

Describe	Present an image of physical reality or a mental image.
Entertain	Amuse, Perform
Inform	Clarify, Explain, State
Narrate	Relate, Tell a story
Persuade	Argue, Convince, Prove

There is no hard and fast rule for identifying the author's purpose. Rely on your informed impression of the passage. Once in a while a passage may overtly state the author's purpose. But you must usually figure it out on your own. Remember, one of the answer choices will be correct. Your job—decide which one it is.

Practice Question

While becoming a teacher, I spent most of my time with books. I read books about the subjects I would teach in school and books that explained how to teach the subjects. As a new teacher, I relied on books to help my students learn. But I learned, and now the basis for my teaching is to help students apply what they have learned to the real world.

1. Which of the following best represents the author's purpose?
   (A) to clarify the duties of a beginning teacher
   (B) to convince people to read in order to learn
   (C) to explain that teaching is extremely rewarding
   (D) to explain the importance of applying learning

Answer on page 33.

DISTINGUISH BETWEEN FACT AND OPINION (B3)

TEST TIP:

You will be asked to classify a statement from a passage as fact or opinion.

There are only two answer choices for this type of multiple-choice question.

These questions ask you to distinguish between statements of fact and statements of opinion. Apply these simple tests to distinguish between fact and fiction.

Facts can be proven true *or* false by some objective means or method. *A fact refers to persons, things, or events that exist now or existed at some time in the past.* Note that a fact does not have to be true. For example, the statement "The tallest human being alive today is 86 feet tall" is false. This statement is a fact because it can be proven false.

Opinions, on the other hand, cannot be proved or disproved by some objective means or method. Opinions are subjective and include opinions, attitudes, and probabilities. Some statements, which seem true, may still be opinions. For example, the statement "A car is easier to park than a bus" seems true. However, this statement is an opinion. There is no way to objectively prove this statement true or false.

Examples:

Fact: <u>Abraham Lincoln was President of the United States during the Civil War.</u> We can check historical records and find out if the statement is true. This statement of fact is true.

Fact: <u>Robert E. Lee went into exile in Canada after the Civil War.</u> We can check historical records. This factual statement is true. Lee later became president of Washington College, now called Washington and Lee University.

Fact: <u>It is more than 90°F. outside.</u> We can use a thermometer to prove or disprove this statement.

Fact: <u>More people are born in November than in any other month.</u> We can check statistical records to prove or disprove this statement.

Opinion: <u>If Lincoln had lived, reconstruction would have been better.</u> This sounds true, but there is no way to prove or disprove this statement.

Opinion: <u>Lee was the Civil War's most brilliant general.</u> Sounds true, but there is no way to prove it.

Opinion: <u>It will always be colder in November than in July.</u> Sounds true! But we can't prove or disprove future events.

Practice Question

Class A had an average grade equivalent of 5.6 on a reading test while Class B had an average grade equivalent of 5.4 on the same test. The research report concluded that Class A had performed better than Class B.

1. The passage represents a statement of
   (A) fact
   (B) opinion

Answer on page 33.

DETECT BIAS (B4)

TEST TIP:

You will be asked to identify a specific example of bias found in a reading passage.

These multiple-choice questions have four answer choices.

Bias

On the CLAST, a statement or passage reveals bias if the author has prejudged or has a predisposition to a doctrine, idea, or practice. Bias means the author is trying to convince or influence the reader through some emotional appeal or slanted writing.

Bias can be positive or negative.

Positive Bias: She is so lovely, she deserves the very best.
Negative Bias: She is so horrible, I hope she gets what's coming to her.

Forms of Bias

Biased writing can often be identified by the presence of one or more of following forms of bias.

Emotional Language	Language that appeals to the reader's emotions, and not to common sense or logic.
	Positive: If I am elected, I will help your family get jobs. Negative: If my opponent is elected, your family will lose their jobs.
Inaccurate Information	Language that presents false, inaccurate, or unproved information as though it were factual.
	Positive: My polls indicate that I am very popular. Negative: My polls indicate that a lot of people disagree with my opponent.
Name Calling	Language that uses negative, disapproving terms without any factual basis.
	Negative: I'll tell you, my opponent is a real jerk.

Slanted Language	Language that slants the facts or evidence toward the writer's point of view.
	Positive: I am a positive person, looking for the good side of people. Negative: My opponent finds fault with everyone and everything.
Stereotyping	Language that indicates that a person is like all the members of a particular group.
	Positive: I belong to the Krepenkle party, the party known for its honesty. Negative: My opponent belongs to the Lerplenkle party, the party of increased taxes.

Reading About Reading

Reading seems to be a natural process. Reading about reading and about steps to taking reading tests can seem contrived and confusing. However, we know that these techniques work. Once you apply them to the practice exercises, your reading ability and scores will improve.

Practice Question

There was a time in the United States when a married woman was expected to take her husband's last name. Most women still follow this practice, but things are changing. In fact, Hawaii has been the only state with a law requiring a woman to take her husband's last name when she marries.

Many women look forward to taking their husband's surname. They may enjoy the bond it establishes with their husband, or want to be identified with their husband's professional status. Other women want to keep their own last name. They may prefer their original last name, or want to maintain their professional identity.

Some women resolve this problem by choosing a last name that hyphenates their surname and their husband's surname. This practice of adopting elements of both surnames is common in other cultures. As the modern American woman increases her social standing, she will no longer need the pseudo support of her husband's surname. The future generations of women will offer their surnames to their new husbands at the nuptial table.

1. In this passage, the author shows a bias against
   (A) being a modern woman.
   (B) women leading professional lives.
   (C) marriage in the twenty-first century.
   (D) women changing surnames after marriage.

Answer on page 33.

RECOGNIZE THE AUTHOR'S TONE (B5)

TEST TIP:

You will be asked to identify the author's tone—frustrated, concerned, and so on—found in a specific passage. You may also be asked to describe the author's tone of voice if the passage were being read aloud.

This type of multiple-choice question has four answer choices. Each of the answer choices is a word that describes a tone or feeling.

Tone

The author's tone is the author's attitude as reflected in the passage. Answering this question means choosing the correct tone word. How do you think the author would sound while speaking? What impression would you form about the speaker's attitude or feeling? The answer to the latter question will usually lead you to the author's tone. A partial list of tone words is given below. Write a brief definition for each word.

absurd	formal
amused	gentle
angry	hard
apathetic	impassioned
arrogant	indignant
bitter	intense
cheerful	intimate
comic	joyous
compassionate	loving
complex	malicious
concerned	mocking
cruel	nostalgic
depressed	objective
distressed	optimistic
evasive	outraged
excited	outspoken

pathetic	sentimental
pessimistic	serious
playful	solemn
prayerful	tragic
reverent	uneasy
righteous	vindictive
satirical	

The choice of the author's tone will be clarified once you see a question. The question gives four answer choices. You have to decide which answer choice is correct.

Practice Question

Japanese students have always been considered to be well-prepared for life in the world's business and engineering communities. The mathematics and science curricula of Japanese schools are considered to be superior to those in American schools. With the daily advancement of Japanese technological prowess, how can American children ever hope to compete with their Japanese counterparts?

1. Which of the following is the best descriptor of the author's tone in this passage?
   (A) disbelief
   (B) anger
   (C) pride
   (D) concern

Answer on page 33.

IDENTIFY THE AUTHOR'S OVERALL ORGANIZATIONAL PATTERN (B2)

TEST TIP:

You will be asked to identify the specific organizational pattern the author used in a passage or paragraph. A passage may have a number of organizational patterns. You should identify the primary organizational pattern used by the author.

These multiple-choice questions have four answer choices.

The organizational pattern is the way the writer structures the material to get across the main idea and details.

Given below are some of the common organizational patterns referred to on the CLAST along with explanations and key words that may help you identify the pattern. Other CLAST objectives refer to these organizational patterns.

Addition	Develop a subject point by point: *further, and, then*
Cause and Effect	Demonstrate how an event came about due to certain conditions or causes: *as a result of, because, therefore*
Classification	Partition a subject into different categories or classes: *division, classification*
Comparison	Point out similarities: *similar to, in common, also*
Contrast	Point out differences: *as opposed to, in contrast to, however*
Definition	Explain or clarify the meaning of a word or term by defining it: *is, defined by, which means*
Generalization/ Example	Make a general statement and support it with specific examples: *for example, that is, for instance*
Simple Listing	List items in which order is NOT important: *including, next, second*
Order	List in order. There are several different types of order that may share common key words:
Order of Importance	Describe events or things in order of importance: *most important, next, last, primarily, finally*
Spatial Order	Describe a thing or event in an orderly way but not related to time: *above, behind, next to*
Time Order	Describe events in time or chronological order: *first, then, next, last*
Statement/ Explanation	Explain more fully what is said earlier in the passage: *that is, in other words*
Summary	Sum up in brief what has already been said at greater length: *in summary, to summarize*

The confusion you may experience with these organizational patterns will disappear when you see a question. The question provides four answer choices and will not include more than one choice which is a reasonable description of the organizational pattern. You just have to decide which of the answer choices is correct.

Practice Question

Remove the jack from the trunk. Set the jack under the car. Use the jack to raise the car. Remove the lug nuts. Remove the tire and replace it with the spare. Reset the lug nuts loosely and use the jack to lower the chassis to the ground. Tighten the lug nuts once the tire is touching the ground.

1. The organizational pattern used by the author to develop this passage could be best described as
   (A) time order.
   (B) simple listing.
   (C) cause and effect.
   (D) definition.

Answer on page 33.

RECOGNIZE RELATIONSHIPS WITHIN SENTENCES (B6)

TEST TIP:

You may be asked to identify a missing word or phrase that completes the meaning of sentences. You may also be asked to identify the structure of a sentence using one of the organizational patterns from Identifying an Author's Overall Organizational Pattern (Objective B2).

This type of multiple-choice question has four answer choices. The choices will be words or phrases that complete the meaning of sentences or the organizational pattern found in a sentence. The questions will always refer to a single sentence within a passage.

Relationships within sentences are small-scale organizational patterns. Relationships within a sentence describe how ideas in the sentence are connected.

Review the organizational patterns and the key words or phrases that accompany them on page 28. Our analysis of previous tests indicates that these organizational patterns are most likely to appear as answers for this question type:

addition
cause and effect
comparison
contrast
generalization/example
statement/explanation
time or spatial order

Any confusion about relationships within a sentence will be clarified when you see a question. The question gives four answer choices. You just have to decide which answer choice is correct.

Practice Questions

The growth of the town lead to a huge increase in the number of students applying for kindergarten admission. Before this time, students had been admitted to kindergarten even if they were technically too young. At first the school administrators considered a testing plan for those applicants too young for regular admission, admitting only those who passed the test. Luckily the administrators submitted a plan that just enforced the official, _____ previously ignored, birth cut-off date for kindergarten admission. This decision set the stage for fairness throughout the school system.

1. The word missing from the empty
   space is
   (A) because
   (B) but
   (C) although
   (D) evidently

   Children can hold onto phobias into their adolescent years. Parents often perpetuate these fixations by denying that they exist. Their children may then feel deserted and be left with unvalidated feelings.

2. Which of the following describes the
   relationship within the second sentence?
   (A) example
   (B) cause and effect
   (C) clarification
   (D) addition

Answers on page 34.

RECOGNIZE RELATIONSHIPS BETWEEN SENTENCES (B7)

TEST TIP:

You may be asked to identify a missing word or phrase that completes the meaning of sentences. You may also be asked to identify the relationship between or among sentences using one of the organizational patterns from Identifying an Author's Overall Organizational Pattern (Objective B2).

This type of multiple-choice question has four answer choices. The choices will be words or phrases that complete the meaning of sentences or the organizational pattern found in a sentence. The questions will always refer to the relationship between or among sentences in a passage.

Review the organizational patterns and the words or phrases that accompany them on page 28. Our analysis of previous tests indicates that these organizational patterns are most likely to appear as answers for this question type:

addition
cause and effect
comparison
contrast
generalization/example
statement/explanation
time or spatial order

Practice Question

During a Stage 4 alert, workers in an energy plant must wear protective pants, a protective shirt, and a helmet except that protective coveralls can be worn in place of protective pants and shirt. When there is a Stage 5 alert, workers must also wear filter masks in addition to the requirements for the Stage 4 alert.

1. What is the relationship between
   sentence 1 and sentence 2?
   (A) generalization and example
   (B) cause and effect
   (C) time order
   (D) addition

Answers on page 34.

RECOGNIZE VALID ARGUMENTS (B8)

TEST TIP:

You will be asked to identify a statement, or an argument in a statement, as valid or invalid.

This type of multiple-choice question has two answer choices.

The terms valid and invalid have very special meanings on the CLAST. Valid arguments are resonable. Valid arguments are objective and supported by evidence. Invalid arguments are *not* reasonable. They are not objective. Invalid arguments usually reflect one of the following fallacies.

Ad hominem	Arguing against a person to discredit their position, rather than an argument against the position itself
Ad populum	An argument that appeals to the emotions of the person
Bandwagon	Arguing for position because of its popularity
Begging the question	Assuming that an argument, or part of an argument, is true without providing proof
Circular logic	Using a statement of a position to argue in favor of that position

Either/or	Stating that the conclusion falls into one of two extremes, when there are more intermediate choices
Faulty analogy	Using an analogy as an argument when the analogy does not match the situation under discussion
Hasty generalization	Reaching a conclusion too quickly, before all the information is known
Non sequitur	A conclusion that does not logically follow from the facts
Post hoc, ergo propter hoc	Falsely stating that one event following another is caused by the first event (faulty cause and effect)
Red herring	An irrelevant point, diverting attention from the position under discussion

A question may ask you to identify a fallacy in a statement. In that case, the test will include this list of fallacies and definitions. Just because a conclusion is true does not mean the argument is valid. Just because you agree or disagree with the conclusion does not mean the conclusion is either true or false. Choose valid when the argument is well-supported. Choose invalid when the argument contains a fallacy.

Practice Question

The way I look at it, Robert E. Lee was the worst general in the Civil War—he was the South's commanding general, and the South lost the war.

1. Is the author's argument logically valid or invalid?
   (A) valid
   (B) invalid

Answer on page 34.

DRAW LOGICAL INFERENCES AND CONCLUSIONS (B9)

TEST TIP:

You will be asked to draw a conclusion based on a passage, to identify a cause-and-effect relationship in the passage, or to determine what can be implied, indicated or inferred from the passage.

This type of multiple-choice question has four answer choices.

You have already learned to make inferences and draw conclusions. You can draw on your previous experiences in this section to help you draw inferences and make conclusions.

Many times the topic or main idea was not stated directly and you had to infer one or the other from information in the passage. You also had to infer the correct replacement for a missing word when the definition of the missing word was not known. You used inference to establish the relationship between sentences, or within a sentence.

You learned how to distinguish between valid and invalid arguments, and so too between valid and invalid conclusions. Every reading comprehension question means reaching some conclusion about which answer is correct.

Still, there are no hard and fast rules for drawing inferences and conclusions from a paragraph or passage. You must use your own common sense. However, you have one significant ally.

You do not have to actually reach a conclusion or draw an inference from the passage. You just have to decide which of four answer choices shows the correct conclusion or inference. Use the answer choices as the basis for responding to this type of question and the percent you get correct will increase markedly.

Remember though that something clearly stated in the passage is a fact, not a conclusion or an inference.

Practice Question

The retired basketball player said that, while modern players were better athletes because there was so much emphasis on youth basketball and increased focus on training, he still believed that the players of his day were better because they were more committed to the game, better understood its nuances, and were more dedicated to team play.

1. The retired basketball player attributes the increased athletic prowess of today's basketball players to
   (A) better nutrition.
   (B) youth basketball programs.
   (C) salary caps.
   (D) more athletic scholarships.

Answer on page 34.

READING PRACTICE EXPLAINED ANSWERS

A1 page 11
1. **D** The person described in the passage was unaware in high school that the soccer team was more successful than the football team he played on.

A2 page 12
1. **B** The shape of the snout is specifically mentioned in the last sentences of the paragraph. Choice (A) might be true; however, it is not mentioned in the passage.

A3 page 13
1. **C** In this context, pledge means apply to join a fraternity or sorority.

B1 page 22
1. **D** The author's purpose is to explain the importance of applying what is learned. All the other choices are too specific to encompass the author's purpose.

B3 page 23
1. **A** The passage indicates that Class A performed better than Class B. This factual statement could be objectively verified.

B4 page 24
1. **D** Choice (D) reflects the obvious bias found in the final paragraph of the passage.

B5 page 26
1. **D** The first section of the passage lays the foundation for the expression of concern found in the last sentence.

B2 page 27
1. **A** Each of the steps must be followed in chronological order. Time order is the only logical answer.

B6 page 29

1. **B** Say the sentence with each answer choice and the word *but* makes the most sense. The first two sentences suggest that the plan was ignored indicating that the word *but* is the correct replacement.

2. **B** The cause and effect relationship is established between parents' actions and children left with unvalidated feelings.

B7 page 30

1. **D** The relationship between the two sentences is addition. Even though each sentence contains a simple listing, it is the relationship between sentences that is important.

B8 page 31

1. **B** Invalid. It is a hasty generalization to say that Lee was the worst general because his army lost in the war. There may be other important factors leading to its defeat.

B9 page 32

1. **B** This answer identifies the cause-and-effect relationship in the passage between youth basketball and the superior athletic ability of modern players.

STEPS FOR PASSING THE READING TEST

The reading test consists primarily of passages followed by multiple-choice questions. You do not have to know what an entire reading passage is about. You just have to know enough to get the answer correct. Less than half, often less than 25 percent, of the information in any passage is needed to answer all the questions.

You do not have to read the passage in detail. In fact, careful slow reading will almost certainly get you in trouble. Strange as it seems, follow this advice—avoid careful, detailed reading at all costs.

Buried among all the false gold in the passage are a few valuable nuggets. Follow these strategies to hit pay dirt and avoid the fool's gold.

Reading seems to be a natural process. Reading about reading and about steps to taking reading tests can seem contrived and confusing. However, we know that these steps and techniques work. Once you apply the steps to the practice exercises, your reading ability and scores will likely improve.

THE SIX STEPS

During a reading test follow these steps.

1. Skim to find the topic of each paragraph.

2. Read the questions and answers.

3. Identify the question type(s).

4. Eliminate incorrect answers.

5. Scan to find the answer.

6. Choose the answer that is absolutely correct.

Skim to Find the Topic of Each Paragraph

Your first job is to find the topic of each paragraph. The topic is what a paragraph or passage is about.

The topic of a paragraph is usually found in the first and last sentences. Read the first and last sentences just enough to find the topic. You can write the topic in the margin next to the passage. Remember, the test booklet is yours. You can mark it up as much as you like.

Reading Sentences

Every sentence has a subject that tells what the sentence is about. The sentence also has a verb that tells what the subject is doing or links the subject to the complement. The sentence may also contain a complement that receives the action or describes what is being said about the subject. The words underlined in the following examples are the ones you would focus on as you read the details.

1. The famous educator <u>John Dewey founded</u> an educational movement called <u>progressive education</u>.

2. Sad to say, we have learned <u>American school children</u> of all ages <u>are poorly nourished</u>.

You may occasionally encounter a paragraph or passage in which the topic can't be summarized from the first and last sentences. This type of paragraph usually contains factural information. If this happens, you will have to read the entire paragraph.

Fact, Opinion, or Fiction

If it is a factural passage, the author will present the fact and support it with details and examples. If the passage presents an opinion, the author will give the opinion and support it with arguments, examples, and other details. Many passages combine fact and opinion. If it is a fiction passage, the author will tell a story with details, descriptions, and examples about people, places, or things.

Once you find the topic, you will probably need more information to answer the questions. But don't worry about this other information and details now. You can go back and find it after you have read the questions.

Read the Questions and the Answers

Now read the questions—one at a time. Read the answers for the question you are working on. Be sure that you understand what each question and its answer mean.

Before you answer a question, be sure you know whether it is asking for a fact or an inference. If the question asks for a fact, the correct answer will identify a main idea or supporting detail. We'll discuss more about main ideas and details later. The correct answer may also identify a cause-and-effect relationship among ideas or be a paraphrase or summary of parts of the passage. Look for these.

If the question asks for an inference, the correct answer will identify the author's purpose, assumptions, or attitude and the difference between fact and the author's opinion. Look for these elements.

Identify the Question Types

There are only twelve question types. Identify the question types as you read to make answering the questions a lot easier.

Two Answer Choices

- Distinguish between fact and opinion

- Recognize valid arguments

Four Answer Choices

- Recognize the main idea

- Identify supporting details

- Determine the meaning of words in context

- Recognize the author's purpose

- Identify the author's overall organizational pattern

- Detect bias

- Recognize the author's tone

- Recognize relationships within sentences

- Recognize relationships between sentences

- Draw logical inferences and conclusions

Eliminate Incorrect Answers

Read the answers and eliminate the ones that you absolutely know are incorrect. Read the answers literally. Look for words such as *always, never, must, all*. If you can find a single exception to this type of sweeping statement, then the answer can't be correct. Eliminate it.

Scan to Find the Answer

Once you have eliminated answers, compare the other answers to the passage. When you find the answer that is confirmed by the passage—stop. That is your answer choice. Follow these other suggestions for finding the correct answer.

You will often need to read details to find the main idea of a paragraph. The main idea of a paragraph is what the writer has to say about the topic. Scan the details about the main idea until you find the answer. Scanning means skipping over information that does not answer the question.

Who Wrote This Answer?

People who write tests go to great lengths to choose a correct answer that cannot be questioned. That is what they get paid for. They are not paid to write answers that have a higher meaning or include great truths.

Test writers want to be asked to write questions and answers again. They want to avoid valid complaints from test takers like you who raise legitimate concerns about their answers.

They usually accomplish this difficult task in one of two ways. They may write answers that are very specific and based directly on the reading. They may also write correct answers that seem very vague.

A Vague Answer Can Be Correct

How can a person write a vague answer that is correct? Think of it this way. If I wrote that a person is 6 feet 5 inches tall, you could get out a tape measure to check my facts. Because I was very specific, you are more likely to be able to prove me wrong.

On the other hand, if I write that the same person is more than 6 feet tall you would be hard pressed to find fault with my statement. So my vague statement was hard to argue with. If the person in question is near 6 feet 5 inches tall, then my vague answer is most likely to be the correct one.

Don't choose an answer just because it seems more detailed or specific. A vague answer may be just as likely to be correct.

Choose the Answer That Is Absolutely Correct

Be sure that your choice answers the question. Be sure that your choice is based on the information contained in the paragraph. Don't choose an answer to another question. Don't choose an answer just because it sounds right. Don't choose an answer just because you agree with it.

There is no room on tests like these for answers that are partially wrong. It is not enough for an answer to be 99.9 percent correct. It must be absolutely, incontrovertibly, unquestionably, indisputably, and unarguably correct.

APPLYING THE STEPS

Let's apply the steps to this passage and questions.

Many vocational high schools in the United States give off-site work experience to their students. Students usually work in local businesses part of the school day and attend high school the other part. These programs have made American vocational schools world leaders in making job experience available to teenage students.

1. According to this paragraph, American vocational high schools are world leaders in making job experience available to teenage students because they
   (A) have students attend school only part of the day.
   (B) were quick to move their students to schools off-site.
   (C) require students to work before they can attend the school.
   (D) involve their students in cooperative education programs.

   Step 1: Skim to find the topic of each paragraph. Both the first and last sentences tell us that the topic is vocational schools and work experience.

   Step 2: Read the questions and answers. Why are American vocational education high schools the world leaders in offering job experience?

   Step 3: Identify the question type. This question asks you to identify supporting details.

   Step 4: Eliminate incorrect answers. Answer (C) is obviously wrong. It has to do with work before high school. Answer (B) is also incorrect. This has to do with attending school off-site. This leaves answers (A) and (D).

   Step 5: Scan to find the answer. Scan the details and find that parts of answer (A) are found in the passage. In answer (D) you have to know that cooperative education is another name for off-site work during school.

   Step 6: Choose the answer that is absolutely correct. It is down to answer (A) or answer (D). But answer (A) contains only part of the reason that vocational education high schools have gained such acclaim. Answer (D) is the absolutely correct answer.

Here's how to apply the steps to the following passage.

Problem Solving   Problem solving has become the main focus of mathematics learning. Students learn problem-solving strategies and then apply them to problems. Many tests now focus on problem solving and limit the number of computational problems. The problem-solving movement is traced to George Polya who wrote several problem-solving books for high school teachers.

Problem Solving Strategies   Problem-solving strategies include guess and check, draw a diagram, and make a list. Many of the strategies are taught as skills, which inhibits flexible and creative thinking. Problems in textbooks can also limit the power of these strategies. However, the problem-solving movement will be with us for some time, and a number of the strategies are useful.

   Step 1: Skim to find the topic of each paragraph. The topic of the first paragraph is problem solving. You find the topic in both the first and last sentences. Write the topic next to the paragraph. The topic for the second paragraph is problem-solving strategies. Write the topic next to the paragraph.

Now we are ready to look at the questions. If the question is about problem solving "in general" we start looking in the first paragraph for the answer. If the question is about strategies, we start looking in the second paragraph for the answer.

   Step 2: Read the questions and answers.

1. According to this passage, a difficulty with teaching problem-solving strategies is:
   (A) The strategies are too difficult for children.
   (B) The strategies are taught as skills.
   (C) The strategies are in textbooks.
   (D) The strategies are part of a movement.

   Step 3: Identify the question type. This question is about details.

   Step 4: Eliminate incorrect answers. Answer (A) can't be right because difficulty is not mentioned in the passage. That leaves (B), (C), and (D) for us to consider.

   Step 5: Scan to find the answer. The question asks about strategies so we look immediately to the second paragraph for the answer. The correct answer is (B). Choice (C) is not correct because the passage does not mention strategies in textbooks. There is no indication that (D) is correct.

   Step 6: Choose the answer that is absolutely correct. The correct choice is (B).

Practice Passage

Apply the steps to this practice passage. Do not look at the answers until you complete your work.

Read the following passage. After reading the passage, choose the best answer to each question from among the four choices. Answer all the questions following the passage on the basis of what is stated or implied in the passage.

Today's students have hand-held calculators that can graph one or even many equations. Students can even type in several equations and the calculator will "solve" them. This is the best way just to see a plotted graph quickly.

Line
(5)   This is the worst way to learn about graphing and equations. The calculator can't tell the student anything about the process of graphing and does not teach them how to plot a graph.

     Left to this electronic graphing process, students will not have the hands-on experience needed to see the patterns and symmetry that characterize graphing and equations. They may become too dependent on the calculator and be unable to reason
(10) effectively about equations and the process of graphing.

     It may be true that graphing and solving equations is taught *mechanically* in some classrooms. There is also something to be said for these electronic devices, which give students the opportunity to try out several graphs and solutions quickly (1) deciding on a final solution.

(15)   For all their electronic accuracy and patience, these graphing calculators cannot replace the process of graphing and solving equations on your own. For mastery of equations and graphing comes not just from seeing the graph automatically displayed on a screen, it also comes from a hands-on involvement with graphing.

1. The main idea of the passage is that
   - (A) a child can be good at graphing equations only through hands-on experience.
   - (B) teaching approaches for graphing equations should be improved.
   - (C) accuracy and patience are the keys to effective graphing instruction.
   - (D) the new graphing calculators have limited ability to teach students about graphing.

2. According to this passage, what negative impact will graphing calculators have on students who use them?
   - (A) They will not have experience with four-function calculators.
   - (B) They will become too dependent on the calculator.
   - (C) They can quickly try out several graphs before coming up with a final answer.
   - (D) They will get too much hands-on experience with calculators.

3. The author's purpose in writing this passage is to
   (A) explain how graphing calculators work.
   (B) describe how students get hands-on experience with graphing calculators.
   (C) show the limitations of using graphing calculators to teach graphing.
   (D) give an overview of how graphing calculators can be used for instruction.

4. In this passage, the word *mechanical* means
   (A) by rote.
   (B) with machines.
   (C) carefully.
   (D) involuntarily.

5. The statement "Students can even type in several equations and the calculator will 'solve' them" is a statement of
   (A) fact.
   (B) opinion.

6. The most appropriate word to place in blank (1) is
   (A) while.
   (B) furthermore.
   (C) before.
   (D) likewise.

7. The organizational pattern used by the author to develop this passage could best be described as
   (A) time order.
   (B) comparison.
   (C) simple listing.
   (D) addition.

8. From this passage, we can conclude that
   (A) the author had a bad experience using graphing calculators to learn about graphing.
   (B) the author is concerned that calculator companies are selling useless calculators.
   (C) the author is an educator.
   (D) the author is a student.

9. Which of the following best describes the relationship between the sentence beginning on line 3, "This is the best . . . ," and the sentence beginning on line 4, "This is the worst . . ."?
   (A) addition
   (B) comparison
   (C) contrast
   (D) cause/effect

10. The author's tone in this passage could best be described as
    (A) angry.
    (B) concerned.
    (C) disappointed.
    (D) melancholy.

11. The author of this passage shows bias when writing
    (A) "This is the worst way to learn about graphing and equations." (Line 4)
    (B) "It may be true that graphing and solving equations is taught mechanically in some classrooms." (Lines 11–12)
    (C) ". . . give students the opportunity to try out several graphs and solutions quickly . . ." (Lines 12–13)
    (D) ". . . it also comes from a hands-on involvement with graphing." (Line 18)

The calculator can't tell the student anything about the process of graphing, so it is the worst way to learn about graphing and equations.

12. Is the argument found in the above statement valid or invalid?
    (A) Valid
    (B) Invalid

Answers on pages 42–48.

Practice Passage Answers

Don't read this section until you have completed the practice passage.
　Here's how to apply the steps.

　　　Step 1: Skim to find the topic of each paragraph. You should have written a topic next
　　　　to each paragraph. Suggested topics are shown next to the following selection. Your
　　　　topics don't have to be identical, but they should accurately reflect the paragraph's
　　　　content.

Graphing Calculators

Today's students have hand-held calculators that can graph one or even many equations. Students can even type in several equations and the calculator will "solve" them. This is the best way to just see a plotted graph quickly.

This is the worst way to learn about graphing and equations. The calculator can't tell the student anything about the process of graphing and does not teach them how to plot a graph.

Problem with Graphing Calculators

Left to this electronic graphing process, students will not have the hands-on experience needed to see the patterns and symmetry that characterize graphing and equations. They may become too dependent on the calculator and be unable to reason effectively about equations and the process of graphing.

Why it's a Problem

It may be true that graphing and solving equations is taught *mechanically* in some classrooms. There is also something to be said for these electronic devices, which give students the opportunity to try out several graphs and solutions quickly (1) deciding on a final solution.

Good Points

For all their electronic accuracy and patience, these graphing calculators cannot replace the process of graphing and solving equations on your own. For mastery of equations and graphing comes not just from seeing the graph automatically displayed on a screen, it also comes from a hands-on involvement with graphing.

Apply Steps 2 through 6 to each of the questions.

1. The main idea of the passage is that
　(A) a child can be good at graphing
　　　equations only through hands-
　　　on experience.
　(B) teaching approaches for graphing
　　　equations should be improved.
　(C) accuracy and patience are the
　　　keys to effective graphing
　　　instruction.
　(D) the new graphing calculators have
　　　limited ability to teach students
　　　about graphing.

Step 2: Read the question and answers.

Step 3: Identify the question type. You have to identify the main idea of the passage. This is a very common question on reading tests. Remember that the main idea is what the writer is trying to say or communicate in the passage.

Step 4: Eliminate incorrect answers. Answers (B) and (C) are not correct. Answer (C) is not at all correct based on the passage. Even though (B) may be true, it does not reflect what the writer is trying to say in this passage.

Step 5: Scan to find the answer. As we review the details we see that answer (A) and answer (D) are both stated or implied in the passage. A scan of the details, alone, does not reveal which is the main idea. We must determine that on our own.

Step 6: Choose the answer that is absolutely correct. Which answer is absolutely correct? The whole passage is about graphing calculators, and they must be an important part of the main idea. The correct answer is (D). The author certainly believes that (A) is true, but uses this point to support the main idea.

2. According to this passage, what negative impact will graphing calculators have on students who use them?
   (A) They will not have experience with four-function calculators.
   (B) They will become too dependent on the calculator.
   (C) They can quickly try out several graphs before coming up with a final answer.
   (D) They will get too much hands-on experience with calculators.

Step 2: Read the question and answers. This is a straightforward comprehension question. What negative impact will calculators have on students who use them? The second and third paragraphs have topics related to problems with calculators. We'll probably find the answer there.

Step 3: Identify the question type.

Step 4: Eliminate incorrect answers. Answer (C) is not a negative impact of graphing calculators. Scan the details to find the correct answer from (A), (B), and (D).

Step 5: Scan to find the answer. The only detail that matches the question is in paragraph 3. The author says that students may become too dependent on the calculator. That's our answer.

Step 6: Choose the answer that is absolutely correct. Answer (B) is the only correct choice.

3. The author's purpose in writing
   this passage is to
   (A) explain how graphing calculators
       work.
   (B) describe how students get hands-on
       experience with graphing
       calculators.
   (C) show the limitations of using
       graphing calculators to teach
       graphing.
   (D) give an overview of how graphing
       calculators can be used for
       instruction.

   Step 2: Read the question and answers.

   Step 3: Identify the question type. The question uses the word *purpose* so we infer that
   this question is about the author's purpose for writing the passage.

   Step 4: Eliminate incorrect answers. The passage does not describe how graphing calculators work, so we can eliminate (A) and (D).

   Step 5: Scan to find the answer. Choices (B) and (C) remain. The whole intent of the
   paragraph is to show the limitations of using graphing calculators for instruction.
   Answer (C) is our choice.

   Step 6: Choose the answer that is absolutely correct. (C) is the only correct answer.

4. In this passage, the word *mechanical*
   means
   (A) by rote.
   (B) with machines.
   (C) carefully.
   (D) involuntarily.

   Step 2: Read the question and answers.

   Step 3: Identify the question type. The question asks for a synonym for *mechanical*.
   This is a word-meaning question.

   Step 4: Eliminate incorrect answers. Choice (C), *carefully* is not a synonym for
   mechanically. The other three choices might be synonyms.

   Step 5: Scan to find the answer. Choices (A), (B), and (D) remain. Say the sentence to
   yourself, substituting these choices for *mechanical*. The answer that makes the
   most sense is (A), by rote.

   Step 6: Choose the answer that is absolutely correct. (A) is the absolutely correct
   answer.

5. The statement "Students can even type
   in several equations, and the calculator
   will 'solve' them" is a statement of
   (A) fact.
   (B) opinion.

   Step 2: Read the question and answers.

   Step 3: Identify the question type. This is a fact or opinion question.

   Step 4: Eliminate incorrect answers. Skip this step for a fact-opinion question.

   Step 5: Scan to find the answer. Can this statement be proven true or false? If so, it is
   a fact. If not, it is an opinion. It would be easy to determine the truth or falsity of
   this statement. It is a fact.

   Step 6: Choose the answer that is absolutely correct. Choice (A) is the absolutely
   correct answer.

6. The most appropriate word to place in
   blank (1) is
   (A) while.
   (B) furthermore.
   (C) before.
   (D) likewise.

   Step 2: Read the question and answers.

   Step 3: Identify the question type. Fill-in-the-blank questions are about relationships
   within a sentence or between sentences. This missing word connects thoughts
   within a sentence.

   Step 4: Eliminate incorrect answers. *Furthermore* and *likewise* make no sense in the
   sentence. Eliminate choices (B) and (D).

   Step 5: Scan to find the answer. Choices (A) and (C) remain. Say the sentence to
   yourself, substituting each of the remaining choices for the blank. Choice (C),
   before, makes the most sense. It would not make sense to try out the graphs while
   you were deciding on a final solution.

   Step 6: Choose the answer that is absolutely correct. Choice (C) is absolutely correct.

7. The organizational pattern used by the
   author to develop this passage could
   best be described as
   (A) time order.
   (B) comparison.
   (C) simple listing.
   (D) addition.

   Step 2: Read the question and answers.

   Step 3: Identify the question type. The question identifies itself. Your answer will be
   an organizational pattern.

Step 4: Eliminate incorrect answers. Choice (C) is incorrect. There is no list in this passage. Choice (A) is incorrect. Time order is not important in this passage.

Step 5: Scan to find the answer. Choices (B) and (D) remain. There is some comparison, but this is not the primary pattern. Choice (D) makes the most sense. The author makes point after point about graphing calculators in the passage.

Step 6: Choose the answer that is absolutely correct. Choice (D) is absolutely correct.

8. From this passage, we can conclude that
   (A) the author had a bad experience using graphing calculators to learn about graphing.
   (B) the author is concerned that calculator companies are selling useless calculators.
   (C) the author is an educator.
   (D) the author is a student.

   Step 2: Read the question and answers.

   Step 3: Identify the question type. The question asks for a conclusion.

   Step 4: Eliminate incorrect answers. Eliminate (B). There is nothing in the passage about the sale of calculators. Eliminate (A). The author never refers to his or her own experience. In fact, the passage is written with an apparent concern for others.

   Step 5: Scan to find the answer. Choice (C) makes the most sense. The passage is written *about* students, not *from* a student's point of view. We can conclude that the author is an educator.

   Step 6: Choose the answer that is absolutely correct. Choice (C) is absolutely correct.

9. Which of the following best describes the relationship between the sentence beginning on line 3, "This is the best . . . ," and the sentence beginning on line 4, "This is the worst . . ."?
   (A) addition
   (B) comparison
   (C) contrast
   (D) cause/effect

   Step 2: Read the question and answers.

   Step 3: Identify the question type. The question asks about a relationship between sentences.

   Step 4: Eliminate incorrect answers. Eliminate (A). Points are not added by the second sentence. Eliminate (D). There is no cause/effect relationship between the sentences.

Step 5: Scan to find the answer. Choices (B) and (C) remain. Comparison points out similarities. Contrast points out differences. Choice (C) is the best. These sentences point out differences.

Step 6: Choose the answer that is absolutely correct. Choice (C) is absolutely correct.

10. The author's tone in this passage could
    best be described as
    (A) angry.
    (B) concerned.
    (C) disappointed.
    (D) melancholy.

    Step 2: Read the question and answers.

    Step 3: Identify the question type. The question asks for the author's tone.

    Step 4: Eliminate incorrect answers. Eliminate choices (A) and (D). There are no words describing either *anger* or *melancholy* in the passage.

    Step 5: Scan to find the answer. Choices (B) and (C) remain. Is the author *concerned* or *disappointed?* Choice (B) is best. The author may be disappointed, but this disappointment leads to the concern that is the predominant tone of this passage.

    Step 6: Choose the answer that is absolutely correct. Choice (B) is absolutely correct.

11. The author of this passage shows bias
    when writing
    (A) "This is the worst way to learn
        about graphing and equations."
        (Line 4)
    (B) "It may be true that graphing and
        solving equations is taught
        mechanically in some classrooms."
        (Lines 11–12)
    (C) "... give students the opportunity
        to try out several graphs and
        solutions quickly ..." (Lines 12–13)
    (D) "... it also comes from a hands-on
        involvement with graphing."
        (Line 18)

    Step 2: Read the question and answers.

    Step 3: Identify the question type. The question asks you to identify an example of bias.

    Step 4: Eliminate incorrect answers. Eliminate (C) and (D). These choices are just descriptions.

Step 5: Scan to find the answer. That leaves choices (A) and (B). (A) is the best choice. The author shows a clear bias against using graphing calculators to learn about graphing and equations. Remember bias means using slanted language to take a stand for or against a particular view or practice. The author uses unproved information and slanted language to support the bias.

Step 6: Choose the answer that is absolutely correct. Choice (A) is absolutely correct.

12. The calculator can't tell the student
     anything about the process of graphing,
     so it is the worst way to learn about
     graphing and equations.

     Is the argument found in the above
     statement valid or invalid?

     (A) Valid
     (B) Invalid

Step 2: Read the question and answers.

Step 3: Identify the question type. We have to identify the passage as valid or invalid.

Step 4: Eliminate incorrect answers. Skip Step 4 for this type of question.

Step 5: Scan to find the answer. The statement tells us that the calculator can't tell the student anything about graphing as the basis for the conclusion that "this . . . is the worst way to learn about graphing and equations." This is a hasty generalization—a conclusion reached with insufficient evidence. The argument is invalid.

Step 6: Choose the answer that is absolutely correct. Choice (B) is the absolutely correct choice.

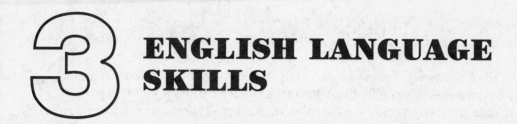

3 ENGLISH LANGUAGE SKILLS

CLAST ENGLISH LANGUAGE SKILLS TEST

Recommended Time: 25 minutes

The CLAST English Language Skills Test consists of 35 multiple-choice questions. There are 15 question types based on the 15 objectives given below. This chapter covers the objectives in the order shown. The number of question types varies, but there are usually 2 or 3 questions of each type on any test. Objective B2 d is often represented by more than 3 questions, while objective B4 c is often represented by just 1 question.

B1 a - Use Words to Convey the Denotative and Connotative Meanings Required by Context
B4 c - Use Proper Pronoun Case Forms
B4 a - Use Standard Verb Forms
B4 f - Avoid Inappropriate Shifts in Tense
B4 b2 - Maintain Agreement Between Pronoun and Antecedent
B4 b1 - Maintain Agreement Between Subject and Verb
B4 e - Use Adjectives and Adverbs Correctly
B4 g - Make Logical Comparisons
B2 a - Place Modifiers Correctly
B5 b - Use Standard Practice for Capitalization and Punctuation
B2 d - Avoid Comma Splices, Fused Sentences and Fragments
B2 c - Use Parallel Expressions for Parallel Ideas
B1 c - Avoid Wordiness
B5 a - Use Standard Practice for Spelling
B2 b - Coordinate and Subordinate Sentence Elements According to their Relative Importance

PASSING THE ENGLISH LANGUAGE SKILLS TEST

You usually must get about 75 percent (26) correct to 80 percent (28) correct to pass the English Language Skills Test. The passing scores vary slightly depending on how all students did on a particular test administration. Approximately 64 percent of all students will pass this test the first time they take it.

REVIEW QUIZ

This English review quiz assesses your knowledge of the English topics included on the CLAST. The quiz also provides an excellent way to refresh your memory about these topics. The first part of the quiz consists of sentences to mark or correct. Make your marks or corrections right on the sentences. This part of the quiz will be more difficult than the CLAST. It is not important to answer all the questions correctly, so don't be concerned if you miss many of them.

The answers are found immediately after the quiz. It's to your advantage not to look until you have completed the quiz. Once you have completed and marked this diagnostic quiz, use the answer check list to decide which sections to study.

PART I—Sentence Correction

> Correct the sentences. Some may not contain errors.

1. Chad was tired after soccer practice. He became a coach for the purpose of helping the college to the soccer finals. During the rein of the former coach, the team had miserable seasons Chad would stay at the job until he could except the first place trophy.

2. Ron and James fathers each sent them to players camp to learn the mysterys of sport.

3. They go to the camp and ridden horses while they were there, and had write letters home.

4. Ron and James called his coach. The operator never answered and they wondered what happened to her.

5. Max and Maxene went to the store and got some groceries.

6. Dad want me to do my homework. My sisters try their best to help me.

> Underline the subject of the sentence.

7. Chad's project, which he showed the teacher, improved his final grade.

> Correct the sentences. Some may not contain errors.

8. Chad was sure correct, the food tastes bad and the singer sang bad but Ryan played really well. Ryan was more happy than Chad who sat closer to the stage than Ryan.

9. The waiter brought food to the table on a large tray. The waiter wanted a job in the suburbs that paid well.

10. Waiting for the food to come, the complaining began.

11. After three weeks in the suburbs, the job was lost.

12. One copy was left only to remind editors of the book.

> Correct the sentence. Some may not contain errors.

13. Ryan hoped his coach, professor Lois Minke, would help him get a tryout with the United States national team. Dr. Minke, a professor of physical education recommended that Ryan read <u>Sports a: Guide to Survival</u>.

14. Chad was satisfied but the players were grumbling. The players wanted to practice less have more free time. The players didn't like their light blue uniforms. The finals began in May 1996. The first game was scheduled for Tuesday May 9 at 1:00 P.M. The time for the game was here the players were on the field. Chad had the essential materials with him player list score book soccer balls and a cup of hope.

15. The coach realized that new selection rules to go into effect in May. She also knew what it would take for Ryan to be selected. Ryan winning every game. But the coach and Ryan had a common goal. To see Ryan on the team.

16. Ryan's parents wanted a success rather than see him fail. They knew he stayed in shape by eating right and exercising daily. Ryan is a person who works hard and has talent.

17. Blaire was getting ready, preparing, to take the examination. She knew that because of the fact that she had prepared would help her immensely. In the final analysis, she was a little concerned about the mathematics test, about mathematics.

18. Blaire had studied the reccommended books and her practice test results had not been disasterous. She was ready to except the final test sceore with all of its impelications.

19. Neither Blaire, or Fannie, Carrie, or Julie, or Ricci was sorry to see the school year end. They all attended the graduation; however, they left the camera at home.

ANSWER CHECKLIST

Review Quiz Part I

The answers are organized by review sections. Study your answers. If you miss any item in a section, check the box and review that section.

❑ *p. 54 B1a*
1. Chad was tired after soccer practice. He became a coach **to help** the college **ascend** to the soccer finals. During the **reign** of the former coach, the team had miserable seasons. Chad would stay at the job until he could **accept** the first place trophy.

❑ *p. 56 B4c*
2. **Ron's** and **James's** fathers each sent them to **players'** camp to learn the **mysteries** of sport.

❑ *p. 58, 61 B4, a,f*
3. They **went** to the camp, **rode** horses while they were there, and had **written** letters home.

❑ *p. 62 B4 b2*
4. Ron and James called **(Ron's, James's, their)** coach. The operator never answered and they wondered what happened to **him or** her.

❑ *p. 65 B4 b1*
5. No error
6. Dad **wants** me to do my homework. My sisters try their best to help me.
7. Chad's **project**, which he showed the teacher, improved his final grade.

❑ *p. 56, 69 B4c, g*
8. Chad was sure**ly** correct, the food tastes bad and the singer sang bad**ly**, but Ryan played really well. Ryan was **happier** than Chad who sat closer to the singer than Ryan **did**.
9. The waiter brought food **on a large tray to the table**. The waiter wanted **a well paying job in the suburbs**.
10. Waiting for the food to come, the **(patrons, diners)** complained. **The (patrons, diners) complained about waiting for the food to come.**
11. After **(he, the waiter)** was in the suburbs for three weeks **(his)** job was lost. **He lost his job after he was in the suburbs for three weeks.**

❑ *p. 71 B2a*
12. Only one copy was left to remind editors of the book.

❑ *p. 73 B5 b*
13. Ryan hoped his coach, **Professor Lois Minke**, would help him get a tryout with the United States National **T**eam. Dr. Minke, a professor of physical education, recommended that Ryan read **Sports: A** Guide to Survival.
14. Chad was satisfied, but the players were grumbling. The players wanted to practice less **and** have more free time. The players didn't like their light blue uniforms. The finals began in May 1996. The first game was scheduled for Tuesday, May 9, at 1:00 P.M. The time for the game was here; the players were on the field. Chad had the essential materials with him: player list, score book, soccer ball**s, (optional)** and a cup of hope.

❏ *p. 78 B2 d*

15. The coach realized that new selection rules **would** go into effect in May. She also knew what it would take for Ryan to be selected. Ryan **would have to win** every game. But the coach and Ryan had a common goal. **They wanted** to see Ryan on the team.

❏ *p. 81 B2 c*

16. Ryan's parents wanted a success rather than **a fail~~ure~~. (wanted success rather than failure**). They knew he stayed in shape by eating right and **by** exercising daily. Ryan is a person who works hard and **who** has talent. (**Ryan is hardworking and talented.**)

❏ *p. 82 B 1c*

17. Blaire was getting ready, ~~preparing,~~ to take the examination. She knew that ~~because of the fact that she had prepared~~ (**her preparation**) would help her immensely. ~~In the final analysis~~ (**Finally**), she was a little concerned about the mathematics test, ~~about mathematics~~.

❏ *p. 84 B5a*

18. Blaire had studie~~s~~(**d**) the recommended books and her practice test results had not been disasterous. She was ready to ~~except~~-(**accept**) the final test score with all of ~~its~~ (**its**) imp~~e~~lications.

❏ *p. 86 B2b*

19. Neither Blaire, **(n)** or Fannie, **(nor)** Carrie, **(n)** or Julie, **(n)** or Ricci was sorry to see the school year end. They all attended the graduation; ~~however~~ (**but**), they left the camera at home.

USE WORDS TO CONVEY THE DENOTATIVE AND CONNOTATIVE MEANINGS REQUIRED BY CONTEXT (B1 a)

TEST TIP:

> You will see a sentence with a word missing and be asked to choose the correct replacement word from three choices.

Context Clues

Many times you can figure out a word from its context. Look at these examples. Synonyms, antonyms, examples, or descriptions may help you figure out the word.

1. The woman's mind wandered as her two friends *prated* on. It really did not bother her though. In all the years she had known them, they had always *babbled* about their lives. It was almost comforting.

2. The wind *abated* in the late afternoon. Things were different yesterday when the wind had *picked up* toward the end of the day.

3. The argument with her boss had been her *Waterloo*. She wondered if the *defeat* suffered by Napoleon *at this famous place* had felt the same.

4. The events swept the politician into a *vortex* of controversy. The politician knew what it meant to be spun around like a toy boat in the *swirl of water* that swept down the bathtub drain.

> Passage 1 gives a synonym for the unknown word. We can tell that *prated* means babbled. *Babbled* is used as a synonym of *prated* in the passage.
>
> Passage 2 gives an antonym for the unknown word. We can tell that *abated* means slowed down or diminished because *picked up* is used as an antonym of *abated*.
>
> Passage 3 gives a description of the unknown word. The description of *Waterloo* tells us that the word means *defeat*.
>
> Passage 4 gives an example of the unknown word. The example of a *swirl of water* going down the bathtub drain gives us a good idea of what a *vortex* is.

Denotation is the dictionary definition or the literal meaning of a word.

Connotation refers to the other meanings of the word, either from its current context, or from the way the word has come to be used over time.

To answer this type of question, read each sentence silently with each of the choices substituted for the missing word. Most frequently, the correct replacement is the word that sounds right as you read.

Practice Questions

> Choose the word or phrase that best fills the blank.

1. Many _____ diseases, including pneumonia and swelling in cuts, are caused by bacteria.
   (A) innocuous
   (B) unfortunate
   (C) infectious

2. Sigmund Freud's views of sexuality had become _____ , and the country entered the sexual revolution.
   (A) well known
   (B) all knowing
   (C) universal

3. After crossing the land bridge near the Bering Strait, groups of Native Americans _____ spread throughout all of North, Central, and South America.
   (A) inclusively
   (B) eventually
   (C) regardless

4. During the early 1500s Cortez and Pizarro opened up Central America to the Spanish who began _____ slaves from Africa.
   (A) importing
   (B) immigrating
   (C) imparting

5. The Stamp Act requiring every legal paper to carry a tax stamp was vehemently _____ and eventually repealed by England.
   (A) denied
   (B) proclaimed
   (C) protested

6. The cognitive domain of Bloom's Taxonomy refers to knowledge, intellectual ability, and the other things _____ with school learning.
   (A) accredited
   (B) associated
   (C) related

7. This decade finds our society beset with _____ problems of crime and violence, alcohol and drug abuse, sex, AIDS, high dropout rates from school, and child abuse.
   (A) unproportioned
   (B) previous
   (C) unprecedented

Answers on page 88.

USE PROPER PRONOUN CASE FORMS (B4 c)

TEST TIP:

> You will see a sentence with three words or phrases underlined and be asked to choose the correct replacement for a pronoun in the wrong case.
>
> This type of question has four answer choices. One of the choices is always "No change is necessary."

Pronoun Cases

Pronouns take three case forms: subjective, objective, and possessive. The personal pronouns *I, he, she, it, we, they, you* refer to an individual or individuals. The relative pronoun *who* refers to these personal pronouns as well as to an individual or individuals. These pronouns change their case form depending on their use in the sentence.

Subjective pronouns I, we, he, it, she, they, who, you

Use the subjective form if the pronoun is, or refers to, the subject of a clause or sentence.

> *He* and *I* studied for the CLAST.
> The proctors for the test were *she* and *I*. [*She* and *I* refer to the subject *proctors*.]
> She is the woman *who* answered every question correctly.
> I don't expect to do as well as *she*. [*She* is the subject for the understood verb *is*.]

Objective pronouns: me, us, him, it, her, them, whom, you

Use the objective form if the pronoun is the object of a verb or preposition.

> Cathy helps both *him* and *me*.
> She wanted *them* to pass.
> I don't know *whom* she helped most.

Possessive pronouns: my, our, his, its, her, their, whose, your

Use the objective form if the pronoun shows possession.

> I recommended they reduce the time they study with *their* friends..
> He was the person *whose* help they relied on.

Practice Questions

1. <u>We</u> need to speak to <u>they</u> about the
     A   B

   changes in <u>their</u> policy.
            C

   (A) us
   (B) them
   (C) there
   (D) No change is necessary.

2. <u>It</u> is impossible for <u>him</u> to please an
    A   B

   audience like <u>she</u>.
           C

   (A) One
   (B) his
   (C) her
   (D) No change is necessary.

3. Religious affiliations have helped <u>there</u>
                               A

   cause maintain <u>its</u> focus during
                 B

   <u>her</u> years in office.
    C

   (A) their
   (B) their
   (C) she
   (D) No change is necessary.

4. <u>She</u> forgetfulness led <u>us</u> to believe that
    A   B

   <u>her</u> marriage was in turmoil.
    C

   (A) Her
   (B) he
   (C) me
   (D) No change is necessary.

5. <u>She</u> went to the performance with <u>him</u>
    A   B

   and <u>I</u>.
      C

   (A) Her
   (B) he
   (C) me
   (D) No change is necessary.

6. <u>Who</u> is responsible for the safety of
    A

   <u>those</u> <u>who</u> travel to foreign nations?
     B   C

   (A) Whom
   (B) they
   (C) whom
   (D) No change is necessary.

Answers on page 88.

USE STANDARD VERB FORMS (B4 a)

TEST TIP:

You will see a sentence with three different words or phrases underlined and be asked to choose the option that corrects the underlined words that are not in standard form.

This type of question has four answer choices. One of the choices is always "No change is necessary."

Verbs must appear in standard form. The review shows how to choose the standard form of a verb.

VERBS

Some verbs are action verbs. Other verbs are linking verbs that link the subject to words that describe it. Here are some examples.

Action Verbs	Linking Verbs
Blaire *runs* down the street.	Blaire *is* tired.
Blaire *told* her story.	The class *was* bored.
The crowd *roared.*	The players *were* inspired.
The old ship *rusted.*	It *had been* a proud ship.

Tense

A verb has three principal tenses: present tense, past tense, and future tense. The present tense shows that the action is happening now. The past tense shows that the action happened in the past. The future tense shows that something will happen. Here are some examples.

Present:	I *enjoy* my time off.
Past:	I *enjoyed* my time off.
Future:	I *will enjoy* my time off.

Present:	I *hate* working late.
Past:	I *hated* working late.
Future:	I *will hate* working late.

Regular and Irregular Verbs

Regular verbs follow the consistent pattern noted previously. However, a number of verbs are irregular. Irregular verbs have their own unique forms for each tense. A partial list of irregular verbs follows. The past participle is usually preceded by *had*, *has*, or *have*.

SOME IRREGULAR VERBS

Present Tense	Past Tense	Past Participle
am, is, are	was, were	been
begin	began	begun
break	broke	broken
bring	brought	brought
catch	caught	caught
choose	chose	chosen
come	came	come
do	did	done
eat	ate	eaten
give	gave	given
go	went	gone
grow	grew	grown
know	knew	known
lie	lay	lain
lay	laid	laid
raise	raised	raised
ride	rode	ridden
see	saw	seen
set	set	set
sit	sat	sat
speak	spoke	spoken
take	took	taken
tear	tore	torn
throw	threw	thrown
write	wrote	written

Practice Questions

1. Most working people <u>would</u> <u>enjoying</u>
                         A   B

   four <u>weeks'</u> vacation last year.
         C

   (A) will
   (B) have enjoyed
   (C) weaks
   (D) No change is necessary.

2. The average ten year old who <u>lives</u> in
                                   A

   the inner city <u>has</u> never <u>go</u> to the
                   B   C

   museum.

   (A) lived
   (B) had
   (C) gone
   (D) No change is necessary.

3. I <u>have talked</u> to my daughter about
        A

   <u>telling</u> the truth countless times
     B

   over the <u>past</u> few weeks.
              C

   (A) had talked
   (B) told
   (C) passed
   (D) No change is necessary.

4. She <u>loves</u> <u>living</u> on her own private
        A   B

   beach <u>in</u> South Florida next summer.
          C

   (A) will love
   (B) having lived
   (C) when
   (D) No change is necessary.

5. Dave <u>hope</u> to <u>receive</u> the <u>most</u> votes
         A   B   C

   in the election.

   (A) hopes
   (B) receiving
   (C) more
   (D) No change is necessary.

6. The cat <u>lies</u> down <u>at</u> the <u>foot</u> of the
            A   B   C

   bed every night.

   (A) lain
   (B) in
   (C) feet
   (D) No change is necessary.

Answers on page 89.

AVOID INAPPROPRIATE SHIFTS IN TENSE (B4 f)

TEST TIP:

You will see a sentence with three different words or phrases underlined and be asked to choose the option that corrects the underlined words that show a tense shift.

This type of question has four answer choices. One of the choices is always "No change is necessary."

The English skills you need for this objective are covered in the previous objective on page 58. However, those question types are different. Examples of the questions for this objective are given below.

Practice Questions

1. The tugboat <u>strains against</u> the ship,
   　　　　　　　　A
   revved up its engines, <u>and was able to</u>
   　　　　　　　　　　　　B
   <u>maneuver</u> the ship into the middle of
   　C
   the channel.
   - (A) strained against
   - (B) and were able
   - (C) maneuvered
   - (D) No change is necessary.

2. After it <u>had snowed</u> steadily for days,
   　　　　　　　A
   the <u>snow plows</u> and snow blowers
   　　　　　　B
   <u>were in need</u> of repairing and
   　C
   reconditioning.
   - (A) had snowed
   - (B) snow plowed
   - (C) was in need
   - (D) No change is necessary.

3. The zoo <u>opens</u> for the day, and
   　　　　　　A
   <u>the children ran</u> to the exhibit
   　　　　B
   <u>that showed</u> the gorillas.
   　　　C
   - (A) opened
   - (B) the children run
   - (C) which had shown
   - (D) No change is necessary.

4. Erik <u>walks</u> three miles every day and
   　　　A
   he <u>rubbed</u> the dirt off his sneakers
   　　　B
   as he <u>went</u>.
   　　　C
   - (A) walked
   - (B) rubs
   - (C) had gone
   - (D) No change is necessary.

5. The taco stand was <u>located</u> in Miami and
                        A

   <u>shared</u> its number one <u>rating</u> with the
     B   C

   fancier taco stand in Lake Placid.

   (A) location in
   (B) shares its
   (C) rates
   (D) No change is necessary.

6. The <u>shower dripped</u> for an hour after
          A

   each person <u>bathed</u> until finally a
                 B

   repairman <u>had been called</u> to fix it.
               C

   (A) shower drips
   (B) baths
   (C) was called
   (D) No change is necessary.

7. The warm spring weather <u>had caused</u>
                             A

   the tulips <u>to shoot up</u> and the
                B

   daffodils <u>to begin</u> to sprout.
               C

   (A) has caused
   (B) shot up
   (C) began to
   (D) No change is necessary.

Answers on page 89.

MAINTAIN AGREEMENT BETWEEN PRONOUN AND ANTECEDENT (B4 b2)

TEST TIP:

You may see a sentence with a portion underlined and be asked to pick the correct replacement if there is faulty agreement. You may also see a sentence with three pronouns underlined and be asked to choose the correct replacement for one of the pronouns.

This type of question has four answer choices. One of the choices is always "No change is necessary."

PRONOUNS

Pronouns take the place of nouns or noun phrases and help avoid constant repetition of the noun or phrase. Here is an example.

> *Blaire* is in law school. *She* studies in *her* room every day.
> [The pronouns *she* and *her* refer to the noun *Blaire.*]

Clear Reference

The pronoun must clearly refer to a particular noun or noun phrase. Here are some examples.

Unclear

Ashley and Blaire took turns feeding *her* cat.
[We can't tell which person *her* refers to.]

Ashley gave *it* to Blaire. [The pronoun *it* refers to a noun that is not stated.]

Clear

Ashley and Blaire took turns feeding Blaire's cat. [A pronoun doesn't work here.]

Ashley got the book and gave it to Blaire. [The pronoun works once the noun is stated.]

Agreement

Each pronoun must agree in number (singular or plural) and gender (male or female) with the noun it refers to. Here are some examples.

Nonagreement in Number

The children played all day, and *she* came in exhausted.
[*Children* is plural, but *she* is singular.]

The child picked up the hat and brought *them* into the house.
[*Child* is singular, but *them* is plural.]

Agreement

The children played all day, and *they* came in exhausted.

The child picked up the hat and brought *it* into the house.

Nonagreement in Gender

The lioness picked up *his* cub. [*Lioness* is female, and *his* is male.]

A child must bring in a doctor's note before she comes to school.
[The child may be a male or female but *she* is female.]

Agreement

The lioness picked up *her* cub.

A child must bring in a doctor's note before *he or she* comes to school.

Practice Questions

1. The teacher was sure that Tom's difficult home life affected <u>his</u> school work.

    (A) their
    (B) her
    (C) him
    (D) No change is necessary.

2. A newspaper columnist <u>promised</u>
                              A
    <u>to print</u> the story about the secret
       B
    negotiations concerning the sports

    stadium in <u>their</u> next column.
                  C

    (A) promise
    (B) printed
    (C) his or her
    (D) No change is necessary.

3. The teacher asked all of <u>her students</u>
                                   A
    to bring in <u>his</u> permission slips
                   B
    <u>to go on</u> the Washington trip.
       C

    (A) whose students
    (B) their
    (C) to go on
    (D) No change is necessary.

4. Marge, the woman <u>whom</u> started the
                        A
    argument, forgot to file the proper

    complaint form with <u>her</u> Senator
                            B
    before <u>she</u> left the office.
              C

    (A) who
    (B) she
    (C) her
    (D) No change is necessary.

5. I am going to visit <u>my</u> aunt so <u>I</u> left a
                           A   B
    message for <u>whoever</u> may need to
                    C
    locate me.

    (A) her
    (B) me
    (C) whomever
    (D) No change is necessary.

6. Small town sheriffs in America, <u>who</u>
                                        A
    were popularized in movies when <u>it</u>
                                        B
    seemed that <u>anyone</u> came from a
                    C
    small town, now face anonymity.

    (A) whom
    (B) they
    (C) everyone
    (D) No change is necessary.

Answers on page 89.

MAINTAIN AGREEMENT BETWEEN SUBJECT AND VERB (B4 b1)

TEST TIP:

You will see a sentence with one or more verbs underlined and be asked to choose the correct replacement for the verb that does not show agreement with the subject.

This type of question has four answer choices. One of the choices is always "No change is necessary."

SUBJECT-VERB AGREEMENT

Singular and Plural

Singular nouns take singular verbs. Plural nouns take plural verbs. Singular verbs usually end in *s*, and plural verbs usually do not. Here are some examples.

Singular: My father wants me home early.
Plural: My parents want me home early.

Singular: Ryan runs a mile each day.
Plural: Ryan and Chad run a mile each day.

Singular: She tries her best to do a good job.
Plural: Liz and Ann try their best to do a good job.

Correctly Identify Subject and Verb

The subject may not be in front of the verb. In fact, the subject may not be anywhere near the verb. Say the subject and the verb to yourself. If it makes sense, you probably have it right.

- Words may come between the subject and the verb.

    Chad's final exam score, which he showed to his mother, improved his final grade.

The verb is *improved*. The word *mother* appears just before improved.

Is this the subject? Say it to yourself. [Mother improved the grade.]

That can't be right. Score must be the subject. Say it to yourself. [Score improved the grade.] That's right. *Score* is the subject, and *improved* is the verb.

    The racer running with a sore arm finished first.

Say it to yourself. [Racer finished first.] *Racer* is the noun, and *finished* is the verb.

It wouldn't make any sense to say the arm finished first.

• The verb may come before the subject.

> Over the river and through the woods romps the merry leprechaun.

Leprechaun is the subject, and *romps* is the verb. [Think: Leprechaun romps.]

> Where are the car keys?

Keys is the subject, and *are* is the verb. [Think: The car keys are where?]

Examples of Subject-Verb Agreement

Words such as *each, neither, everyone, nobody, someone,* and *anyone* are singular pronouns. They always take a singular verb.

> Everyone needs a good laugh now and then.

> Nobody knows more about computers than Bob.

Words that refer to number such as *one-half, any, most,* and *some* can be singular or plural.

> One-fifth of the students were absent. [*Students* is plural.]

> One-fifth of the cake was eaten. [There is only one cake.]

Practice Questions

> Choose the change that makes the
> sentence correct.

1. Throughout the ages, human beings <u>has learned</u> to communicate by nonverbal means.

   (A) learning
   (B) have learned
   (C) has learn
   (D) No change is necessary.

2. All married couples <u>had fought</u> at one time or another during their time together.

   (A) had fight
   (B) have fought
   (C) will fought
   (D) No change is necessary.

3. *Jonathan Livingston Seagull* <u>was</u>
                           A
   a book <u>written</u> <u>to express</u> one
         B   C
   man's quest for freedom.

   (A) were
   (B) writing
   (C) expressing
   (D) No change is necessary.

4. The flower shop <u>is pleasant</u> and <u>possess</u>
                     A   B
   an aroma that <u>welcomes</u> its customers.
                    C

   (A) is pleased
   (B) possesses
   (C) welcomed
   (D) No change is necessary.

5. Office World, the office supply store, <u>claim to be</u> the quintessential supplier of office machines in Florida.

    (A) claiming to be
    (B) claims to be
    (C) has claim to be
    (D) No change is necessary.

6. Charles Monroe III and his family <u>enjoys</u>
                   A
    yachting, swimming, and polo,
    <u>when on holiday</u>, <u>delighting</u> in the
        B   C
    South of France.

    (A) enjoy
    (B) on holiday
    (C) delights
    (D) No change is necessary.

Answers on page 89.

USE ADJECTIVES AND ADVERBS CORRECTLY (B4 e)

TEST TIP:

> You will see a sentence with three adjectives or adverbs underlined and be asked to pick the correct replacement.
>
> This type of question has four answer choices. One of the choices is always "No change is necessary."

ADJECTIVES AND ADVERBS

Adjectives

Adjectives modify nouns and pronouns. Adjectives add detail and clarify nouns and pronouns. Frequently, adjectives come immediately before the nouns or pronouns they are modifying. At other times, the nouns or pronouns come first and are connected directly to the adjectives by linking verbs. Here are some examples.

Direct	With a Linking Verb
That is a *large* dog.	That dog is *large*.
He's an *angry* man.	The man seems *angry*.

Adverbs

Adverbs are often formed by adding *ly* to an adjective. However, many adverbs don't end in *ly* (for example, *always*). Adverbs modify verbs, adjectives, and adverbs. Adverbs can also modify phrases, clauses, and sentences. Here are some examples.

Modify verb:	Ryan *quickly* sought a solution.
Modify adjective:	That is an *exceedingly* large dog.
Modify adverb:	Lisa told her story *quite* truthfully.
Modify sentence:	*Unfortunately*, all good things must end.
Modify phrase:	The instructor arrived *just* in time to start the class.

Avoiding Adjective and Adverb Errors

- Don't use adjectives in place of adverbs.

Correct	Incorrect
Lynne read the book quickly.	Lynne read the book quick.
Stan finished his work easily.	Stan finished the book easy.

- Don't confuse the adjectives *good* and *bad* with the adverbs *well* and *badly*.

Correct	Incorrect
Adverbs	
She wanted to play the piano well.	She wanted to play the piano good.
Bob sang badly.	Bob sang bad.

Adjectives	
The food tastes good.	The food tastes well.
The food tastes bad.	The food tastes badly.

- Don't confuse the adjectives *real* and *sure* with the adverbs *really* and *surely*.

Correct	Incorrect
Chuck played really well.	Chuck played real well.
He was surely correct.	He was sure correct.

Practice Questions

> Identify the correct choice to fix the sentence.

1. The <u>incredible</u> <u>intense</u> seminar held all
        A   B
   the participants in a <u>hypnotic</u> trance.
                  C

   (A) incredibly
   (B) intensify
   (C) hypnosis
   (D) No change is necessary.

2. All <u>tenured</u> professors have been
      A
   stereotyped as being <u>stuffy</u> and
                 B
   overly <u>literary</u>.
        C

   (A) tenure
   (B) stuffed
   (C) literate
   (D) No change is necessary.

Answers on page 89.

3. The <u>retired</u> baseball player haggled
        A
   <u>unexpectedly</u> with the younger child
      B
   over who played <u>good</u>.
              C

   (A) retire
   (B) unexpected
   (C) well
   (D) No change is necessary.

4. <u>Succulent</u> crab, <u>plentiful</u> shrimp, and
     A   B
   meaty lobster are the <u>mainly</u> dishes
               C
   advertised by the Lobster Hut.

   (A) succulently
   (B) plenty
   (C) main
   (D) No change is necessary.

MAKE LOGICAL COMPARISONS (B4 g)

TEST TIP:

You will see three sentences and be asked to identify the sentence that shows a logical comparison.

Questions based on this objective usually ask you to distinguish between the comparative and superlative forms.

Use the comparative form to compare two items.
The comparative form includes happier, younger, older, more tired, and more interesting.

Comparison

Adjectives and adverbs can show comparisons. Avoid clumsy modifiers.

Correct	Incorrect
Jim is more clingy than Ray.	Jim is clingier than Ray.
Ray is taller than Jim.	Ray is more taller than Jim.
Jim is more interesting than Ray.	Jim is interesting than Ray.
Ray is happier than Jim.	Ray is more happy than Jim.

Use the **superlative form** to compare more than two items.
The superlative form includes happiest, youngest, oldest, most tired, and most interesting.

Correct	Incorrect
Bob got the highest test score.	Bob got the higher test score.
Doris is the most tired teacher in Florida.	Doris is the more tired teacher in Florida.
He is their most enthusiastic fan.	He is their enthusiastic fan.

Word comparisons carefully to be sure that the comparison is clear.

Unclear:	Chad lives closer to Ryan than Blaire.
Clear:	Chad lives closer to Ryan than Blaire does.
Clear:	Chad lives closer to Ryan than he does to Blaire.
Unclear:	The bus engine is bigger than a car's.
Clear:	The bus engine is bigger than a car's engine.

Practice Questions

1. Choose the sentence that shows a logical comparison.
    (A) Joe remained the fast runner after the track meet.
    (B) Joe remained the faster runner after the track meet.
    (C) Joe remained the fastest runner after the track meet.

2. Choose the sentence that shows a logical comparison.
    (A) The humerus is the most delicate bone in the arm.
    (B) The humerus is the more delicate bone in the arm.
    (C) The humerus is the delicate bone in the arm.

3. Choose the sentence that shows a logical comparison.
    (A) The small of the two fish gets caught in the filter on a regular basis.
    (B) The smaller of the two fish gets caught in the filter on a regular basis.
    (C) The smallest of the two fish gets caught in the filter on a regular basis.

4. Choose the sentence that shows a logical comparison.
    (A) Carry the light boxes if you are afraid of hurting your back.
    (B) Carry the lighter boxes if you are afraid of hurting your back.
    (C) Carry the lightest boxes if you are afraid of hurting your back.

5. Choose the sentence that shows a
   logical comparison.
   (A) Giovanni chocolate is my most
   favorite treat during exams.
   (B) Giovanni chocolate is my more
   favorite treat during exams.
   (C) Giovanni chocolate is my favorite
   treat during exams.

6. Choose the sentence that shows a
   logical comparison.
   (A) The third aria is the longer song
   of the entire opera.
   (B) The third aria is the long song
   of the entire opera.
   (C) The third aria is the longest song
   of the entire opera.

Answers on page 89.

PLACE MODIFIERS CORRECTLY (B2 a)

TEST TIP:

You will see three sentences, two of which include incorrectly placed modifiers.
You will be asked to choose the sentence with all modifiers placed correctly.

Modifiers must be correctly placed near the words they modify. Questions based
on this objective ask you to choose the sentence without misplaced or dangling
modifiers.

Misplaced and Dangling Modifiers

Modifiers may be words or groups of words. Modifiers change or qualify the meaning of another word or group of words. Modifiers belong near the words they modify. Misplaced modifiers appear to modify words in a way that doesn't make sense.

The modifier in the following sentence is *in a large box*. It doesn't make sense for *in a
large box* to modify *house*. Move the modifier near *pizza* where it belongs.

> Misplaced: Les delivered pizza to the house in a large box.
> Revised: Les delivered pizza in a large box to the house.

The modifier in the next sentence is *paid well. Paid well* can't modify *city*. Move it next to
the job where it belongs.

> Misplaced: Gail wanted the job in the city that paid well.
> Revised: Gail wanted the well-paying job in the city.

Dangling modifiers modify words not present in the sentence. The modifier in the following
sentence is *waiting for the concert to begin*. This modifier describes the audience, but
audience is not mentioned in the sentence. The modifier is left dangling with nothing to
attach itself to.

> Dangling: Waiting for the concert to begin, the chanting started.
> Revised: Waiting for the concert to begin, the audience began chanting.
> Revised: The audience began chanting while waiting for the concert to begin.

The modifier in the next sentence is *after three weeks in the country.* The modifier describes the person, not the license. But the person is not mentioned in the sentence. The modifier is dangling.

> Dangling: After three weeks in the country, the license was revoked.
> Revised: After he was in the country for three weeks, his license was revoked.
> Revised: His license was revoked after he was in the country three weeks.

Practice Questions

> Choose the sentence that expresses the content most clearly and has no structural errors.

1. (A) The weather forecaster said that people living near the shore should be prepared in the event that the storm headed for land.
   (B) In the event that the storm headed for land, the weather forecaster said that people living near the shore should be prepared.
   (C) "People living near the shore should be prepared in the event that the storm headed for land" the weather forecaster said.

2. (A) The players on the national team were supposed, by some of their countrymen, to have almost superhuman ability.
   (B) Some of their countrymen supposed the players on the national team had almost superhuman ability.
   (C) Superhuman ability was said to have had by the national team by some of their countrymen.

3. (A) Judge Conklin had managed to stay popular with the media, even though his demeanor seems to be quite abrasive.
   (B) Even though his demeanor seems quite abrasive, Judge Conklin has managed to stay popular with the media.
   (C) He has managed to stay popular with the media even though Judge Conklin's demeanor seems to be quite abrasive.

4. (A) It would be easier than putting it off for another day and risk experiencing excess stress for the man who knew how to solve the problem now can be easier.
   (B) Rather than risk experiencing excess stress, the man knew that to solve the problem now can be easier than putting it off for another day.
   (C) The man knew that solving the problem now can be easier than putting it off for another day and risk experiencing excess stress.

5. (A) The soccer coach concluded that women soccer players were more aggressive than men who played soccer after years of observation.
   (B) After years of observation, the soccer coach concluded that women soccer players were more aggressive than men who played soccer.
   (C) Women soccer players were more aggressive than men who play soccer, concluded the soccer coach after years of observation.

6. (A) If a person had musical ability then he should try to develop the ability by taking music lessons.
   (B) He should try to develop his musical ability, if he has musical ability, by taking music lessons.
   (C) By taking music lessons, he should try to develop this ability, if he has musical ability.

7. (A) The otherwise grand-sounding, unintelligible speeches to the undergraduate population were what the dean was famous for delivering.
   (B) The dean was famous for delivering grand-sounding, otherwise unintelligible speeches to the undergraduate population.
   (C) The undergraduate population to the dean who is famous for delivering grand-sounding but otherwise unintelligible speeches.

Answers on page 90.

USE STANDARD PRACTICE FOR CAPITALIZATION AND PUNCTUATION (B5 b)

TEST TIP:

You may see a sentence with a portion underlined and be asked to pick the replacement with correct punctuation. You may also see a sentence with three parts underlined and be asked to choose the replacement for the incorrect part.

These questions have four answer choices. One of the answer choices is always "No change is necessary."

CAPITALIZATION

- Capitalize the first word in each sentence.
- Capitalize *I*.
- Capitalize proper nouns. In a title, capitalize proper and common nouns, but not articles or short prepositions. Proper nouns are specific names for people, places, or things.
- Capitalize proper adjectives. Proper adjectives can be formed from some proper nouns.

PROPER NOUNS

Bill Clinton	Taj Mahal
Bob Postman	Thanksgiving
Alabama	July
North America	Wednesday

COMMON NOUNS

president	building
author	fall
state	month
continent	day

PROPER NOUNS AND PROPER ADJECTIVES

Pennsylvania	Pennsylvanian
California	Californian
New York	New Yorker
Italy	Italian

PROPER NOUNS WITH COMMON NOUNS AND ARTICLES

United States of America
the Mississippi River
Lake Michigan

- Capitalize titles before, but not after, proper nouns.

Professor Jeremy Smails	Jeremy Smails, professor of history
President Otto Smart	Otto Smart, president of Limelight Ltd.

Titles, alone, may be capitalized if they indicate a very high rank.

President of the United States

Secretary of State

- Capitalize titles of books except for short articles, prepositions, and conjunctions unless they are the first or last words or follow a colon (:).

How to Prepare for the CLAST

The How to Survive in College Book

Derek: A Study in Perseverance

PUNCTUATION

The Period (.)

Use a period to end every sentence, unless the sentence is a direct question, a strong command, or an interjection.

>You will do well on the CLAST.

The Question Mark (?)

Use a question mark to end every sentence that is a direct question.

>What is the passing score for the CLAST?

The Exclamation Point (!)

Use an exclamation point to end every sentence that is a strong command or interjection. Do not overuse exclamation points.

>Interjection: Pass that test!
>Command: Avalanche, head for cover!

The Comma (,)

The comma may be the most used punctuation mark. This section details a few of these uses. If a clause begins with a conjunction, use a comma before the conjunction. A clause is part of a sentence that could be a sentence itself.

>Incorrect: I was satisfied with the food but John was grumbling.
>Correct: I was satisfied with the food, but John was grumbling.

>Incorrect: Larry was going fishing or he was going to paint his house.
>Correct: Larry was going fishing, or he was going to paint his house.

A clause or a phrase often introduces a sentence. Introductory phrases or clauses should be set off by a comma. If the introductory element is very short, the comma is optional. Here are some examples.

>However, there are other options you may want to consider.

>When the de-icer hit the plane's wing, the ice began to melt.

>To get a driver's license, go to the motor vehicle bureau.

>It doesn't matter what you want, you have to take what you get.

Parenthetical expressions interrupt the flow of a sentence. Set off the parenthetical expression with commas. Do not set off expressions that are essential to understanding the sentence. Here are some examples.

Tom, an old friend, showed up at my house the other day.

I was traveling on a train, in car 8200, on my way to Florida.

John and Ron, who are seniors, went on break to Florida.
[Use a comma. The phrase "who are seniors" is extra information]

All the students who are seniors take an additional course.
[Don't use a comma. The phrase "who are seniors" is essential information.]

Commas are used to set off items in a list or series. Here are some examples.

Jed is interested in computers, surfing, and fishing.
[Notice the comma before the conjunction *and*]

Mario drives a fast, red car.
[The sentence would make sense with *and* in place of the commas.]

Andy hoped for a bright, sunny, balmy day.
[The sentence would make sense with *and* in place of the commas.]

Lucy had a pale green dress.
[The sentence would not make sense with *and*. The word *pale* modifies *green*. Don't use a comma.]

Randy will go to the movies, pick up some groceries, and then go home.
[Notice the comma before *and*.]

Commas are used in other writing. Here are some examples.

Dates

Tuesday, February 8, 1994

July 4, 1776, was the first Independence Day.

School begins on Wednesday, September 6, at 8:00 A.M.

His parents immigrated in October 1936.
[No comma is needed.]

Addresses

Closter, New Jersey 07624

321 Forest Street, Phoenix, Arizona

The distance to Hauppauge, Long Island is 37 miles.

16 Martins Avenue

The Semicolon (;)

Use the semicolon to connect main clauses not connected by a conjunction. Include a semicolon with very long clauses connected by a conjunction. Here are some examples.

> The puck was dropped; the hockey game began.

> The puck was dropped, and the hockey game began.

> The general manager of the hockey team was not sure what should be done about the player who was injured during the game; but he did know that the player's contract stipulated that his pay would continue whether he was able to play or not.

The Colon (:)

Use the colon after a main clause to introduce a list. Here are some examples.

> Liz kept these items in her car: spare tire, jack, flares, and a blanket.

> Liz kept a spare tire, jack, flares, and a blanket in her car.

Practice Questions

> Choose the correct replacement.

1. Dan is deciding which event to compete in. <u>He is a strong swimmer but he is best known for his diving.</u>

   (A) He is a strong swimmer; but, he is best known for his diving.
   (B) He is a strong swimmer, but he is best known for his diving.
   (C) He is a strong swimmer, but, he is best known for his diving.
   (D) No change is necessary.

2. <u>Key West to the best of my knowledge is farther</u> south than any other point in the mainland United States.

   (A) Key West, to the best of my knowledge is farther
   (B) Key West to the best of my knowledge, is farther
   (C) Key West, to the best of my knowledge, is farther
   (D) No change is necessary.

3. David is going on <u>vacation he may not come back</u>.

   (A) vacation, he may not come back
   (B) vacation; he may not come back
   (C) vacation: he may not come back
   (D) No change is necessary.

4. <u>His</u> boat was badly damaged after the
          A
   <u>manufacturers</u> warranty expired
          B
   when <u>its</u> propeller struck a rock.
          C

   (A) His'
   (B) manufacturer's
   (C) its'
   (D) No change is necessary.

5. Kitty and Harry said to their <u>friends</u> <u>"We're just about through studying for</u> <u>the CLAST"</u>.

    (A) friends ",We're just about through studying for the CLAST".

    (B) friends, "We're just about through studying for the CLAST".

    (C) friends, "We're just about through studying for the CLAST."

    (D) No change is necessary.

6. Matthew and Tim were frustrated. <u>They</u> <u>asked the professor for the president's</u> <u>phone number.</u>

    (A) They asked the Professor for the president's phone number.

    (B) They asked the professor for the President's phone number.

    (C) They asked the Professor for the President's phone number.

    (D) No change is necessary.

Answers on page 90.

AVOID COMMA SPLICES, FUSED SENTENCES, AND FRAGMENTS (B2 d)

TEST TIP:

You may see a sentence with a portion underlined and be asked to pick the correct replacement. You may also be shown a sentence with three parts underlined and be asked to choose the correct replacement for one of the parts.

These types of questions have four answer choices. One of the choices is always "No change is necessary."

Most of the questions for this objective feature fragments.

SENTENCE FRAGMENTS

English sentences require a subject and a verb. Fragments are parts of sentences written as though they were sentences. Fragments are writing mistakes that lack a subject, a predicate, or both subject and predicate. Here are some examples.

    Since when.

    To enjoy the summer months.

    Because he isn't working hard.

    If you can fix old cars.

    What the principal wanted to hear.

    Include a subject and/or a verb to rewrite a fragment as a sentence.

Fragment	Sentence
Should be coming up the driveway now.	The *car* should be coming up the driveway now.
Both the lawyer and her client.	Both the lawyer and her client *waited* in court.
Which is my favorite subject.	*I took math,* which is my favorite subject.
If you can play.	If you can play, *you'll improve with practice.*

Verbs such as *to be, to go, winning, starring,* etc., need a main verb.

Fragment	Sentence
The new rules to go into effect in April.	The new rules *will* go into effect in April.
The team winning every game.	The team *was* winning every game.

Often, a fragment is related to a complete sentence. Combine the two to make a single sentence.

Fragment: Reni loved vegetables. *Particularly corn, celery, lettuce, squash, and eggplant.*

Revised: Reni loved vegetables, particularly corn, celery, lettuce, squash, and eggplant.

Fragment: *To see people standing on Mars.* This could happen in the 21st century.

Revised: To see people standing on Mars is one of the things that could happen in the 21st century.

Sometimes short fragments can be used for emphasis. However, you should not use fragments in your essay. Here are some examples.

Stop! Don't take one more step toward that apple pie.

I need some time to myself. *That's why.*

COMMA SPLICES AND FUSED SENTENCES

An *independent clause* is a clause that could be a sentence.
Independent clauses should be joined by a semicolon, or by a comma and a conjunction.

A *comma splice* consists of two independent clauses joined by just a comma.

A *fused (run-on)* sentence consists of two independent clauses not joined in any way.

Correct: The whole family went on vacation; the parents took turns driving.
[Two independent clauses are joined by a semicolon.]

The whole family went on vacation, and the parents took turns driving.
[Two independent clauses are joined by a comma and a conjunction.]

Incorrect: The whole family went on vacation, the parents took turns driving.
[Comma splice. Two independent clauses are joined by just a comma.]

The whole family went on vacation the parents took turns driving.
[Fused sentence. Two independent clauses are not joined at all.]

Practice Questions

| Choose the correct replacement. |
---

1. Many students <u>prefer to</u> gain
              A
   <u>life experience</u> outside of
        B
   <u>college. Such</u> as the Peace Corps
         C
   or travel overseas.

   (A) prefer, to
   (B) life. Experiences
   (C) college such
   (D) No change is necessary.

2. <u>Ashley, the</u> daughter of the
      A
   <u>governor, attends</u> the private
         B
   <u>school called</u> the Hastings
       C
   School for Girls.

   (A) Ashley the
   (B) governor. Attends
   (C) school, called
   (D) No change is necessary.

3. The following stores will be new to the
   Greenburgh <u>Mall: Sterns</u>, Jasper's
   Bar & Grill, and Sports Warehouse.

   (A) Mall, Sterns
   (B) Mall Sterns
   (C) Mall. Sterns
   (D) No change is necessary.

Answers on page 90.

4. The <u>dairy farm is</u> maintained by the
        A
   support of sixty new <u>cows in</u> addition
             B
   there are thirty-five original <u>cows who</u>
              C
   still supply some milk.

   (A) dairy farm, is
   (B) cows. In
   (C) cows. Who
   (D) No change is necessary.

5. Among the many diplomats at the
   <u>party. She</u> was the most polite <u>to the</u>
      A, B   C
   catering staff.

   (A) party she
   (B) party, she
   (C) to. The
   (D) No change is necessary.

6. Roseanna, Lisa, and <u>Jenn, are</u> preparing
               A
   for the coming <u>summer camp</u>
            B
   <u>session with</u> great expectation.
      C

   (A) Jenn are
   (B) summer. Camp
   (C) session, with
   (D) No change is necessary

USE PARALLEL EXPRESSIONS FOR PARALLEL IDEAS (B2 c)

TEST TIP:

You will see three sentences and be asked to choose the sentence using the correct parallel structure.

PARALLELISM

When two or more ideas are connected, use a parallel structure. Parallelism helps the reader follow the passage more clearly. Here are some examples.

Not Parallel:	Toni stayed in shape by eating right and exercising daily.
Parallel:	Toni stayed in shape by eating right and *by* exercising daily.
Not Parallel:	Lisa is a student who works hard and has genuine insight.
Parallel:	Lisa is a student who works hard and *who* has genuine insight.
Not Parallel:	Art had a choice either to clean his room or take out the garbage.
Parallel:	Art had a choice either to clean his room or *to* take out the garbage.
Not Parallel:	Derek wanted a success rather than failing.
Parallel:	Derek wanted a success rather than a failure.
Parallel:	Derek wanted success rather than failure.

Practice Questions

1. Choose the correct parallel form.
   (A) Liz went to the softball game and she saw her favorite team play.
   (B) Ryan is a reliable person and has a bright future.
   (C) Chad has to decide if he is going on vacation or staying home.

2. Choose the correct parallel form.
   (A) The repairman fixed the dishwasher and adjusted the thermostat.
   (B) Bob kept physically fit by jogging and by swimming.
   (C) Catherine wanted a boy rather than a girl.

3. Choose the correct parallel form.
   (A) This picture was taken either in Miami or Lake Placid.
   (B) Jeffrey can either work in the lab or he can work in the emergency room.
   (C) Blaire saw a chance to succeed and grabbed the opportunity.

4. Choose the correct parallel form.
   (A) Ron wanted to be a psychologist or a doctor when he grew up.
   (B) John takes the bus or rides his bike to work.
   (C) Liz can either call Kathy or call Ila.

5. Choose the correct parallel form.
   (A) Ralph stayed to wait for Ginger and call his mother.
   (B) Jack is a person who works hard and has fun.
   (C) Colleen likes to fish and to play cards on vacation.

Answers on page 90.

AVOID WORDINESS (B1 c)

TEST TIP:

You will see a paragraph with five parts underlined and be asked to choose the correct replacement for the part that is wordy or unnecessary.

This type of question has five answer choices.

Avoid words or phrases that are redundant or repetitive.

DICTION

Diction is choosing and using appropriate words. Good diction conveys a thought clearly without unnecessary words. Good diction develops fully over a number of years; however, there are some rules and tips you can follow.

- Do not use slang, colloquialisms, or other non-standard English. One person's slang is another person's confusion. Slang is often regional, and slang meanings change rapidly. We do not give examples of slang here for that very reason. Do not use slang words in your formal writing.

    Colloquialisms are words used frequently in spoken language. This informal use of terms such as *dog tired*, *kids*, and *hanging around*, is not generally accepted in formal writing. Save these informal terms for daily speech and omit or remove them from your writing except as quotations.

    Omit any other non-standard English. Always choose standard English terms that accurately reflect the thought to be conveyed.

- Avoid wordy, redundant, or pretentious writing. Good writing is clear and economical.

    Wordy: I chose my career as a teacher because of its high ideals, the truly self-sacrificing idealism of a career in teaching, and for the purpose of receiving the myriad and cascading recognition that one can receive from the community as a whole and from its constituents.

    Revised: I chose a career in teaching for its high ideals and for community recognition.

Given below is a partial list of wordy phrases and the replacement word.

WORDY PHRASES AND REPLACEMENTS

at the present time	now	because of the fact that	because
for the purpose of	for	in the final analysis	finally
in the event that	if	until such time as	until

Practice Questions

> Choose the lettered portion that is unnecessary in the passage.

1. No goal is more noble —
   A   B
   no feat more revealing — than the
        C
   strikingly brave exploration of space.
        D   E

   (A) No
   (B) more noble
   (C) no feat more revealing
   (D) strikingly brave
   (E) exploration of space

2. As many as a ton of bananas may have
      A   B   C
   spoiled when the ship was stuck
            D
   and delayed in the Panama Canal.
      E

   (A) As many
   (B) a ton of
   (C) may have
   (D) the ship
   (E) and delayed

3. He was concerned about crossing the
         A   B
   bridge, but the officer said that it was
         C   D
   all right to cross and he need not worry.
              E

   (A) was concerned
   (B) crossing
   (C) but the officer
   (D) that
   (E) and he need not worry

4. A professional golfer told the
       A
   novice beginning golfer that
      B
   professional instruction or more
           C
   practice improves most golfer's scores.
           D   E

   (A) professional
   (B) novice
   (C) professional instruction
   (D) improves
   (E) most golfer's scores

5. The soccer player's slight strain from
             A
   the shot on goal that won the game led
              B
   to a pulled muscle that would keep her
       C   D
   from playing the next match.
          E

   (A) slight
   (B) that won the game
   (C) pulled
   (D) would
   (E) playing

6. It was difficult for the farmer
         A
   to comprehend the unhappiness he
       B
   encountered among so many of the rich
          C
   and successful produce buyers in
       D   E
   the city.

   (A) difficult for
   (B) to comprehend
   (C) encountered among
   (D) and successful
   (E) produce

Answers on page 90.

USE STANDARD PRACTICE FOR SPELLING (B5 a)

TEST TIP:

You will see a sentence with three words underlined and be asked to identify the word that is **not** spelled correctly.

This type of question has four answer choices. One of the choices is always "No change is necessary."

English words can be difficult to spell. Spelling rules can be inconsistent and contradictory. Use the information below to help you answer the CLAST questions that follow.

Here is a list of commonly misspelled words.

absence	exaggerate	omission
accommodate	extremely	opinion
across	fascinate	parallel
aggressive	February	possession
all right	foreign	precede
already	government	prejudice
argument	grammar	prevalent
armies	guarantee	primitive
basically	harass	privilege
believe	height	recommend
benefited	hindrance	referring
calendar	illiterate	reminisce
category	infinite	rhythm
cemetery	interfere	ridiculous
certain	jealousy	seize
column	judgment	separate
condemn	laboratory	sergeant
conscious	leaped	shield
controversial	leisurely	succeed
descendant	length	technique
desperate	license	thorough
dining	maneuver	unnecessary
disastrous	miniature	vacuum
dries	necessary	vengeance
embarrass	noticeable	villain
emphasize	occasion	Wednesday
entirely	occurred	weird
environment	occurrence	yield

Homonyms

Homonyms are words that sound alike but do not have the same meaning. These words can be confusing and you may use the incorrect spelling of a word. If words are homonyms, be sure you choose the correct spelling for the meaning you intend.

HOMONYMS

accept (receive)	ascent (rise)
except (other than)	assent (agreement)
board (wood)	fair (average)
bored (uninterested)	fare (a charge)
led (guided)	lessen (make less)
lead (metal)	lesson (learning experience)
past (gone before)	peace (no war)
passed (moved by)	piece (portion)
rain (precipitation)	to (toward)
reign (rule)	too (also)
rein (animal strap)	two (a number)
their (possessive pronoun)	its (shows possession)
there (location)	it's (it is)
they're (they are)	

Practice Questions

> Select the word that is spelled incorrectly in each sentence.

1. The <u>labratory</u> was <u>sterile</u> and was
         A   B
    highly <u>regarded</u> by those in the industry.
         C

    (A) laboratory
    (B) sterrile
    (C) reguarded
    (D) No change is necessary.

2. The <u>arrangements</u> for the funeral <u>rites</u>
            A   B
    were made by the <u>mortican</u>.
                    C

    (A) arangements
    (B) rights
    (C) mortician
    (D) No change is necessary.

3. <u>Weather</u> conditions have a controlling
       A
    <u>affect</u> on air <u>traffic</u>.
       B   C

    (A) Whether
    (B) effect
    (C) trafic
    (D) No change is necessary.

4. Gold <u>remains</u> among the most
           A

<u>valueable</u> <u>commodities</u> in the stock
  B   C

market.

  (A) remanes
  (B) valuable
  (C) comodity
  (D) No change is necessary.

5. The guest <u>speaker</u> was the
           A

<u>renowned</u> <u>orator</u> F. Leonard Breeland.
  B   C

  (A) speaker
  (B) reknowned
  (C) orater
  (D) No change is necesary.

Answers on page 90.

COORDINATE AND SUBORDINATE SENTENCE ELEMENTS ACCORDING TO THEIR RELATIVE IMPORTANCE (B2 b)

TEST TIP:

You will see a passage with a sentence underlined. You will be asked to choose the correctly coordinated sentence.

This type of question has four answer choices. The sentence as it appears in the passage is always one of the choices.

Coordination and Subordination

Coordinate ideas are thoughts that have equal importance. Use the conjunctions *and, but, nor, or, for, so,* and *yet* and the adverbs *however, moreover,* and *therefore* to coordinate words, phrases, and clauses. Using parallel construction (see page 81) also coordinates sentence elements.

Correct: The CLAST has four parts *and* it is given three times a year.
[Each of these facts about the CLAST is equally important.]

The mathematics part of the CLAST is most difficult; *however,* you can increase your chances of passing.
[The adverb *however* is used to coordinate these equally important elements.]

These conjunctive pairs also coordinate sentence elements: *either-or, neither-nor, not only-but also.* Words in these pairs should not be mixed.

Neither Joel *nor* his brother is going to the beach this weekend.
The picnickers come back to the picnic table *not only* when they are hungry *but also* when they are thirsty.

Coordinate related ideas that appear in separate, simple sentences.

Incorrect: The weather was warm. They did not go swimming.

Correct: The weather was warm; *however*, they did not go swimming.

[The adverb *however* is the correct choice to coordinate these elements.]

Incorrect: The natural beauty of Florida includes the Everglades. The ocean is another of Florida's natural beauties.

Correct: Florida's natural beauty includes the Everglades *and* the ocean.

[The conjunction *and* correctly coordinates these sentence elements.]

Provide enough information to sensibly connect coordinated elements.

Incorrect: The manatee was found in a river and had to be treated for deep cuts.

Correct: The manatee found in the river had been cut by a boat propeller and had to be treated for deep cuts.

(The incorrect sentence does not provide enough information to coordinate the sentence elements. Why did the manatee have to be treated for deep cuts? The correct sentence corrects this problem.)

Subordinate ideas of lesser importance to those of greater importance. Use the conjunctions *although, because, if, when, where,* and *while* or the pronouns *who, which,* and *that* to introduce subordinate ideas.

The crew worked to clean up the oil spill, *while* a small crowd watched from shore.

[The conjunction *while* subordinates the watching crowd to the crew cleaning up the oil spill.]

Because the school bus was late, she missed early morning practice.

[The conjunction *because* subordinates the missed practice to the late arrival of the school bus.]

That professor is the one *who* wrote the CLAST book.

[The pronoun *who* introduces and subordinates "wrote the CLAST book."]

Practice Questions

As a child he read the Hardy Boys *series of books and was in awe of the author Franklin Dixon. As an adult, he read a book titled* Ghost of the Hardy Boys, *and revealed there was no Franklin Dixon. Ghost writers* had authored the books. The authors were apparently working for a large publishing syndicate.

1. Choose the correct coordinating sentence.
   (A) As a child he read the *Hardy Boys* series of books and was in awe of the author Franklin Dixon.
   (B) As a child he read the *Hardy Boys* series of books but was in awe of the author Franklin Dixon.
   (C) As a child he read the *Hardy Boys* series of books; however, was in awe of the author Franklin Dixon.
   (D) As a child he read the *Hardy Boys* series of books but was also in awe of the author Franklin Dixon.

2. Choose the correct coordinating sentence.
   (A) As an adult, he read a book titled *Ghost of the Hardy Boys*, and revealed there was no Franklin Dixon.
   (B) As an adult, he read a book titled *Ghost of the Hardy Boys*; however, there was no Franklin Dixon.
   (C) As an adult, he read a book titled *Ghost of the Hardy Boys*, which revealed there was no Franklin Dixon.
   (D) As an adult he read a book titled *Ghost of the Hardy Boys*, yet it revealed there was no Franklin Dixon.

The Iroquois nation consisted of five main tribes—Cayuga, Mohawk, Oneida, Onondaga, and Seneca. Called the Five Nations or the League of Five Nations, these tribes occupied much of New York State. Since the tribes were arranged from east to west, the region they occupied was called the long house of the Iroquois.

The Iroquois economy was based mainly on agriculture. *The main crop was corn, but they also grew pumpkins, beans, and fruit.* The Iroquois used wampum (hollow beads) for money, and records were woven into wampum belts.

3. Choose the correct coordinating sentence.
   (A) The main crop was corn, but they also grew pumpkins, beans, and fruit.
   (B) The main crop was corn, but, however, they grew pumpkins, beans, and fruit.
   (C) Either the main crop was corn or they grew pumpkins.
   (D) Not only did they grow corn, but they also grew pumpkins, beans, and fruit.

Answers on page 90.

ENGLISH LANGUAGE SKILLS PRACTICE EXPLAINED ANSWERS

B1 a page 54

1. **C** *Infectious* means a disease caused by bacteria. While the disease may be unfortunate the context of the sentence calls for a word that means *caused by bacteria.*
2. **A** *Well known* means known by many people. *Universal* means known everywhere, which does not fit the context of this sentence.
3. **B** *Eventually* means over a period of time. The other words do not make sense in this context.
4. **A** *Importing* means to bring in, which fits the context of this sentence.
5. **C** The act could only be *protested* in this context. It was not denied and it does not make sense to say that an act was *vehemently* denied.
6. **B** *Associated* means having to do with, and it is the only word that makes sense in this context.
7. **C** *Unprecedented* means more than ever before. *Previous* does not make sense because it means before this time.

B4 c page 56

1. **B** This word is the object of the verb *speak*. The objective case is the correct choice.
2. **C** *Her* is the correct pronoun form. This word is an object.
3. **A** *Their* is the correct possessive form of this pronoun.
4. **A** *Her* is the correct possessive form and tells us whose forgetfulness it is.
5. **C** *Me* is the correct objective form of this pronoun.
6. **D** All the pronouns are correct. Choice C is correct because it is the subject of the clause *who travel to foreign nations.*

B4 a page 58
1. **B** The past participle *have enjoyed* is correct.
2. **C** The past participle *gone* is correct. The full form of the verb is *has gone*. The word *never* is an adverb that modifies gone.
3. **D** All verbs have the correct form.
4. **A** The future tense *will love* is correct. The sentence talks about next summer.
5. **A** The present tense *hopes* is correct. Dave is a singular noun and requires a singular verb.
6. **D** All verbs are in the correct form.

B4 f page 61
1. **A** This past tense *strained* agrees with the other verbs.
2. **D** Each verb has the correct tense.
3. **A** The past tense *opened* agrees with the other verbs.
4. **A** The past tense *walked* agrees with the other verbs.
5. **D** Each verb has the correct tense.
6. **C** The past tense *called* agrees with the other verbs.
7. **A** The present tense *has caused* agrees with the other verbs.

B4 b2 page 62
1. **D** No change, because the pronoun *his* agrees with the antecedent *Tom*.
2. **C** *His or her* agrees with the antecedent *columnist*. We know there is one columnist but we do not know the sex of the columnist.
3. **B** *Their* agrees with the antecedent.
4. **A** *Who* correctly shows the subjective case.
5. **D** All the pronouns are correct.
6. **C** *Everyone* is correct.

B4 b1 page 65
1. **B** *Have learned* is the present plural verb.
2. **B** *Have fought* is the present plural verb.
3. **D** No change is necessary.
4. **B** *Flower shop* is singular and takes the singular verb *possesses*.
5. **B** *Office World* is singular and takes the singular verb *claims*.
6. **A** The subject is plural and takes the plural verb *enjoy*.

B4 e page 67
1. **A** The adverb *incredibly* modifies the adjective *intense*.
2. **D** There are no errors.
3. **C** The adverb *well* is correct.
4. **C** The adjective *main* is correct.

B4 g page 69
1. **C** The superlative form is used because it is assumed that more than two people are being compared.
2. **A** The superlative is used to compare more than two items.
3. **B** The comparative is used to compare two fish.
4. **C** Use the superlative form to compare more than two boxes.
5. **C** Neither the comparative nor superlative form is used. This form describes a noun or pronoun without comparing it to anything else.
6. **C** Use the superlative form because we know that there are more than two arias.

B2 a page 71
1. **A** In choices B and C we can't tell what the weather forecaster was saying.
2. **A** In choices B and C we can't tell who has superhuman ability.
3. **B** In A and C we can't tell who his and he, respectively, refer to.
4. **C** In A and B the modifiers are confused or dangling.
5. **B** Both B and C place the modifier near the words they modify, but choice C shows a dangling modifier.
6. **A** Both B and C have misplaced modifiers.
7. **B** Both A and C have dangling or misplaced modifiers.

B5 b page 73
1. **B** A comma is used before a conjunction that joins these two independent clauses.
An independent clause can stand on its own as a sentence
2. **C** A comma is needed on each side of words that interrupt the flow of the sentence.
3. **B** A semicolon is used to join two independent clauses when there is no conjunction joining them.
4. **B** Use the apostrophe before the *s* to show possession. The word its shows possession without the apostrophe.
5. **C** Generally speaking, punctuation before a quote goes outside the quotation marks, while punctuation following a quote goes inside the quotation marks.
6. **D** No change is necessary. Words such as *professor* and *president* are capitalized only when they appear as a title.

B2 d page 78
1. **C** *Such as the Peace* ... is not a sentence.
2. **D** All the punctuation is correct.
3. **D** The colon is the correct way to introduce the list of stores.
4. **B** The original sentence is a fused or run-on sentence.
5. **B** The first "sentence" is actually a phrase. There is no verb.
6. **A** The comma is unnecessary.

B2 c page 81
1. **A** The pronoun *she* substitutes for Liz and creates a parallel form.
2. **B** The word *by* is used twice to create a parallel form.
3. **B** The pronoun *he* substitutes for Jeffrey and creates a parallel form.
4. **C** The word *call* used twice creates a parallel form.
5. **B** The rhythm of *works hard/has fun* reveals the parallel form.

B1 c page 82
1. **D** The word *strikingly* is unnecessary.
2. **E** It is enough to know that the ship is stuck. The words *and delayed* are redundant.
3. **E** The phrase *and he need not worry* is redundant.
4. **B** *Novice* and *beginning* mean the same thing. *Novice* is redundant.
5. **B** This information has nothing to do with her ability to play the next match.
6. **D** The words *and successful* are redundant.

B5 a page 84
1. **A** *Laboratory* is the correct spelling.
2. **D** No change is necessary.
3. **B** For this meaning, the correct spelling is *effect*.
4. **B** *Valuable* is the correct spelling.
5. **A** *Speaker* is the correct spelling.

B2 b page 86
1. **A** The conjunction *and* coordinates the two clauses.
2. **C** The pronoun *which* introduces and subordinates the second clause in the sentence.
3. **A** The word pair *not only but ... also* coordinates each clause in the sentence.

STRATEGIES FOR PASSING THE ENGLISH LANGUAGE SKILLS TEST

The English Skills test consists primarily of passages followed by sentences from the passages to correct. Follow these simple strategies to pass the English Skills test.

The Test Questions Will Be Like the Questions in This Book

The test questions will be familiar. Relax and answer them as you learned to do in this book. Each question will be based on one of the fifteen English objectives.

Don't Read the Passages

Reading the passages before the questions will not help you. In fact, it just wastes time. Go directly to the questions, then refer to the passage.

Remember to Fill in the Correct Circle

Concentrate on filling in the correct circle. If you get the right answer but fill in the wrong circle, the machine will mark it wrong. Try to follow this strategy:

Write the letter for your answer big in the test booklet next to the number of the problem. If you change your mind about an answer, cross out the first letter and write the new one. At the end of each set of questions, transfer all the answers at once from the test booklet to the answer sheet.

Save the Hard Questions for Last

You're not supposed to get all the questions correct and some of them will be too difficult for you. Work through the questions and answer the easy ones. Pass by the other ones. Work on these questions the second time through. If a question seems *really* hard, circle the question number in the test booklet. Save these questions for the very end.

Eliminate the Incorrect Answers

If you can't figure out which answer is correct, then decide which answers *can't* be correct and cross them off in the test booklet. Only one left? That's the correct answer.

Guess, Guess, Guess

If there are still two or more answers left, then guess. Guess the answer from those remaining. *Never* leave any item blank. There is no penalty for guessing.

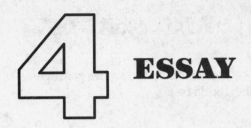

ESSAY

| CLAST ESSAY TEST |

Time: 60 minutes

You will write an essay on one of two topics presented on the test. Your essay is scored holistically by two raters using the six-point scale described on page 97. Your final score is the sum of the raters' score. Holistic grading means the raters' scoring is based on their informed sense about your writing and not on a detailed analysis of the essay. *A total score of 6* is passing for the essay.

Raters use the objectives for the English Language Skills Test as a basis for their rating. However, you should base your writing on the following key elements.

Introduction
Begin the essay with an introduction to orient the reader to the topic.

Thesis Statement
Write a thesis statement early in the essay that clearly states the main idea of the entire essay.

Paragraphs
Topic Sentence Begin each paragraph with a clear topic sentence.
Thesis Support Use each paragraph to support the thesis statement.
Details Provide details, examples, and arguments to support the topic sentence.
Relevant Present material that is relevant to the thesis and the topic sentence.

Sentences
Grammar, Punctuation, Spelling Edit sentences to conform with standard usage.
Avoid Passive Construction Write actively and avoid the passive voice.

Conclusion
End the essay with a conclusion that briefly summarizes the main points in the essay.

PASSING THE ESSAY TEST

In practice, raters classify essays as top third (5–6), middle third (3–4) and lower third (1–2). Then the raters assign one of the two scores in that third. Your goal is to write an essay that is guaranteed to fall into the middle third for a potential score of 6, 7, or 8. If you can write an essay that falls into the upper third, that's great. Approximately 83 percent of all students pass this test the first time they take it.

Using This Section

This section will show you how to write a passing essay. Complete the English Language Skills section before reading this section. Follow the Steps for Writing a Passing Essay on the following pages.

STEPS FOR WRITING A PASSING ESSAY

Follow these steps to write a passing essay. You have one hour to complete all the steps. Manage your time wisely.

1. **Choose the topic.** (1 minute)
   The CLAST gives you two essay topics. Choose the topic you know something about or are most interested in.

2. **Understand the topic.** (1 minute)
   Each topic provides a subject and then describes the subject in more detail. Read the topic carefully to ensure that you understand each of these parts.

3. **Choose your thesis statement. Write it down.** (3 minutes)
   Readers expect you to have one clear main point of view about the topic. Choose yours; make sure it addresses the entire topic, and stick to it.

4. **Write an outline.** (5 minutes)
   Write a brief outline summarizing the following essay elements.

   • Thesis statement

   • Introduction

   • Topic sentence and details for each paragraph

   • Conclusion

Using this time to plan your essay. The outline will not be graded.

5. **Write the essay.** (30 minutes)
   Essays scoring 3 or higher typically have five paragraphs totaling 300–600 words. Writing an essay this long does not guarantee a passing score, but most passing essays are about this long. Use this time to write well.

6. **Proofread and edit.** (10 minutes)
   Review your essay and correct any errors in usage, spelling, or punctuation. *The readers understand that your essay is a first draft and they expect to see corrections and cross-outs. Do not attempt to copy your essay; you will not have time.*

APPLYING THE STEPS

Let's see how to apply these steps for a particular topic. Remember, for any topic, there are many different thesis statements and essays that would receive a passing score.

TOPIC: A machine that helps people

1. **Choose the topic.** (1 minute)
   This topic has been prechosen for the purposes of this activity.

2. **Understand the topic.** (1 minute)
   Subject: machine.
   Description: that helps people

   A complete response to the topic is an essay about a machine that helps people. Your essay will discuss one machine that helps people. There are many machines to choose from. An incomplete response will significantly lower your score.

3. **Choose a thesis statement. Write it down.** (3 minutes)
   This is an important step that sets the stage for your entire essay. Work through this section actively.
       Write down the names of several machines that help people. There is no one correct answer, so it does not have to be an exhaustive list.

   Computer
   Dialysis machine
   Escalator
   Car (may not be a machine)
   Heart-lung machine
   Fax machine

Add your own machines to this list.

_____

_____

_____

_____

_____

I'll choose *heart-lung machines*.

Now I write how, what, and why, heart-lung machines help people.

    How: Circulate blood in place of the heart.
    What: Replaces the heart during heart surgery.
    Why: The heart is unable to pump blood when it is being operated on.

Write your choice from the lists of machines: _____

Write the how, what, and why of the way in which the machine you chose helps people.
    How: _____
    What: _____
    Why: _____

My thesis statement is:

> Heart-lung machines are machines that help people by taking the place of the heart during heart surgery.
>
> [The thesis statement identifies the heart-lung machine as a machine that helps people and explains the basis for my choice of the heart-lung machine. Both parts are needed for an effective thesis statement.]

Write your thesis statement:_____

4. **Write an outline.** (5 minutes)

   - Introduction including the thesis statement

   - A heart-lung machine saves lives.
     [People would die if the machines were not available.]

   - The machine circulates and filters blood during operations.
     [Special membranes filter the blood, removing impurities.]

   - The heart can literally stop while the heart-lung machine is in use.
     [Doctors have to restart the heart.]

   - Conclusion

   Note that my outline consists of an introduction, conclusion, and topic sentences, along with supporting details for three paragraphs.

Write an outline for your essay.

_____
_____
_____
_____
_____

5. **Write the essay.** (30 minutes)
   Use a separate sheet of paper. Write an essay on my topic: <u>heart lung machines</u>. Don't forget to proofread. Compare this essay to the sample essays on pages 98–101. Rate your essay 1–6. Use the essay scoring scale on page 97.

At a later time, write an essay on your topic. Show both essays to an English professor or an English teacher. Ask them to rate your essays 1–6. They should base the rating on the scoring scale and the sample essays.

Need more help? Keep writing essays until you can consistently write a middle third essay. Go to the college's tutoring center for additional help.

SCORING OBJECTIVES USED BY CLAST ESSAY RATERS

☐ 1. selects a subject that lends itself to development;

☐ 2. determines the purpose and the audience for writing;

☐ 3. limits the subject to a topic that can be developed within the requirements of time, purpose, and audience;

☐ 4. formulates a thesis or statement of main idea that focuses the essay;

☐ 5. Develops the thesis or main idea statement by:
    ☐ a. providing adequate support that shows the ability to distinguish between generalized and specific evidence;
    ☐ b. arranging the ideas and supporting details in a logical pattern appropriate to the purpose and focus;
    ☐ c. writing unified prose in which all supporting material is relevant to the thesis or main idea statement; and
    ☐ d. writing coherent prose and providing effective transitional devices that clearly reflect the organizational pattern and the relationships of the parts.

☐ 6. Demonstrates effective word choice by:
    ☐ *a. using words that convey the denotative and connotative meanings required by context;
    ☐ b. avoiding inappropriate use of slang, jargon, clichés, and pretentious expressions; and
    ☐ *c. avoiding wordiness.

☐ 7. Employs conventional sentence structure by:
    ☐ *a. placing modifiers correctly;
    ☐ *b. coordinating and subordinating sentence elements according to their relative importance;
    ☐ *c. using parallel expressions for parallel ideas; and
    ☐ *d. avoiding fragments, comma splices, and fused sentences.

☐ 8. Employs effective sentence structure by:
    ☐ a. using a variety of sentence patterns, and
    ☐ b. avoiding overuse of passive constructions;

☐ 9. Observes the conventions of standard American English grammar and usage by:
    ☐ *a. using standard verb forms;
    ☐ *b. maintaining agreement between subject and verb, pronoun and antecedent;
    ☐ *c. avoiding inappropriate shifts in tense;
    ☐ *d. using proper case forms;
    ☐ e. maintaining a consistent point of view;
    ☐ *f. using adjectives and adverbs correctly; and
    ☐ *g. making logical comparisons.

☐ *10. Uses standard practice for spelling, punctuation, and capitalization.

☐ 11. Revises, edits, and proofreads units of discourse to ensure clarity, consistency, and conformity to the conventions of standard written American English.

* covered in the English Language Skills section

ESSAY SCORING SCALE

The essay subtest is scored independently by two evaluators, each of whom assigns the composition a score on a scale of 1 to 6. The scores are then combined for a total score of from 2 to 12, which is reported to the student. Papers judged to be off topic are assigned an OT instead of a numerical score. Below are the scoring criteria for the essay subtest according to the 6-point scale.

Score of 1   The paper generally presents a thesis that is vaguely worded or weakly asserted. Support, if any, tends to be rambling and/or superficial. The writer uses language that often becomes tangled, incoherent, and thus confusing. Errors in sentence structure, usage, and mechanics occur frequently.

Score of 2   The paper usually presents a thesis. The writer provides support that tends to be sketchy and/or illogical. Sentence structure may be simplistic and disjointed. Errors in sentence structure, usage, and mechanics frequently interfere with the writer's ability to communicate the purpose.

Score of 3   The paper presents a thesis and often suggests a plan of development, which is usually carried out. The writer provides support that tends toward generalized statements or a listing. In general, the support in a 3 paper is neither sufficient nor clear enough to be convincing. Sentence structure tends to be pedestrian and often repetitious. Errors in sentence structure, usage, and mechanics sometimes interfere with the writer's ability to communicate the purpose.

Score of 4   The paper presents a thesis and often suggests a plan of development, which is usually carried out. The writer provides enough supporting detail to accomplish the purpose of the paper. The writer makes competent use of language and sometimes varies the sentence structure. Occasional errors in sentence structure, usage, and mechanics do not interfere with the writer's ability to communicate the purpose.

Score of 5   The paper presents or implies a thesis and provides convincing, specific support. The writer's ideas are usually fresh, mature, and extensively developed. The writer demonstrates a command of language and uses a variety of structures. Control of sentence structure, usage, and mechanics, despite an occasional flaw, contributes to the writer's ability to communicate the purpose.

Score of 6   The paper presents or implies a thesis that is developed with noticeable coherence. The writer's ideas are usually substantive, sophisticated, and carefully elaborated. The writer's choice of language and structure is precise and purposeful, often to the point of being polished. Control of sentence structure, usage, and mechanics, despite an occasional flaw, contributes to the writer's ability to communicate the purpose.

SAMPLE ESSAYS

ESSAY 1

Heart-lung machines are a medical miracle. Heart-lung machines are used in hospitals all over the country. Doctors rely on this machine during surgery. Heart-lung machines keep people alive during surgery and they use them to do open heart surgery. Lots of people can thank the heart-lung machine for keeping them alive. Some people say that there are too many bypass surgeries done every year and this may cause more problems than it fixes. However lots of people would die without the machine. It is a good thing that the heart-lung machine was invented.

Likely Score: Lower third—1
Discussion: This essay does not develop any theme or idea. It is incomplete. The essay is relatively free of grammatical errors. However, the lack of effort and development assures this essay and any like it the lowest grade. Any essay this short will never receive a passing evaluation.

ESSAY 2

Heart-lung machines are use in hospital all over the world. They get use every day. People are hook up to them when they are having surgry like if they are in open heart surgery.

I will now present one of way heart lung-machines are use. Once we did't have heart-lung machines to help a doctor. When the machine was invent we see lots of changes in surgry that a doctor can do. The doctor can oprate during the person heart not work. My granmothr went to the hospital for have surgry and they use the machine. Where she would have been without the machine.

And the machine keep blood move through the body. The doctor can take their time to fix a person heart while they are laying their on the operating room. I know someone who work in a hospital and they said don't know how it was possible befour the machine.

Last, that machine clean a bodies blood as it foes through. The blood won't poison the person who blood it is. But it wood be better if the body could clean it's own blood. A body is better than a machine.

I did tell about how the machine work and what it did. The machine can save a lifes.

Likely Score: Lower third — 2
Discussion: This essay does present a thesis and provides some details and explanations to support the thesis. However, there are many errors in standard English, spelling, and structure, which relegate this essay to the lower third. Elimination of a number of errors might raise this essay to the middle third. Note that many of these changes could have been accomplished during proofreading.

ESSAY 3

Heart lung machines are a medical miracle. They are used in hospitals all over the world. Heart lung machines are used during open heart surgery to circulate a patients blood and clean the blood. These machines can save lots of lives.

Heart-lung machines have made open heart surgery possible. Before they were invented, many people died because of disaese or during surgery. Surgery would not have been possible before then. And many people are alive today because of them. Besides surgery can now go on for hours. Sometimes the surgry can last as long as 12 hours. The heart lung machine makes things possible and saves lives.

Heart-lung machines circulate blood through the body. It pumps like a heart. The heart can stop and the heart lung machine will pump instead. Then the blood moves through the body just like the heart was pumping. So the blood gets to all the viens. It is unbelievable how the heart-lung machine can work and to keep people from dying.

The heart-lung machine can clean a persons blood. All the bad stuff gets taken out of the blood before it goes back into the body. That way the body won't get poison. I know of someone who had their blood cleaned by the machine while they were operated on. The person was unconscious. The doctor fixed his heart. Because the machine was going the persons heart was stopped. The doctor had to start it up again. It was pretty scary to think about that happening to a person. But the machine took all the bad stuff out of the blood and the person lived.

To conclude, I believe that the heart lung machine is great for people who need open heart surgery. It pumps and cleans their blood too. They are a medical miracle.

Likely Score: Middle third—3 or 4

Discussion: This essay has a thesis and ample examples and details to support the thesis. The English grammar and usage are essentially correct, although there are some errors. You should set this essay as your minimum standard. You should not write an essay any shorter or with any less thesis support.

ESSAY 4

Every day the heart-lung machine saves someone's life. Each day we walk by someone who is alive because of a heart-lung machine. Each day in hospitals throughout the world, skilled surgeons perform difficult surgery with the aid of a heart-lung machine. Some day, we may be kept alive by a heart-lung machine. The heart-lung machine is a wonderful machine that makes open-heart surgery possible by pumping and cleaning a person's blood. Surgeons use the machine during open heart surgery.

The heart-lung machine makes open-heart surgery possible. Open-heart surgery means the doctor is operating on the inside of the heart. In order to operate on the inside of a heart, the flow of blood through the heart must be stopped. But without blood flow, the patient will die. Researchers worked for decades to find a way to keep a person alive while the heart was stopped. Many of their early attempts failed; however, during this century the researchers and inventors were successful. They named their invention the heart-lung machine. The first heart-lung machines were probably very primitive, but to-day's machines are very sophisticated.

The heart-lung machine circulates blood while the heart is not pumping. The machine is hooked up to a person's circulatory system and acts just like a heart. The blood is taken from the body into one side of the machine and pumped back into the body through the other side of the machine. Blood returning to the heart is taken into the machine. The blood pumped out travels to every part of the body. The heart-lung machine helps the patient by replacing blood while the heart is stopped during open-heart surgery.

However, just pumping blood is not enough. As blood passes through a person's body, the body takes oxygen stored in the blood. Blood starts through the body full of oxygen and returns from the body without much oxygen. Normally, the lungs would take in oxygen and place that oxygen in the blood. But since the person's heart is stopped, the lungs are not working. The heart-lung machine does the lung's work and places oxygen in the blood as the blood passes through the machine.

The heart-lung machine makes open-heart surgery possible. The machine circulates and oxygenates a person's blood while their heart is stopped. Without the machine, many people would die from heart disease or would die during surgery. The heart-lung machine is a machine that helps people by keeping them alive and holds the promise for even more amazing machines to come.

Likely Score: Upper third—5 or perhaps 6.

Discussion: This essay is about the best one might expect in an hour's writing. The thesis is well developed and well supported by examples and details. You will not have to write an essay of this quality to pass the CLAST.

HANDWRITTEN ESSAY

This is what Essay 3 looked like in handwritten form. This is the essay that the raters would actually see. Note the editorial changes that the student has made during writing and proof-reading. The raters expect to see these changes and marks.

Review the essay. Make further editorial changes to improve the quality of the essay.

Heart lung machines are a ~~medcine~~ _medical_ miracle. They are used in hospitals all over the world. Heart lung machines are used during open heart surgery to circulate a patients blood and clean the blood. These machines can save lots of ~~lifes~~ _lives_.

Heart-lung machines have made open heart surgery possible. Before they were invented, many people died because of disease or during surgery. Surgery would not have been ~~impossible~~ before then. And many people are alive ~~here~~ today because of them. Besides surgery can now go on for hours. Sometimes the surgery can last as long as 12 hours. The heart lung machine makes things ~~very~~ possible and saves lives.

Heart-lung machines circulate blood ~~about~~ _through_ a body. It pumps like a heart. The heart can stop and the heart lung machine will pump instead. Then the blood moves through the body just like the heart ~~is~~ _was_ pumping. So the blood gets to all the viens. It is ~~too~~ unbelievable ~~why~~ _how_ the heart lung machine can work and to keep people from dying.

The heart-lung machine can clean a persons blood. All the bad stuff gets taken out of the blood before it goes back into the body. That way the body won't get poison. I know of someone who had their blood cleaned by the machine while they were operated on. The person was ~~unconscience~~ _unconscious_. The doctor fixed his heart. ~~Since~~ _Because_ the machine was going the persons heart was stopped. The doctor had to start it up again. It was pretty scary to think about that happening to a person. But the machine took all the bad stuff out of the blood and the person lived.

To conclude, I believe that the heart lung machine is great for people who need open heart surgery. It pumps and cleans their blood too. They are a medical miracle.

5 MATHEMATICS

Time: 90 minutes

The CLAST mathematics test has 50 scored multiple-choice questions. There are many question types based on the following 57 objectives. The number of questions for any one objective varies widely from test to test. The objectives are covered in the order shown below.

Arithmetic (12 scored items per test)
I A1 a - Add and Subtract Positive and Negative Fractions
I A1 b - Multiply and Divide Positive and Negative Fractions
I A2   - Add, Subtract, Multiply, and Divide Positive and Negative Decimals
II A3   - Identify Equivalent Decimals, Percents, and Fractions
I A3   - Calculate Percent Increase and Percent Decrease
I A4   - Solve for One Variable of the Equation; $a\%$ of b is c
II A1   - Recognize the Meaning of Exponents
II A2   - Identify the Place Value of a Digit in a Decimal Numeral and Identify the Expanded Notation for a Decimal Numeral
II A4   - Use >, <, and = to Compare Real Numbers
II A5   - Estimate the Sum, Average, or Product of Numbers in a Word Problem
III A1 - Find Missing Numbers in a Pattern
IV A1 - Solve Real-World Word Problems Not Involving Variables or Percent
IV A2 - Solve Real-World Word Problems That Involve Percent
IV A3 - Solve Problems That Involve the Structure and Logic of Arithmetic

Geometry and Measurement (8 scored items per test)
I B1   - Round Measurements to the Nearest Given Unit
I B2   - Calculate Distance, Area, and Volume
II B1   - Identify Relationships Between Angle Measures
II B2   - Classify Simple Plane Figures According to Their Properties
II B3   - Recognize Similar Triangles and Their Properties
II B4   - Identify Appropriate Units of Measurement for Geometric Objects
III B1 - Infer Formulas for Measuring Geometric Figures
III B2 - Select Formulas for Computing Measures of Geometric Figures
IV B1 - Solve Real-World Word Problems About Measures of Geometric Figures
IV B2 - Solve Real-World Word Problems Involving the Pythagorean Theorem

Algebra (16 scored items per test)

I C1   - Add, Subtract, Multiply and Divide Real Numbers
I C2   - Use the Correct Order-of-Operations to Compute
I C3   - Use Scientific Notation in Calculations of Very Large or Very Small Numbers
I C4   - Solve Linear Equations and Inequalities
I C5   - Use Nongeometric Formulas
I C6   - Find Values of a Function
I C7   - Factor a Quadratic Expression
I C8   - Find the Roots of a Quadratic Equation
I C9   - Solve a System of Two Linear Equations in Two Unknowns
II C1 - Use Properties of Operations
II C2 - Determine If a Number Is a Solution to an Equation or Inequality
II C3 - Recognize Statements and Conditions of Proportionality and Variation
II C4 - Match Regions of the Coordinate Plane with Equations and Inequalities
III C2 - Identify Equivalent Equations and Inequalities
IV C1 - Solve Nongeometric Word Problems Involving Variables
IV C2 - Solve Problems That Involve the Structure and Logic of Algebra

Statistics and Probability (8 scored items per test)

I D1   - Identify Information Contained in Bar, Line, and Circle Graphs
I D2   - Find the Mean, Median, and Mode of a Set of Numbers
I D3   - Use the Fundamental Counting Principle
II D1 - Recognize Relationships Among the Mean, Median, and Mode
II D2 - Choose the Most Appropriate Procedure for Selecting an Unbiased Sample
II D3 - Identify the Probability of an Outcome
III D1 - Infer Relations and Make Predictions from Statistical Data
IV D1 - Interpret Real-World Data from Frequency Tables
IV D2 - Solve Real-World Word Problems Involving Probability

Logic (6 scored items per test)

I E1   - Deduce Facts of Set Inclusion or Set Noninclusion from a Diagram
II E1 - Identify Negations of Simple and Compound Statements
II E2 - Determine the Equivalence or Nonequivalence of Statements
II E3 - Draw Logical Conclusions from Data
II E4 - Recognize Invalid Arguments with True Conclusions
III E1 - Recognize Valid Reasoning Patterns in Everyday Language
III E2 - Select Rules Used to Transform Statements
IV E1 - Draw Logical Conclusions When Facts Warrant

PASSING THE MATHEMATICS TEST

You must usually get 66 percent (33) correct to 70 percent (35) correct to pass the Mathematics Test. Passing scores vary slightly depending on how the other students do on your test administration. Approximately 47 percent of all students pass this test the first time they take it.

MATHEMATICS REVIEW QUIZ

This mathematics diagnostic quiz tests your knowledge of the mathematics topics included on the CLAST. This quiz is not like a CLAST Test. It does not use a multiple choice format. The idea here is to find out what you know and don't know. So don't guess answers on this review quiz.

This quiz will be more difficult than the questions on the actual CLAST. It is not important to answer all of these questions correctly and don't be concerned if you miss many of them.

The answers are found immediately after the quiz. It's to your advantage not to look until you have completed the quiz. Once you have completed and scored this review quiz, use the checklist to decide which sections of the review to study.

You don't have to finish this quiz in one sitting.

Write the answers in the space provided or on a separate piece of paper.

1. $\frac{1}{2} + (-\frac{1}{6}) =$

2. $\frac{1}{4} + 2 =$

3. $\frac{1}{2} - \frac{1}{2} =$

4. $-\frac{2}{3} \div \frac{1}{6} =$

5. $\frac{2}{5} \times \frac{3}{4} =$

6. $-\frac{5}{6} \div -5 =$

7. $19.25 + (-9.75) =$

8. $-2.36 - (-9.24) =$

9. $1.24 \times 2.36 =$

10. $-10.08 \div 3.15 =$

11. The price is decreased from $50 to $35. What is the percent of decrease?

12. A sale marks down an $85 dress by 20%. What is the sale price of the dress?

13. 35 is what percent of 75?

14. 15% of 90 is what number?

15. 25 is 20% of what number?

16. $4^2 + 0^3 =$

17. $(3^2)^5 =$

18. $(5 - 2)^4 =$

19. $(3^3)\,(9^2) =$

20. What is the place value of the underlined digit?

    (A) 30.1<u>6</u>2

    (B) <u>3</u>1.24

21. What is the correct numeral for (5×10^3) $+ (6 \times 10^1) + (4 \times \frac{1}{10^2})$?

22. Complete to show the missing decimal, percent, or fraction.

	Fraction	Decimal	Percent
(A)			16%
(B)		.25	
(C)	$\frac{1}{2}$		

23. Use >, <, or = to compare the numbers.

    (A) $\sqrt{64}$ ☐ 8

    (B) 9.145 ☐ 9.143

    (C) −10 ☐ −20

    (D) |−9| ☐ |3|

    (E) 9.5 ☐ $9\frac{3}{4}$

    (F) 10^2 ☐ 100

    (G) |−18| ☐ 18

24. Jim plays basketball for his high school team. In his past five games he has scored 18, 25, 13, 8, and 30 points. What is a reasonable estimate of Jim's average scoring in the past 5 games?

25. It takes 15 minutes for Alice to walk to school and 10 minutes to walk home from school. If Alice goes to school 24 days a month, how many hours does she walk back and forth to school each month?

26. There are 12 ounces of soda in every soda can. If I need 200 ounces of soda, what is a good estimate of how many soda cans I need?

27. Find the missing term in each pattern below.

    (A) 1, 3, 5, 7, ____
    (B) (2,4), (5,25), (9,81), (10,____)
    (C) 1600, 400, 100, 25, ____
    (D) 1, 4, 8, 13, ____

28. If Jim spends $100 a month (May–September) for air conditioning and $40 a month (October–April), what is Jim's average air-conditioning bill for the whole year?

29. Ryan gets paid $10 an hour when he works alone, and $6 an hour when he works with someone else. How much money does Ryan earn in a week if he works 15 hours by himself and 25 hours with someone else?

30. If Erin makes $3,500 a month and 15% goes to pay off college loans, how much money does she have left each month?

31. A car is being sold by two car dealers for $5,000. At Jim's Used Car Dealer, the salesperson is offering 15% off. At Mike's Used Car Lot, the salesperson is offering $500 off the $5,000 listed price. Which dealer is giving you the better deal?

32. What are the factors of 24?

33. List five multiples of 8.

34. Round 11 lbs. 16 oz. to the nearest pound.

35. Round 68.58 km. to the nearest km.

36. Round 4:36 PM to the nearest hour.

37. A circle has a diameter of 16 meters. What is the area of the circle?

38. Each side of an octagon is 7 feet long. What is the distance around the octagon?

39. A cylinder has a height of 6 feet and a radius of 2 feet. What is the surface area of the cylinder?

40. The volume of a rectangular solid is 2,000 cubic meters. Knowing that the width is 5 meters, and the length is 20 meters, what is the height of the rectangular solid?

41. The radius of a sphere is 5 feet. What is the volume of the sphere?

42.

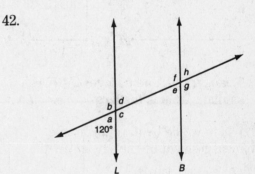

If L ‖ B, which of the following is true?

    (A) angle c = 120 degrees
    (B) angle a + angle b = 360 degrees
    (C) angle h = angle a
    (D) angle d is ≠ to angle a

43. How many sides does a pentagon have?

44. In a triangle two of the angles are 30 degrees and 60 degrees. What is the measure of the third angle?

45. What 4-sided polygon has one pair of parallel sides?

46.

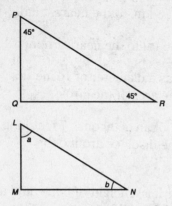

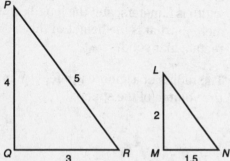

Triangle *PQR* and triangle *LMN* are similar. What is the measurement of angle *b*?

47.

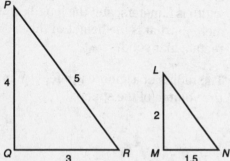

Triangle *PQR* and triangle *LMN* are similar. What is the length of side *LN*?

48. Which would be the appropriate measurement of one's height?

(A) square yards
(B) feet
(C) gallons
(D) ounces

49. What would be the appropriate measurement of liquid in a glass?

(A) gallons
(B) square meters
(C) fluid ounces
(D) hours

50. Calculate *P* if $x = 2$, $y = 5$

X	Y	P
1	1	4
1	2	6
1	3	8
2	4	12
2	5	

51.

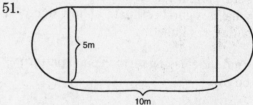

What is the area of the above figure?

52.

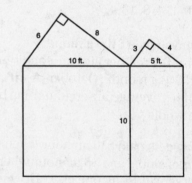

What is the area of the house drawn above?

53. It takes 1 pound of fertilizer to fertilize 1,000 square feet. According to the diagram below, how many pounds of fertilizer will be needed?

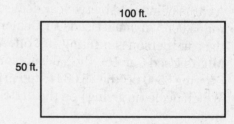

54. A gas tank holds 20 gallons of gas. If there are already 8 gallons in the tank, and gas costs $1.25 per gallon, how much will it cost to fill the tank?

55. A flag pole 30 meters high casts a shadow of 10 meters. How long is a straight line from the tip of the flagpole to the end of the shadow?

56. $\sqrt{18} - \sqrt{2} =$

57. $\sqrt{16} \div \sqrt{2} =$

58. $(2 + 5) - 6 \times 30 =$

59. $8 - 4 + 2 - 6 =$

60. $m^k \times m^p =$
(Use scientific notation to write the answer.)

61. $5.25 \times 10^5 \div 2.5 \times 10^{-6} =$

62. $8y + 6 = 2y - 2$: Solve for y

63. Solve for t : $2t > t + 4$

64. Solve for z : $-z < 4$

65. Using $I = PRT$, how much interest will be paid on a $10,000 loan at 13% interest for 5 years?

66. What is the interest rate on an $8,000 loan for 5 years if the borrower has to pay $2,000 interest?

67. Evaluate the functions.
(A) $f(x) = 2x^2 - 8x + 9$ Find $f(2)$
(B) $f(x) = 3x^4 + 2(x)^3$ Find $f(-3)$

68. What are the linear factors of $x^2 = x + 6$?
(A) $(x - 6)(x + 1)$
(B) $(x + 2)(x - 3)$
(C) $(x + 4)(x + 2)$
(D) $(x - 2)(x + 3)$

69. Find the roots, the solution, of $2x^2 = -3x + 9$

70. Choose the correct solution for the system of equations.
$$2x + 4y = 8$$
$$-3x + 2y = -4$$
(A) $(^9\!/_4, 0)$
(B) $(3, 2)$
(C) $(2, 1)$
(D) the empty set

71. What property is illustrated by $(2 + 5) + 3 = 2 + (5 + 3)$?

72. What property is illustrated by $x(x + 2) = x^2 + 2x$?

73. Write an expression equivalent to $6x - 3x$.

74. What property is illustrated by $2a + 5b = 5b + 2a$?

75. Which statement(s) below have $x = 2$ as a solution?
(A) $2x + 5 = 9$
(B) $x + 3 = 6$
(C) 4 divided by $x = 2$
(D) none of the above

76. Jack scores a goal every 12 times he shoots. How many times must Jack shoot to score 15 goals?

77. Which is the correct graph of the inequality $y \leq 2x - 4$?

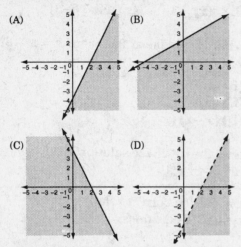

(A) (B)

(C) (D)

78. Write an equation equivalent to $-3x = 4$.

79. Write an inequality equivalent to $x + 1 > 2$.

80. If a store makes a profit of $1.50 for every $15 sold, what would their profit be if they sold $90 worth of goods?

81. The formula for calculating distance is:
distance = rate × time.
If Jills rate is 5 mph for 2 hours, how far has she gone?

82. The product of three consecutive numbers is five times the smallest integer. Write an equation to show this relationship.

83.

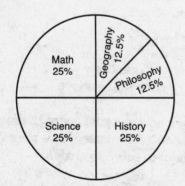

The above pie graph represents the percentage of money that is given to each department at Ryan's college. If there is $3,000,000 in available funds, how much does the math department get?

84.

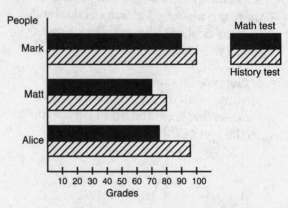

What did Mark get on his math test?

Use this data for questions 85 and 88.

$\{1, 4, 5, 6, 11, 2, 6, 10, 9\}$

85. (A) What is the mode?
    (B) What is the mean?
    (C) What is the median?

86. If there are five people, how many different ways can they line up single file?

87. If ten people are on a basketball team and only five can play at a time, how many different five-people teams can there be?

88. What is the relationship of the mean, median, and mode of the data at question 85?

89. A recreation center is going to be built. The builders randomly poll people in town of various ages, male and female, to find out what is wanted in the recreation center. Is this an appropriate or inappropriate form of sampling?

90. There are ten marbles in a bag, two white, three blue, and five red. What is the probability that you will pick a white marble?

91.

Year	Yearly Salary
1990	$20,000
1991	$21,000
1992	$22,050
1993	$23,152.50
1994	$24,310.13

Write a statement for the relationship found in the above table.

92.

Score	Percent of Students
90–100	10
80–89	34
70–79	28
60–69	8
0–16	20

From the table above, what percent of the students scored below 80?

93.

Score	Percentile Rank
90	99
80	80
70	70
60	39
50	20
40	12
30	2

From the table above, what percent of the scores are below 60?

94.

	Air Express	Rail	Truck
10 pounds or more	.06	.34	.26
Under 10 pounds	.05	.15	.14

Using the above table, what is the probability that a package goes by truck?

95.

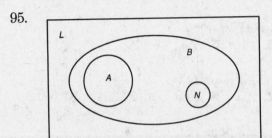

Using the above diagram, which of the following statements are true?

(A) Any element of N is an element of L.
(B) Any element of A is an element of N.
(C) Any element of B is an element of N.
(D) Any element of L is an element of B.

ANSWER CHECKLIST

The answers are organized by review sections. If you miss any answers in a section, check that box and review that section.

☐ *I A1 a page 112*
1. $\frac{1}{3}$ 2. $2\frac{1}{4}$ 3. 0

☐ *I A1 b page 115*
4. –4   5. $\frac{3}{10}$ 6. $\frac{1}{6}$

☐ *I A2 page 117*
7. 9.5   8. 6.88   9. 2.9264   10. –3.2

☐ *I A3 page 121*
11. 30%   12. $68

☐ *I A4 a page 122*
13. $46\frac{2}{3}$% (46.$\overline{6}$%)   14. 13.5   15. 125

☐ *II A1 page 124*
16. 16   17. 59,049   18. 81   19. 2,187

☐ *II A2 page 125*
20. A. hundredths B. tens   21. 5,060.04

☐ *II A3 page 119*
22. A. $\frac{4}{25}$—0.16 B. $\frac{1}{4}$—25% C. 50%—0.5

☐ *II A4 page 126*
23. A. = B. > C. > D. > E. < F. = G. =

☐ *II A5 page 129*
24. 20 points a game   25. 10 hours
26. 20 soda cans

☐ *III A1 page 130*
27. A. 9 B. 100 C. 6.25 D. 19

☐ *IV A1 page 132*
28. $65.00 a month   29. $300.00 a week

☐ *IV A2 page 133*
30. $2,975
31. Jim's used car is the better deal

☐ *IV A3 page 134*
32. 1, 2, 3, 4, 6, 8, 12, 24   33. 8, 16, 24, 32, 40

☐ *I B1 page 136*
34. 12   35. 69   36. 5:00 PM

☐ *I B2 page 139*
37. 200.96 square meters
38. 56 feet
39. 100.48 square feet
40. 20 meters   41. 523.$\overline{3}$ (523$\frac{1}{3}$) cubic feet

☐ *II B1 page 143*
42. C

☐ *II B2 page 147*
43. 5   44. 90° 45. trapezoid

☐ *II B3 page 149*
46. 45°   47. 2.5

☐ *II B4 page 151*
48. B   49. C

☐ *III B1 page 152*
50. 14

☐ *III B2 page 153*
51. 69.625 square meters
52. 180 square feet

☐ *IV B1 page 155*
53. 5 pounds of fertilizer   54. $15.00

☐ *IV B2 page 156*
55. 31.62 meters (rounded to the nearest hundredth.)

☐ *I C1 page 158*
56. $2\sqrt{2}$ 57. $2\sqrt{2}$

☐ *I C2 page 160*
58. –173   59. 0

☐ *I C3 page 160*
60. m^{k+p} 61. 2.1×10^{11}

❏ *I C4 page 162*
62. $y = -1\frac{1}{3}$ **63.** $t > 4$ **64.** $z > -4$

❏ *I C5 page 165*
65. 6,500 **66.** 5%

❏ *I C6 page 166*
67. A. $f(2) = 1$ B. $f(-3) = 189$

❏ *I C7 page 167*
68. B

❏ *I C8 page 168*
69. $x = 1\frac{1}{2}$, $x = -3$

❏ *I C9 page 170*
70. C

❏ *II C1 page 173*
71. associative **72.** distributive
73. $3x$ **74.** commutative

❏ *II C2 page 174*
75. A and C

❏ *II C3 page 175*
76. 180 times

❏ *II C4 page 176*
77. A

❏ *III C2 page 179*
78. Examples: $x = -\frac{4}{3}$; $3x = -4$; $-\frac{3}{4}x = 1$;
   $-3x - 4 = 0$
79. Examples: $x + 2 > 3$; $x > 1$; $-x < -1$

❏ *IV C1 page 181*
80. A profit of $9.00 **81.** 10 miles

❏ *IV C2 page 182*
82. $(x)(x + 1)(x + 2) = 5x$

❏ *I D1 page 184*
83. $750,000 **84.** 90

❏ *I D2 page 186*
85. A. 6 B. 6 C. 6

❏ *I D3 page 187*
86. 120 ways **87.** 252

❏ *II D1 page 189*
88. They are all the same—6

❏ *II D2 page 190*
89. Appropriate

❏ *II D3 page 192*
90. $\frac{1}{5}$

❏ *III D1 page 193*
91. Salary increases 5% each year

❏ *IV D1 page 196*
92. 56% **93.** 39%

❏ *IV D2 page 198*
94. 40% (0.4)

❏ *I E1 page 200*
95. Only A is true.

ARITHMETIC

ADD AND SUBTRACT POSITIVE AND NEGATIVE FRACTIONS (I A1 a)

TEST QUESTION EXAMPLES:

CLAST questions look something like this:

A. $\frac{1}{3} + (-\frac{1}{5}) =$ B. $-2\frac{5}{16} - 1\frac{3}{8} =$

Add Fractions and Mixed Numbers

Add $\frac{1}{3} + \frac{1}{6}$

$$\frac{1}{3} = \frac{2}{6}$$
$$+\frac{1}{6} = \frac{1}{6}$$

Write fractions with common denominators.

$$\frac{1}{3} = \frac{2}{6}$$
$$\frac{1}{6} = \frac{1}{6}$$
$$\frac{3}{6}$$

Add the numerators. Keep the denominator.

$$\frac{1}{3} = \frac{2}{6}$$
$$\frac{1}{6} = \frac{1}{6}$$
$$\frac{3}{6} = \frac{1}{2}$$

Write in simplest form.

Add $3\frac{3}{4} + 1\frac{5}{12}$

$$3\frac{3}{4} = 3\frac{9}{12}$$
$$+1\frac{5}{12} = 1\frac{5}{12}$$

Write fractions with common denominators.

$$3\frac{3}{4} = 3\frac{9}{12}$$
$$+1\frac{1}{3} = 1\frac{5}{12}$$
$$\frac{14}{12} = 1\frac{2}{12}$$

Add fractions.

$$3\frac{3}{4} = 3\frac{9}{12}$$
$$+1\frac{1}{3} = 1\frac{5}{12}$$
$$5\frac{2}{12}$$

Add whole numbers.

$$3\frac{9}{12}$$
$$1\frac{5}{12}$$
$$5\frac{2}{12} = 5\frac{1}{6}$$

Write in simplest form.

Write fractions with common denominators. Add and then write in simplest form.

Add: $\dfrac{3}{8} + \dfrac{1}{4}$

$$\dfrac{3}{8} = \dfrac{3}{8}$$
$$+\dfrac{1}{4} = \dfrac{2}{8}$$
$$\overline{\qquad\dfrac{5}{8}}$$

Add: $\dfrac{7}{8} + \dfrac{5}{12}$

$$\dfrac{7}{8} = \dfrac{21}{24}$$
$$+\dfrac{5}{12} = \dfrac{10}{24}$$
$$\overline{\qquad\dfrac{31}{24} = 1\dfrac{7}{24}}$$

Add: $2\dfrac{1}{3} + \dfrac{5}{7}$

$$2\dfrac{1}{3} = 2\dfrac{7}{21}$$
$$+\dfrac{5}{7} = \dfrac{15}{21}$$
$$\overline{\qquad 2\dfrac{22}{21} = 3\dfrac{1}{21}}$$

Write fractions with common denominators. Subtract and then write in simplest form.

Subtract: $\dfrac{5}{6} - \dfrac{1}{3}$

$$\dfrac{5}{6} = \dfrac{5}{6}$$
$$\dfrac{1}{3} = \dfrac{2}{6}$$
$$\overline{\qquad\dfrac{3}{6} = \dfrac{1}{2}}$$

Subtract: $\dfrac{3}{8} - \dfrac{1}{5}$

$$\dfrac{3}{8} = \dfrac{15}{40}$$
$$\dfrac{1}{5} = \dfrac{8}{40}$$
$$\overline{\qquad\dfrac{7}{40}}$$

Subtract: $3\dfrac{1}{6} - 1\dfrac{1}{3}$

$$3\dfrac{1}{6} = 3\dfrac{1}{6} = 2\dfrac{7}{6}$$
$$1\dfrac{1}{3} = 1\dfrac{2}{6} = 1\dfrac{2}{6}$$
$$\overline{\qquad 1\dfrac{5}{6}}$$

Practice Questions: Add and Subtract Fractions

1. $\frac{1}{4} + \frac{1}{6}$

2. $\frac{1}{3} - (\frac{1}{6})$

3. $\frac{1}{5} + \frac{6}{7}$

4. $\frac{1}{8} + \frac{5}{6}$

5. $6 - \frac{3}{5}$

6. $6\frac{1}{2} - 4\frac{3}{4}$

7. $3\frac{1}{3} + 2\frac{4}{5}$

8. $\frac{4}{5} + 5\frac{1}{6}$

9. $6\frac{7}{12} - 4$

10. $5\frac{2}{5} - 2\frac{1}{4}$

11. $\frac{7}{12} + 2\frac{5}{8}$

12. $3\frac{3}{4} - 2\frac{4}{5}$

Answers on page 212.

Adding and Subtracting Integers and Rational Numbers

Addition

When the signs are the same keep the sign and add.

$$\begin{array}{r} {}^{+}7 \\ +{}^{+}8 \\ \hline {}^{+}15 \end{array}$$

$$\dfrac{-5}{6} = \dfrac{-20}{24}$$
$$+\dfrac{-5}{8} = \dfrac{-15}{24}$$
$$\overline{\qquad\dfrac{-35}{24} = -1\dfrac{11}{24}}$$

When the signs are different, disregard the signs, subtract the smaller number, and keep the sign of the larger number.

$$\frac{-4}{9} = \frac{-28}{63}$$

$$+\frac{^{+}28}{^{-}49}$$
$$\overline{^{-}21}$$

$$+\frac{^{+}5}{7} = \frac{^{+}45}{63}$$
$$\overline{+\frac{17}{63}}$$

Subtraction

Change the sign of the number being subtracted. Then add using the preceding rules.

$$\begin{array}{r} ^{+}13 \\ -18 \\ \Downarrow \\ ^{+}13 \\ + \, ^{+}18 \\ \hline ^{+}31 \end{array}$$

$$\begin{array}{r} ^{-}43 \\ -\,^{-}17 \\ \Downarrow \\ ^{-}43 \\ + \, ^{+}17 \\ \hline ^{-}26 \end{array}$$

$$\begin{array}{r} \dfrac{-7}{16} \\[4pt] -\,\dfrac{+3}{16} \\[4pt] \Downarrow \\[4pt] \dfrac{-7}{16} \\[4pt] +\,\dfrac{-3}{16} \\[4pt] \hline \dfrac{-10}{16} = \dfrac{-5}{8} \end{array}$$

$$\begin{array}{r} \dfrac{+7}{8} \\[4pt] -\,\dfrac{+3}{4} \\[4pt] \Downarrow \\[4pt] \dfrac{+7}{8} \\[4pt] +\,\dfrac{-6}{8} \\[4pt] \hline \dfrac{+1}{8} \end{array}$$

Completed Examples

A. $\frac{1}{3} + (-\frac{1}{5}) = \frac{5}{15} - \frac{3}{15} = \frac{2}{15}$

B. $-2\frac{5}{16} - 1\frac{3}{8} = -2\frac{5}{16} - 1\frac{6}{16} = -3\frac{11}{16}$

Practice Questions: Add and Subtract Integers

1. +9	2. +10	3. −17	4. −25	5. +37	6. − 124
+ +6	+ − 7	− +12	− − 9	− +19	+ + 48

Add and Subtract Positive and Negative Fractions

7. $+\frac{1}{2}$	8. $-\frac{3}{8}$	9. $+\frac{7}{10}$	10. $-2\frac{1}{2}$	11. $+4\frac{1}{5}$	12. $-4\frac{6}{7}$
$+-\frac{1}{4}$	$+-\frac{1}{4}$	$--\frac{1}{5}$	$-+5\frac{1}{4}$	$-+3\frac{1}{4}$	$--5\frac{2}{5}$

Answers on page 212.

MULTIPLY AND DIVIDE POSITIVE AND NEGATIVE FRACTIONS (I A1 b)

TEST QUESTION EXAMPLES:

CLAST questions look something like this:

$$\text{A. } (-3) \times 4\tfrac{1}{2} = \qquad\qquad \text{B. } 3\tfrac{2}{3} \div (-\tfrac{1}{5}) =$$

Multiply and Divide Fractions and Mixed Numbers

Multiply $\dfrac{3}{4} \times \dfrac{2}{3}$

$$\frac{3}{4} \times \frac{2}{3} = \frac{6}{12} \qquad\qquad \frac{3}{4} \times \frac{2}{3} = \frac{6}{12} = \frac{1}{2}$$

Multiply numerators.
Multiply denominators.   Write in lowest terms.

Divide $\dfrac{5}{8} \div \dfrac{3}{4}$

$$\frac{5}{8} \times \frac{4}{3} \qquad\qquad \frac{5}{8} \times \frac{4}{3} = \frac{20}{24} \qquad\qquad \frac{5}{8} \times \frac{4}{3} = \frac{20}{24} = \frac{5}{6}$$

Invert the divisor.   Multiply numerators.   Write in lowest terms.
Multiply.   Multiply denominators.

Multiplying, Dividing, Adding, and Subtracting Fractions and Mixed Numbers

Write any mixed number as an improper fraction. Multiply numerator and denominator. Write the product in simplest form.

Multiply $3\tfrac{1}{3}$ times $\tfrac{3}{5}$: $\qquad 3\dfrac{1}{3} \times \dfrac{3}{5} = \dfrac{10}{3} \times \dfrac{3}{5} = \dfrac{30}{15} = 2$

To divide $1\tfrac{4}{5}$ by $\tfrac{3}{8}$:

$$1\frac{4}{5} \div \frac{3}{8} \;=\; \frac{9}{5} \div \frac{3}{8} \;=\; \frac{9}{5} \times \frac{8}{3} \;=\; \frac{72}{15} \;=\; 4\frac{12}{15} \;=\; 4\frac{4}{5}$$

Write mixed numbers as   Invert the divisor   Write the   Write in
improper fractions.   and multiply.   product.   simplest form.

Practice Questions: Multiply and Divide Fractions

1. $\frac{3}{4} \times \frac{3}{4}$

2. $\frac{2}{5} \times 3$

3. $\frac{4}{5} \times \frac{10}{16}$

4. $\frac{5}{12} \times \frac{4}{7}$

5. $4\frac{1}{4} \times 2\frac{2}{5}$

6. $2\frac{4}{5} \times 1\frac{3}{7}$

7. $\frac{5}{7} \div \frac{1}{2}$

8. $\frac{6}{8} \div \frac{16}{20}$

9. $+\frac{5}{10} \div 1\frac{1}{2}$

10. $\frac{7}{8} \div \frac{5}{6}$

11. $5\frac{3}{5} \div 3\frac{3}{5}$

12. $10 \div \frac{4}{6}$

Answer on page 213.

Multiplying and Dividing Integers and Rational Numbers

Multiply

Multiply as you would whole numbers. The product is *positive* if there are an even number of negative factors. The product is *negative* is there are an odd number of negative factors.

$$^-2 \times {}^+4 \times {}^-6 \times {}^+3 = {}^+144 \qquad {}^-2 \times {}^-4 \times {}^+6 \times {}^-3 = {}^-144$$

Divide

Forget the signs and divide. The quotient is *positive* if both integers have the same sign. The quotient is *negative* if the integers have different signs.

$$^+24 \div {}^+4 = {}^+6 \qquad {}^-24 \div {}^-4 = {}^+6 \qquad {}^+24 \div {}^-4 = {}^-6 \qquad {}^-24 \div {}^+4 = {}^-6$$

$$\frac{-3}{4} \div \frac{+5}{8} = \frac{-3}{4} \times \frac{+8}{5} = \frac{-24}{20} = -1\frac{1}{5} \qquad \frac{-1}{3} \div \frac{-1}{5} = \frac{-1}{3} \times \frac{-5}{1} = \frac{+5}{3} = {}^+1\frac{2}{3}$$

Completed Examples

A. $(-3) \times 4\frac{1}{2} = -\frac{3}{1} \times \frac{9}{2} = -\frac{27}{2} = -13\frac{1}{2}$

B. $3\frac{2}{3} \div (-\frac{1}{5}) = \frac{11}{3} \div -\frac{1}{5} = \frac{11}{13} \times -\frac{5}{1} = -\frac{55}{3} = -18\frac{1}{3}$

Practice Questions: Multiply and Divide Integers and Positive and Negative Fractions

1. -1×-10

2. $-5 \times +6$

3. $-2 \times +3 \times -4 \times +5$

4. $+15 \times -3 \times -4$

5. $-\frac{3}{4} \times +\frac{5}{6}$

6. $-1\frac{3}{7} \times -2\frac{1}{2}$

7. $-48 \div -8$

8. $-120 \div +12$

9. $-156 \div +3$

10. $+\frac{5}{8} \div -\frac{6}{12}$

11. $-3\frac{4}{5} \div -2$

12. $-12 \div +\frac{3}{4}$

Answers on page 213.

ADD, SUBTRACT, MULTIPLY, AND DIVIDE POSITIVE AND NEGATIVE DECIMALS (I A2)

TEST QUESTION EXAMPLES:

CLAST questions look something like this:

A. $(-14.4) \div 0.9 =$ B. $(-12.34) \times 6.8 =$

C. $14.324 + (-7.2) =$ D. $8.07 - (-6.738) =$

Add and Subtract Decimals

Line up the decimal points and add or subtract.

Add: $14.9 + 3.108 + 0.16$ Subtract: $14.234 - 7.14$

$$
\begin{array}{r}
14.9 \\
3.108 \\
+0.16 \\
\hline
18.168
\end{array}
\qquad
\begin{array}{r}
14.234 \\
-7.14 \\
\hline
7.094
\end{array}
$$

Multiply Decimals

Multiply as with whole numbers. Count the total number of decimal places in the factors. Put that many decimal places in the product. You may have to write leading zeros.

Multiply: 17.4×1.3 Multiply: 0.016×1.7

$$
\begin{array}{r}
17.4 \\
\times 1.3 \\
\hline
522 \\
174 \\
\hline
22.62
\end{array}
\qquad
\begin{array}{r}
0.016 \\
\times \ 1.7 \\
\hline
112 \\
16 \\
\hline
.0272
\end{array}
$$

Divide Decimals

Move the decimal point to make the divisor a whole number. Match the movement in the dividend and then divide. Write the decimal point in the answer over the decimal point in the dividend.

$$
0.16\overline{)1.328} \qquad 0.16\overline{)1.328} \qquad
\begin{array}{r}
8.3 \\
16\overline{)132.8} \\
128 \\
\hline
48 \\
48 \\
\hline
0
\end{array}
$$

Completed Examples—Multiplication and Division

A. $(-14.4) \div 0.9 = -144 \div 9 = -16$
B. $(-12.34) \times 6.8 = -83.912$

Practice Questions: Multiply and Divide Decimals

1. $-16.3 \div -0.5$

2. $+8.94 \div -1.2$

3. $-100.5 \div -25$

4. -3.5×-4.7

5. $+25.4 \times -13$

6. $-0.359 \times + 0.12$

Answers on page 213.

Add and Subtract Positive and Negative Decimals

Addition

When the signs are the same, keep the signs and add.

When the signs are different, disregard the signs, subtract the smaller decimal and keep the sign of the larger decimal.

$$
\begin{array}{r}
-3.6 \\
+ -0.75 \\
\hline
-4.35
\end{array}
\qquad
\begin{array}{r}
1.08 \\
+ 0.3 \\
\hline
1.38
\end{array}
\qquad\qquad
\begin{array}{r}
-4.8 \\
+ +0.7 \\
\hline
-4.1
\end{array}
\qquad
\begin{array}{r}
+1.8 \\
+ -0.6 \\
\hline
+1.2
\end{array}
$$

Subtraction

Change the sign of the number being subtracted. Then add using the rules above.

$$
\begin{array}{r}
-5.6 \\
- -1.35 \\
\Downarrow
\end{array}
\qquad
\begin{array}{r}
2.07 \\
- 0.8 \\
\Downarrow
\end{array}
\qquad
\begin{array}{r}
-5.3 \\
- +1.2 \\
\Downarrow
\end{array}
\qquad
\begin{array}{r}
+2.4 \\
- -0.9 \\
\Downarrow
\end{array}
$$

$$
\begin{array}{r}
-5.6 \\
+ +1.35 \\
\hline
-4.25
\end{array}
\qquad
\begin{array}{r}
2.07 \\
+ -0.8 \\
\hline
+1.27
\end{array}
\qquad
\begin{array}{r}
-5.3 \\
+ -1.2 \\
\hline
-6.5
\end{array}
\qquad
\begin{array}{r}
+ +2.4 \\
+ +0.9 \\
\hline
+3.3
\end{array}
$$

Completed Examples—Addition and Subtraction

C. $14.324 + (-7.2) = 14.324 - 7.2 = 7.124$
D. $8.07 - (-6.738) = 8.07 + 6.738 = 14.808$

Practice Questions: Add and Subtract Decimals

1. -8.9 $-\ -7.1$	2. $+5.7$ $+\ -3.3$	3. $+3.05$ $+\ -0.3$	4. $+45.3$ $-\ -5.40$	5. -0.74 $-\ +25.6$	6. -487.2 $-\ -9.32$
7. $+315$ $+\ \ -0.35$	8. $+0.369$ $+\ +.9$	9. -6.9 $+\ -0.7$	10. $+74.3$ $+\ +5.6$	11. -2.76 $+\ +8.1$	12. -9.82 $-\ +2.11$

Answers on page 213.

IDENTIFY EQUIVALENT DECIMALS, PERCENTS, AND FRACTIONS (II A3)

TEST QUESTION EXAMPLES:

CLAST questions look something like this:

A. 16/20 =   B. 18% =   C. 0.026 =

Percent

Percent comes from *per centum*, which means per hundred. Whenever you see a number followed by a percent sign it means that number out of 100.

Decimals and Percents

To write a decimal as a percent, move the decimal point two places to the right and write the percent sign.

$$0.34 = 34\% \qquad 0.297 = 29.7\% \qquad 0.6 = 60\% \qquad 0.001 = 0.1\%$$

To write a percent as a decimal, move the decimal point two places to the left and delete the percent sign.

$$51\% = 0.51 \qquad 34.18\% = 0.3418 \qquad 0.9\% = 0.009$$

Fractions and Percents

Writing Fractions as Percents

• Divide the numerator by the denominator. Write the answer as a percent.

Write $\frac{3}{5}$ as a percent.   Write $\frac{5}{8}$ as a percent.

$$5\overline{)3.0} \quad \begin{array}{c} 0.6 \end{array} \qquad 0.6 = 60\%$$

$$8\overline{)5.00} \quad \begin{array}{c} 0.625 \end{array} \qquad 0.625 = 62.5\%$$

- Write an equivalent fraction with 100 in the denominator. Write the numerator followed by a percent sign.

Write $^{13}\!/_{25}$ as a percent.

$$\frac{13}{25} = \frac{52}{100} = 52\%$$

- Use these equivalencies.

$$\frac{1}{4} = 25\% \qquad \frac{1}{2} = 50\% \qquad \frac{3}{4} = 75\% \qquad \frac{4}{4} = 100\%$$

$$\frac{1}{5} = 20\% \qquad \frac{2}{5} = 40\% \qquad \frac{3}{5} = 60\% \qquad \frac{4}{5} = 80\%$$

$$\frac{1}{6} = 16\frac{2}{3}\% \qquad \frac{1}{3} = 33\frac{1}{3}\% \qquad \frac{2}{3} = 66\frac{2}{3}\% \qquad \frac{5}{6} = 83\frac{1}{3}\%$$

$$\frac{1}{8} = 12\frac{1}{2}\% \qquad \frac{3}{8} = 37\frac{1}{2}\% \qquad \frac{5}{8} = 62\frac{1}{2}\% \qquad \frac{7}{8} = 87\frac{1}{2}\%$$

Writing Percents as Fractions

Write a fraction with 100 in the denominator and the percent in the numerator. Simplify.

$$18\% = \frac{18}{100} = \frac{9}{50} \qquad 7.5\% = \frac{7.5}{100} = \frac{75}{1000} = \frac{3}{40}$$

Completed Examples

A. $^{16}\!/_{20}$ = $^{80}\!/_{100}$ = 0.8 = 80%

B. 18% = 0.18 = $^{18}\!/_{100}$ = $^{9}\!/_{50}$

C. 0.026 = 2.6% = $^{2.6}\!/_{100}$ = $^{26}\!/_{1000}$ = $^{3}\!/_{500}$

Practice Questions

Complete to show the missing decimal, percent, and fraction.

1. 20%

2. 0.16

3. $^{6}\!/_{20}$

4. 0.035

5. 40%

6. $^{4}\!/_{25}$

7. $^{6}\!/_{50}$

8. 70%

9. $^{3}\!/_{10}$

10. 35%

11. 0.45

12. 0.80

Answers on page 213.

CALCULATE PERCENT INCREASE AND PERCENT DECREASE (I A3)

TEST QUESTION EXAMPLES:

CLAST questions look something like this:

A. The price increased from $30 to $36. What is the percent increase?

B. An $80 item goes on sale for 25% off. What is the sale price?

Percent of Increase

A price increases from $50 to $65. What is the percent of increase?

Subtract to find the amount of increase.

$65 − $50 = $15
$15 is the amount of increase

Write a fraction. The amount of increase is the numerator. The original amount is the denominator.

$$\frac{\$15}{\$50} \quad \frac{\text{Amount of increase}}{\text{Original amount}}$$

Write the fraction as a percent. The percent of increase is 30%.

$$50\overline{)15.00} \quad 0.3 = 30\%$$

Percent of Decrease

A price decreases from $35 to $28. What is the percent of decrease?

Subtract to find the amount of decrease.

$35 − $28 = $7
$7 is the amount of decrease

Write a fraction. The amount of decrease is the numerator. The original amount is the denominator.

$$\frac{\$7}{\$35} \quad \frac{\text{Amount of decrease}}{\text{Original amount}}$$

Write the fraction as a percent. The percent of decrease is 20%.

$$\frac{7}{35} = \frac{1}{5} = 20\%$$

Completed Examples

A. The price increased from $30 to $36. What is the percent increase?

$$\$36 − \$30 = \$6$$

$$\frac{6}{30} = \frac{1}{5} = 20\%$$

B. An $80 item goes on sale for 25% off. What is the sale price?

$$\$80 \times 25\% = \$80 \times .25 = \$20$$

$$\$80 − \$20 = \$60. \quad \$60 \text{ is the sale price.}$$

Practice Questions

1. The price increased from $25 to $35. What is the percent of increase?

2. A sale marks down a $100 item 25%. What is the sale price?

3. The price decreases from $80 by 15%. What is the new price?

4. The price increased from $120 to $150. What is the percent of increase?

5. A sale marks down a $75 item 10%. What is the sale price?

6. The price decreases from $18 to $6. What is the percent of decrease?

7. A sale marks down a $225 item to $180. What is the percent of decrease?

8. A sale price of $150 was 25% off the original price. What was the original price?

Answers on page 213.

SOLVE FOR ONE VARIABLE OF THE EQUATION:
a% of b is c (I A4)

TEST QUESTION EXAMPLES:

CLAST questions look something like this:

A. What percent of 70 is 28?

B. 30% of 60 is what number?

C. 40% of what number is 16?

Three Types of Percent Problems

Finding a Percent of a Number

To find a percent of a number, write a number sentence with a decimal for the percent and solve.

$$\text{Find } 40\% \text{ of } 90.$$
$$0.4 \times 90 = 36$$

It may be easier to write a fraction for the percent.

$$\text{Find } 62\frac{1}{2}\% \text{ of } 64.$$

$$\frac{5}{8} \times 64 = 5 \times 8 = 40$$

Finding What Percent One Number Is of Another

To find what percent one number is of another, write a number sentence and solve to find the percent.

What percent of 5 is 3?

$$n \times 5 = 3$$

$$n = \frac{3}{5} = 0.6 = 60\%$$

Finding a Number When a Percent of It Is Known

To find a number when a percent of it is known, write a number sentence with a decimal or a fraction for the percent and solve to find the number.

5% of what number is 2?

$$0.05 \times n = 2$$

$$n = 2 \div 0.05$$

$$n = 40$$

Completed Examples

A. What percent of 70 is 28?

$$\square \times 70 = 28$$

$$\square = \frac{28}{70} = \frac{4}{10}$$

$$\square = 40\%$$

B. 30% of 60 is what number?

$$30\% \times 60 = \square$$

$$.3 \times 60 =$$

$$\square = 18$$

C. 40% of what number is 16?

$$.40 \times \square = 16$$

$$\square = \frac{16}{.4}$$

$$\square = 40$$

Practice Questions

1. 120 is what percent of 240?

2. 15% of 70 is what number?

3. 60% of 300 is what number?

4. What percent of 60 is 42?

5. What percent of 25 is 2.5?

6. 40% of what number is 22?

7. 70% of what number is 85?

8. 25% of 38 is what number?

9. 35% of what number is 24?

Answers on page 214.

RECOGNIZE THE MEANING OF EXPONENTS (II A1)

Test Question Examples:

> CLAST questions look something like this:
>
> A. $4^3 + 6^2 =$ B. $(2^3)(4^2) =$ C. $(3^2)^2 =$ D. $(10 - 9)^2 =$

Positive Exponents

You can show repeated multiplication as an exponent. The exponent shows how many times the factor appears.

$$\text{Base} \rightarrow 3^{\overset{\text{[Exponent]}}{5}} = 3 \times 3 \times 3 \times 3 \times 3 = 243$$
$$\text{[Factors]}$$

Rules for Exponents

$a^0 = 1 \quad a^1 = a$

Use these rules to multiply and divide exponents with the *same base*.

$7^8 \times 7^5 = 7^{13} \quad a^n \times a^m = a^{m+n}$
$7^8 \div 7^5 = 7^3 \quad a^n \div a^m = a^{n-m}$

Completed Examples

A. $4^3 + 6^2 \quad = \quad 4 \times 4 \times 4 + 6 \times 6 \quad = \quad 64 + 36 \quad = \quad 100$

B. $(2^3)(4^2) \quad = \quad (2 \times 2 \times 2) \times (4 \times 4) \quad = \quad 8 \times 16 \quad = \quad 128$

C. $(3^2)^2 \quad = \quad 3^4 \quad = \quad 3 \times 3 \times 3 \times 3 \quad = \quad 81$

D. $(10 - 9)^2 \quad = \quad 1^2 \quad = \quad 1$

Practice Questions

1. $5^2 + 6^3 =$

2. $(3^2)^2 =$

3. $(8 - 6)^3 =$

4. $(5^2)(6^2) =$

5. $3^3 + 2^3 =$

6. $10^2 - 7^2 =$

7. $(4^3)^2 =$

8. $(2^1)^5 =$

9. $6^2 + 2^3 =$

10. $(25 - 15)^3 =$

11. $(4^2)^2 =$

12. $(2^3)(3^2) =$

Answers on page 214.

IDENTIFY THE PLACE VALUE OF A DIGIT IN A DECIMAL NUMERAL AND IDENTIFY THE EXPANDED NOTATION FOR A DECIMAL NUMERAL (II A2)

TEST QUESTION EXAMPLES:

CLAST questions look something like this:

A. What is the place value of the underlined digit? 14.67$\underline{2}$

B. What is the correct numeral for $(6 \times 10^3) + (4 \times 10) + (3 \times \frac{1}{10}^2)$?

Place Value

We use ten digits, 0–9, to write out numerals. We also use a place-value system of numeration. The value of a digit depends on the place it occupies. Each place value can be written using a power of 10. Look at the following place-value chart.

10^6	10^5	10^4	10^3	10^2	10^1	10^0
millions	hundred thousands	ten thousands	thousands	hundreds	tens	ones
3	5	7	9	4	1	0

The value of the 9 is 9,000. The 9 is in the thousands place. The value of the 5 is 500,000. The 5 is in the hundred thousands place. Read the number three million, five hundred seventy-nine thousand, four hundred ten.

	$\frac{1}{10^1}$	$\frac{1}{10^2}$	$\frac{1}{10^3}$	$\frac{1}{10^4}$	$\frac{1}{10^5}$	$\frac{1}{10^6}$	$\frac{1}{10^7}$
ones	tenths	hundredths	thousandths	ten thousandths	hundred-thousandths	millionths	ten-millionths
0 .	3	6	8	7			

The value of 3 is three tenths. The 3 is in the tenths place. The value of 8 is eight thousandths. The 8 is in the thousandths place. Read the numeral three thousand, six hundred, eighty-seven ten-thousandths.

Expanded Form

Multiply each digit by the exponential place value to write a numeral in expanded form.

Write the numeral 3,457.032 in expanded form.

$$(3 \times 10^3) + (4 \times 10^2) + (5 \times 10^1) + (7 \times 10^0) + (0 \times \frac{1}{10^1}) + (3 \times \frac{1}{10^2}) + (2 \times \frac{1}{10^3})$$

Write the correct numeral for $(6 \times 10^3) + (4 \times 10) + (3 \times \frac{1}{10}^2) = 6{,}040.03$

Completed Examples

A. What is the place value of the underlined digit? 14.67$\underline{2}$
   The digit 2 is in the **thousandths** place.

B. What is the correct numeral for $(6 \times 10^3) + (4 \times 10) + (3 \times \frac{1}{10}^2)$?
   $6 \times 1000 + 4 \times 10 + 3 \times 0.01 = 6{,}040.0\,3$

Practice Questions

1. What is the place value of the underlined digit? 5.3$\underline{6}$1

2. What is the correct numeral for $(4 \times 10^2) + (5 \times 10)$?

3. What is the place value of the underlined digit? 6$\underline{4}$3.25

4. What is the correct numeral for $(6 \times 10^4) + (8 \times 10^3) + (4 \times 10^2) + (3 \times \frac{1}{10}^2)$?

5. What is the place value of the underlined digit? 2.447$\underline{9}$

6. What is the correct numeral for $(7 \times \frac{1}{10}^2) + (8 \times \frac{1}{10}^3) + (1 \times \frac{1}{10}^4)$?

7. What is the place value of the underlined digit? 337.99$\underline{0}$

8. What is the correct numeral for $(3 \times \frac{1}{10}) + (5 \times \frac{1}{10}^3) + (7 \times \frac{1}{10}^5) + (9 \times \frac{1}{10}^7)$?

Answers on page 214.

USE >, <, AND = TO COMPARE REAL NUMBERS (II A4)

TEST QUESTION EXAMPLES:

CLAST questions look something like this:

Which symbol (<, >, or =) belongs in the box between the two numbers?

A. $6.\overline{387}$ □ $6.\overline{4}$ B. $5\frac{1}{3}$ □ $-6\frac{5}{8}$ C. $\sqrt{27}$ □ 4.9   D. 4.25 □ $4\frac{1}{4}$

Real numbers are just about all the numbers you can think of. They include rational numbers as well as numbers such as π and $\sqrt{8}$. You can visualize real numbers on a number line. Here are some examples.

$-7\frac{1}{3}$ $-\sqrt{25}$ $-\pi$ $\sqrt{2}$ $3\frac{1}{2}$ $|-8|$

-10 -9 -8 -7 -6 -5 -4 -3 -2 -1 0 $+1$ $+2$ $+3$ $+4$ $+5$ $+6$ $+7$ $+8$ $+9$ $+10$

Use this rule to compare two numbers: The number further left on the number line is the smaller number. The number further right on the number line is the larger number.

Use these other approaches to compare numbers.

Two Numbers Have Different Signs (–5.9 < +1.8)

The number with the negative sign is always the smaller number.

Both Numbers Are Positive

To compare two numbers line up the place values. Start at the left and keep going until the digits in the same place are different.

Compare	9,879 and 16,459	23,801 and 23,798	58.1289 and 58.132
Line up the place values	9,879	23,**8**01	58.1289
	16,459	23,798	58.1**3**2
	9,879 < 16,459	23,801 > 23,798	58.1289 < 58.132
	Less than	Greater than	Less than

Repeating Decimals

Compare $3.\overline{3}$ and $3.\overline{289}$

A line over the digits in a decimal indicates that these decimals repeat.

$3.\overline{3} = 3.33333\ldots$

$3.\overline{289} = 3.289289289\ldots$

Line up the place values $3.\mathbf{3}3333333\ldots$
                                $3.\mathbf{2}89289289\ldots$

$3.\overline{3} > 3.\overline{289}$

Equivalent Fractions

Two fractions that stand for the same number are called equivalent fractions. Multiply or divide the numerator and denominator by the same number to find an equivalent fraction.

$$\frac{2 \times 3}{5 \times 3} = \frac{6}{15} \qquad \frac{6 \div 3}{9 \div 3} = \frac{2}{3} \qquad \frac{6 \times 4}{8 \times 4} = \frac{24}{32} \qquad \frac{8 \div 2}{10 \div 2} = \frac{4}{5}$$

Fractions can also be written and ordered on a number line. You can use the number line to compare fractions. Fractions get smaller as we go to the left and larger as we go to the right. We use the terms equivalent to (=), less than (<), greater than (>), and between to compare fractions.

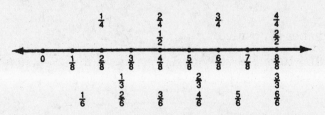

½ is equivalent to ²⁄₄   ⅔ is less than ¾   ⅝ is greater than ½   ⅓ is between ¼ and ⅜

$$\frac{1}{2} = \frac{2}{4} \qquad\qquad \frac{2}{3} < \frac{3}{4} \qquad\qquad \frac{5}{8} > \frac{1}{2} \qquad\qquad \frac{1}{4} < \frac{1}{3} < \frac{3}{8}$$

Compare Two Fractions

Use this method to compare two fractions. For example, compare $\frac{13}{18}$ and $\frac{5}{7}$. First, write the two fractions and cross multiply as shown. The larger cross product appears next to the larger fraction. If cross products are equal then the fractions are equivalent.

$$91 = \overbrace{13 \times 5} = 90$$
$$\underbrace{18 \times 7}$$

$$91 > 90 \text{ so } \frac{13}{18} > \frac{5}{7}$$

Comparing With Square Roots

The square root of a given number, when multiplied by itself, equals the given number. This symbol means the square root of $25\sqrt{25}$. The square root of 25 is 5. $5 \times 5 = 25$.

Some Square Roots Are Whole Numbers

Compare $\sqrt{36}$ and 5.
The numbers with whole-number square roots are called perfect squares.

$$\sqrt{1} = 1 \quad \sqrt{4} = 2 \quad \sqrt{9} = 3 \quad \sqrt{16} = 4 \quad \sqrt{25} = 5 \quad \sqrt{36} = 6$$

$$\sqrt{49} = 7 \quad \sqrt{64} = 8 \quad \sqrt{81} = 9 \quad \sqrt{100} = 10 \quad \sqrt{121} = 11 \quad \sqrt{144} = 12$$

$\sqrt{36} = 6$. So $\sqrt{36} > 5$.

Other Times You May Have To Approximate the Square Root

Compare 9.6 and $\sqrt{92}$
Find the square root of 92. We know that $\sqrt{81} = 9$ and $\sqrt{100} = 10$. So we know that the square root of 92 is between 9 and 10. 92 is closer to 100 so let's try 9.6.

$$\text{Try } 9.6 \times 9.6 = 92.16$$

So, $9.6 > \sqrt{92}$

Comparing with Absolute Value

$$|-5| = 5 \quad |5| = 5 \quad |-\sqrt{25}| = \sqrt{25} = 5$$

Compare 16 and $|-18|$.
The absolute value of a number is positive.

$|-18| = 18 \quad 18 > 16 \text{ so } |-18| > 16$

Comparing when Both Numbers Are Negative

Disregard the negative signs. Compare the numbers using the following methods.
Numbers that were larger when both signs were positive are smaller when both signs are negative.
+6.3 > 5.9, so −6.3 < −5.9.

Numbers that were smaller when both signs were positive are larger when both signs are negative.
$+3\frac{1}{5} < +4\frac{3}{8}$, so $-3\frac{1}{5} > -4\frac{3}{8}$.

Completed Examples

A. $6.\overline{387} \leq 6.\overline{4}$ B. $5\frac{1}{3} \geq -6\frac{5}{8}$ C. $\sqrt{27} \geq 4.9$ D. $4.25 = 4\frac{1}{4}$

Practice Questions

> Use >, <, or = to compare the numbers.

1. 89.753 ☐ 89.755   2. $\sqrt{81}$ ☐ 9.5   3. |−7| ☐ |−3| 4. 10^3 ☐ 1000
5. $7\frac{3}{4}$ ☐ 7.75   6. −56.7 ☐ −56.9   7. −604 ☐ −610   8. |−25.5| ☐ −25.5

Answers on page 214.

ESTIMATE THE SUM, AVERAGE, OR PRODUCT OF NUMBERS IN A WORD PROBLEM (II A5)

TEST QUESTION EXAMPLE:

CLAST questions look something like this:

It takes a person about $7\frac{1}{2}$ minutes to run a mile. The person runs 174 miles in a month. What is a reasonable estimate of the time it takes for the person to run that distance?

Follow these steps.

1. Round the numbers.

2. Use the rounded numbers to estimate the answer.

Completed Example

1. Round $7\frac{1}{2}$ to 8.
   Round 174 to 180.

2. 180 × 8 = 1440 minutes or 24 hours.
   24 hours is a reasonable estimate of the answer.

Practice Questions

1. A class took a spelling quiz and the grades were 93, 97, 87, 88, 98, 91. What is a reasonable estimate of the average of these grades?

2. To build a sandbox, you need lumber in the following lengths: 12 ft., 16 ft., 18 ft., and 23 ft. What is a reasonable estimate of the total length of the lumber?

Answers on page 215.

3. Each batch of cookies yields 11 dozen. You need 165 dozen. What is a reasonable estimate for the number of batches you will need?

4. It takes 48 minutes for a commuter to travel back and forth from work each day. If the commuter drives back and forth 26 days a month, what is a reasonable estimate of the number of hours that spent driving?

FIND MISSING NUMBERS IN A PATTERN (III A1)

TEST QUESTION EXAMPLES:

CLAST items based on this objective will look something like this:

A. What term is missing in this number pattern?

B. These points are all on the same line.

Find the missing term

A. 2   5   10   17   ___

B. $(-7, -15)$ $(\frac{2}{3}, \frac{1}{3})$ $(2, 3)$ $(4, 7)$ $(8, \_\_)$

Sequences

Arithmetic Sequence

A sequence of numbers formed by adding the same nonzero number.

3, 11, 19, 27, 35, 42, 50   Add 8 to get each successive term
53, 48, 44, 40, 36, 32   Add (–4) to get each successive term

Geometric Sequence

A sequence of numbers formed by multiplying the same nonzero number.

3, 15, 75, 375   Multiply by 5 to get each successive term.
160, 40, 10, $2\frac{1}{2}$ Multiply by $\frac{1}{4}$ to get each successive term.

Harmonic Sequence

A sequence of fractions with a numerator of 1 in which the denominators form an arithmetic sequence.

$\frac{1}{2}$ $\frac{1}{9}$ $\frac{1}{16}$ $\frac{1}{23}$ $\frac{1}{30}$ Each denominator is 1. The denominators form an arithmetic sequence.

Relationships

Linear Relationships

Linear relationships are pairs of numbers formed by adding or multiplying the same number to the first term in a pair. Here are some examples.

(3, 12), (5, 14), (11, 20), (15, 24) Add 9 to the first term to get the second.

(1, 6), (2, 12), (3, 18), (4, 24), (5, 30) Multiply the first term by 6 to get the second.

(96, 12), (72, 9), (56, 7), (24, 3), (16, 2) Multiply the first term by $\frac{1}{8}$ to get the second.

Quadratic Relationships

Quadratic relationships are pairs of numbers formed by squaring one of the terms.

$(\frac{1}{2}, \frac{1}{4}), (\frac{1}{3}, \frac{1}{9}), (\frac{1}{4}, \frac{1}{16}), (\frac{1}{7}, \frac{1}{49})$ Square the first term to get the second.

$(4, 2), (19, \sqrt{19}), (36, 6), (2, \sqrt{2})$ Square the second term to get the first.

Completed Examples

A. What term is missing in this number pattern?

2   5   10   17   __
  +3   +5   +7   +9

26 is the missing term.

B. These points are all on the same line. Find the missing term.

$(-7, -15) (\frac{2}{3}, \frac{1}{3}) (2, 3) (4, 7) (8, \_)$

Multiply the first term by 2 and subtract 1. The missing term is (8, 15).

Practice Questions

Find the missing term in each pattern below.

1. 4, 2, 0, –2, –4, __ –8, –10
2. 4, 6.5, 9, 11.5, __
3. 120, 60, 30, 15, __
4. 1, 2, 6, 24, 120, __
5. 1/5, 1/9, 1/17, 1/33 __
6. 5 9 13 17 __

The points in each sequence below are on the same line. Find the missing term.

7. (4, 12), (2, 10), (10, 18), (18, 26), (22, __)
8. (100, 11), (70, 8), (90, 10), (40, 5), (30, __)
9. (3, 9), (7, 49), (2, 4), (100, 10000), (5, __)
10. $(\frac{1}{12}, \frac{1}{4}), (\frac{1}{15}, \frac{1}{5}), (\frac{1}{24}, \frac{1}{8}), (\frac{1}{9}, \_)$
11. $(\sqrt{8}, 16), (2, 8), (\sqrt{3}, 6), (\sqrt{\frac{1}{4}}, \frac{1}{2}), (\sqrt{5}, \_)$

Answers on page 215.

SOLVE REAL-WORLD WORD PROBLEMS NOT INVOLVING VARIABLES OR PERCENT (IV A1)

TEST QUESTION EXAMPLE:

CLAST questions look something like this:

A car gets 20 miles per gallon of gas going downhill and 18 miles per gallon of gas going uphill. About how many gallons of gas would the car use going 81 miles uphill and 54 miles downhill?

Follow these problem-solving steps.

1. Choose the operations.

2. Write and solve the number sentence(s).

3. Interpret the meaning of the solution.

Key Words

Addition	sum, and, more, increased by
Subtraction	less, difference, decreased by
Multiplication	of, product, times
Division	per, quotient, shared ratio
Equals	is, equals

You can't just use these key words without thinking. You must check to be sure that the operation makes sense when it replaces the key word. For example,

19 and 23 is 42	16 is 4 more than 12	What number times 19 is 5.7
19 + 23 = 42	16 = 4 + 12	___ × 19 = 5.7

Completed Example

1. Divide to find the number of gallons used.
   Then add to find the total number of gallons used.

2. 81 ÷ 18 = 4.5 (About 4.5 gallons going uphill)

   54 ÷ 20 = 2.7 (About 2.7 gallons going downhill)

   2.7 + 4.5 = 7.2

3. About 7.2 gallons total

Practice Questions

1. It costs $115 to print 100 pamphlets. It costs an additional $2.50 for each pamphlet in excess of 100. If 120 pamphlets are needed, how much would it cost to print them ?

2. An apartment house has six apartments. During the warm months the average electric bill for the six apartments was $37 . During the winter months (November-March) the average electric bill for the six apartments was $55. What is the average monthly bill for the year for the six apartments?

Answers on page 215.

3. Samantha drinks four cups of instant coffee per day. In each cup she uses exactly $1\frac{1}{2}$ teaspoons of coffee. If there are 135 teaspoons of coffee in each jar, in how many days will Samantha use a jar of coffee?

4. A pilot makes a salary of $2,100.00 per week based on 20,000 miles flown. He receives a bonus of $25 for every extra 50 miles flown more than the initial 20,000 miles. If the pilot makes 8 inter-continental flights per week, averaging 2700 miles each, and 6 continental flights, averaging 575 miles each, how much bonus money would he earn for the week?

SOLVE REAL-WORLD WORD PROBLEMS THAT INVOLVE PERCENT (IV A2)

Test Question Example:

CLAST questions look something like this:

The Tallahassee bookstore accounted for 23% of the book company's revenues. The bookstore in Miami accounted for 31% of the book company's revenues. If the book company's revenues were $750,000, how much revenue did the other bookstores account for?

To solve percent word problems, change percents to decimals or fractions.
See page 119 to see how to change percents to decimals and fractions.

Completed Example

- The Tallahassee and Miami bookstores accounted for 54% of the book company's sales.
- That leaves 46% for the rest of the bookstores.
- Change 46% to 0.46.
- Multiply .46 × $750,000 = $345,000.
- The other bookstores accounted for $345,000 in sales.

Practice Questions

1. Thirty-five percent of Cathy's monthly salary goes to paying the rent. Twenty-five percent goes to her car payment. If her monthly salary is $3,200.00, what amount of money does she have left per month?

2. Mark Messier scored 33 goals for the New York Rangers in 1994. Adam Graves scored 52. If the total goals scored for the entire Ranger team was 340, what percent of the goals did the rest of the team score?

Answers on page 215.

3. On a busy night a seafood and steak house sells 80 pounds of beef in 16-oz. steak dinners, and 65 lobster dinners. If 200 dinners are served, what percentage of them are lobster dinners?

4. A trust fund of $100,000.00 is opened in 1996. If the money gets 5 percent interest every year, how much money is in the trust after two years?

5. A stereo system's retail price is $249.00. It goes on sale at Berdine's department store for $225.00. At Zoom Electronics it is on sale for 15% off. What is the difference between the sale prices?

SOLVE PROBLEMS THAT INVOLVE THE STRUCTURE AND LOGIC OF ARITHMETIC (IV A3)

TEST QUESTION EXAMPLE:

CLAST questions look something like this:

Find all the single digit numbers that divide 230,616 without a remainder.

Factors and Multiples

The **factors** of a number are those numbers that evenly divide it.
Look at the factors of some numbers.

Factors of 12	→	1, 2, 3, 4, 6, 12
Factors of 20	→	1, 2, 4, 5, 20

The **multiples** of a number are those numbers it evenly divides.
Look at the multiples of some numbers.

Multiples of 4	→	0, 4, 8, 12, 16, 20, 24, ...
Multiples of 6	→	0, 6, 12, 18, 24, 30, 36 ...

Divisibility Rules

Use these rules to find out if a number is divisible by the given number. *Divisible* means the given number divides evenly with no remainder.

2 Every even number is divisible by 2.

3 If the sum of the digits is divisible by 3, the number is divisible by 3.

347    $3 + 4 + 7 = 14$ 14 is not divisible by 3 so 347 is not divisible by 3.

738    $7 + 3 + 8 = 18$ 18 is not divisible by 3 so 738 is divisible by 3.

4 If the last two digits are divisible by 4, the number is divisible by 4.

484,8<u>42</u>   42 is not divisible by 4 so 484,842 is not divisible by 4.

371,9<u>56</u>   56 is divisible by 4 so 372,956 is divisible by 4.

5 If the last digit is 0 or 5, then the number is divisible by 5.

6 If the number meets the divisibility rules for both 2 *and* 3 then it is divisible by 6.

8 If the last three digits are divisible by 8, then the number is divisible by 8.

208,513,<u>114</u>   114 is not divisible by 8 so 208,513,114 is not divisible by 8.

703,628,<u>920</u>   920 is divisible by 8 so 703,628,920 is divisible by 8.

9 If the sum of the digits is divisible by 9 then the number is divisible by 9.

93,163 $9 + 3 + 1 + 6 + 3 = 22$ 22 is not divisible by 9 so 93,163 is not divisible by 9.

86,715 $8 + 6 + 7 + 1 + 5 = 27$ 27 is divisible by 9 so 86,715 is divisible by 9.

Completed Example

Apply the divisibility rules to 230,616

2 YES The number is even.
3 YES $2 + 3 + 0 + 6 + 1 + 6 = 18$—18 is divisible by 3.
4 YES 16 is divisible by 4.
5 NO   The number does not end in 0 or 5.
6 YES The number is divisible by 2 and 3.
7 NO   We have to work this one out.
8 YES 616 is divisible by 8.
9 YES $2 + 3 + 0 + 6 + 1 + 6 = 18$—18 is divisible by 9.

230,616 is evenly divisible by 2, 3, 4, 6, 8 and 9.

Practice Questions

1. List the factors of 25.

2. List the factors of 32.

3. List the first five nonzero multiples of 3.

Answers on page 216.

4. List the first five nonzero multiples of 7.

5. List all the single digit numbers that divide 40,329 without a remainder.

6. Find all the single digit numbers that divide 103,259 without a remainder.

GEOMETRY AND MEASUREMENT

ROUND MEASUREMENTS TO THE NEAREST GIVEN UNIT (I B1)

TEST QUESTION EXAMPLES:

CLAST questions look something like this:

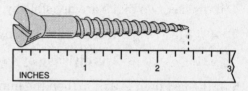

A. Round 483.65 meters to the nearest meter.

B. Round the measure of the screw to the nearest ¼ inch.

Customary (English) Units

Length

12 inches (in.) = 1 foot
3 feet = 1 yard (yd)
36 inches = 1 yard
1,760 yards = 1 mile (mi)
5,280 feet = 1 mile

Weight

16 ounces (oz) = 1 pound (lb)
2,000 pounds = 1 ton (T)

Capacity

2 cups = 1 pint (pt)
2 pints = 1 quart (qt)
4 quarts = 1 gallon (gal)

Metric System

The metric system used common units of measure. The system uses prefixes that are powers of 10 or 0.1.

The common units used in the metric system follow:

Length—meter
Mass—gram
Capacity—liter

The prefixes used in the metric system follow:

1000	100	10	Unit	0.1	0.01	0.001
Kilo	Hecto	Deka		Deci	Centi	Milli

Notice that the prefixes less than one end in *i*.

Customary Rulers

Measure the length of a line segment to the nearest $\frac{1}{16}$ of an inch. Put one end of the line segment at the 0 point on the ruler. Read the mark closest to the end of the line.

The line segment is $1\frac{11}{16}$ inches long. Rounded to the nearest quarter inch, the line segment is $1\frac{3}{4}$ inches long. The end of the line segment is closer to $1\frac{3}{4}$ inches than to $1\frac{1}{2}$ inches.

Metric Rulers

Measure the length of the line segment to the nearest millimeter. Put one end of the line segment at the 0 point on the ruler. Read the mark closest to the end of the line.

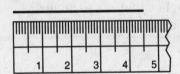

The line segment is 45 mm long. Rounded to the nearest cm, the line segment is 5 cm long. The end of the line segment is closer to 5 cm than to 4 cm.

Rounding Whole Numbers and Decimals

Follow these steps to round a number to a place.

- Look at the digit to the right of that place.

- If the digit to the right is 5 or more, round up. If the digit is less than 5, leave the numeral to be rounded as written.

Round 859,465 to the thousands place.

Underline the thousands place.

Look to the right. The digit 4 is less than 5 so leave as written.

859,465 rounded to the *thousands* place is 859,000.

859,465 rounded to the *ten-thousands* place is 860,000.

Round 8.647 to the hundredths place.

Underline the hundredths place.

Look to the right. The digit 7 is 5 or more so you round up.

8.647 rounded to the *hundredths* place is 8.65.

8.647 rounded to the *tenths* place is 8.6.

Completed Examples

A. Round 483.65 meters to the nearest meter.

- •Underline the meters place. 483.65

- •Look to the right. The digit 6 is 5 or more.

- •Round up. 484

483.65 meters rounded to the nearest meter is 484.

B. Round the length of the screw to the nearest $\frac{1}{4}$ inch.

The measure is closer to $2\frac{1}{2}$ inches than to $2\frac{1}{4}$ inches.
The measure rounded to the nearest $\frac{1}{4}$ inch is $2\frac{1}{2}$ inches.

Practice Questions

1. Round 101 lbs. 12 oz. to the nearest pound.

2. Round 684.37 meters to the nearest tenth of a meter.

3. Round 10,093 yards to the nearest 100 yards.

4. Round the measure below to the nearest cm.

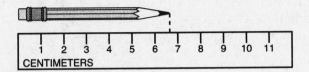

5. Round 12:56 AM to the nearest hour.

6. Round 407.65 km to the nearest kilometer.

Answers on page 216.

CALCULATE DISTANCE, AREA, AND VOLUME (I B2)

TEST QUESTION EXAMPLES:

CLAST questions look something like this:

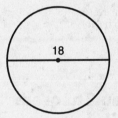

A. How many meters is it around a regular hexagon with a side of 87 centimeters?

B. What is the area of this figure?

C. A circular cone has a radius of 8 cm and a height of 10 cm. What is the volume?

Distance and Area

Perimeter   The distance around a figure. The perimeter of a circle is called the circumference.

Area   The amount of space occupied by a two-dimensional figure.

Formulas for Perimeter and Area

Figure	Formula	Description
Triangle	Area = $\frac{1}{2} bh$ Perimeter = $s_1 + s_2 + s_3$	
Square	Area = s^2 Perimeter = $4s$	
Rectangle	Area = lw Perimeter = $2l + 2w$	
Parallelogram	Area = bh Perimeter = $2b + 2s$	
Trapezoid	Area = $\frac{1}{2}h\,(b_1 + b_2)$ Perimeter = $b_1 + b_2 + s_1 + s_2$	
Circle	Area = πr^2 Circumference = $2\pi r$ or $\quad = \pi d$	

Pythagorean Theorem

The Pythagorean Theorem for right triangles states that the sum of the square of the legs equals the square of the hypotenuse:

$$a^2 + b^2 = c^2$$

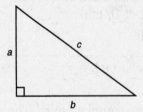

Other Polygons

Pentagon	5 sides	Octagon	8 sides
Hexagon	6 sides	Nonagon	9 sides
Heptagon	7 sides	Decagon	10 sides

Regular Polygon — All sides are the same length.

Completed Examples—Distance and Area

Let's solve the distance-and-area problems.

A. How many meters is it around a regular hexagon with a side of 87 centimeters?

A hexagon has 6 sides. It's a regular hexagon, so all the sides are the same length.

$6 \times 87 = 522$. The perimeter is 522 centimeters, which equals 5.22 meters.

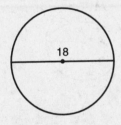

B. What is the area of this figure?

The formula for the area of a circle is πr^2.
The diameter is 18, so the radius is 9. Use 3.14 for π.
$A = 3.14 \times (9)^2 = 3.14 \times 81 = 254.34$ or about 254.

Practice Questions

1. A circle has a radius of 9 inches. What is the area?

2. The sides of a 4-sided pyramid are equilateral triangles. What is the surface area of the pyramid if the sides of the triangles equal 3 three inches and the height is 2.6 inches?

3. A regular hexagon has one side 5 feet long. What is the distance around its edge?

4. What is the surface area of the side of a cylinder (not top and bottom) with a height of 10 cm and a diameter of 2.5 cm?

5. A rectangle has a width x and a length $(x + 5)$. If the perimeter is 90 feet, what is the length?

6. The perimeter of one face of a cube is 20 cm. What is the surface area?

Answers on page 216.

Volume

Volume—The amount of space occupied by a three-dimensional figure

Formulas for Volume

Figure	Formula	Description
Cube	Volume = s^3	
Rectangular Prism	Volume = lwh	
Sphere	Volume = $\frac{4}{3} \pi r^3$	
Cone	Volume = $\frac{1}{3}\pi r^2 h$	
Cylinder	Volume = $\pi r^2 h$ Surface Area = $2\pi r(h+r)$	

Completed Example—Volume

C. A circular cone has a radius of 8 cm and a height of 10 cm. What is the volume?

Formula for the volume of a cone = $\frac{1}{3} \pi r^2 h$.

$V = (\frac{1}{3}) (3.14) (8^2) (10) = (\frac{1}{3}) (3.14) (64) (10) = (\frac{1}{3}) (3.14) (640) = 669.87$

The volume of the cone is 669.87 cubic centimeters or about 670 cubic centimeters.

Practice Questions

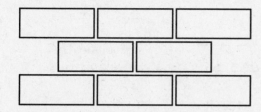

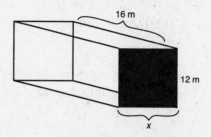

3. The official basketball has a radius of 6.5 inches. What is the volume?

1. The bricks in the wall pictured here measure 2 inches by 4 inches by 8 inches. What is the volume of the bricks in this section of the wall?

2. A circular cone has a radius of 4 cm. If the volume is 134 cm², what is the height?

4. The rectangular solid shown here has a volume of 1920m³. What is the area of the shaded side?

Answers on page 216.

IDENTIFY RELATIONSHIPS BETWEEN ANGLE MEASURES (II B1)

TEST QUESTION EXAMPLE:

CLAST questions look something like this:

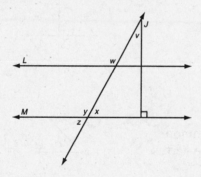

Lines *L* and *M* are parallel. Line *J* is perpendicular to line *M*.
What statements can we make about ∠*v*, ∠*w*, ∠*x*, ∠*y* and ∠*z*?

Definition	Model	Symbol
Point—a location	.A	A
Plane—a flat surface that extends infinitely in all directions		plane ABC
Space—occupies three dimensions and extends infinitely in all directions		space xyz
Line—a set of points in a straight path that extends infinitely in two directions		$\overleftrightarrow{AB}$
Line segment—part of a line with two endpoints		$\overline{AB}$
Ray—part of a line with one endpoint		$\overrightarrow{AB}$
Parallel lines—lines that stay the same distance apart and never touch		
Perpendicular lines—lines that meet at right angles		
Angle—two rays with a common endpoint, which is called the vertex.		∠ABC
Acute angle—angle that measures between 0° and 90°		
Right angle—angle that measures 90°		
Obtuse angle—angle that measures between 90° and 180°		
Complementary angles—angles that have a total measure of 90°		

Supplementary angles—angles that
have a total measure of 180°

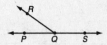
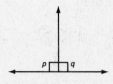

Congruent angles have the same
angle measure.
∠p and ∠q measure 90°.
∠p and ∠q are congruent.
m∠p = m∠q

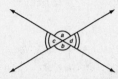

Vertical angles are formed when
two lines intersect. Angles opposite
each other are vertical angles. Vertical
angles are the same size.

∠ a and b are vertical angles.   ∠ c and ∠ d are vertical angles.

The measures of vertical angles are equal. m∠a = m∠ b m∠c = m∠d

Parallel lines cut by a transversal
form congruent angles.
Line A and line B are parallel.
Line C is the transversal.

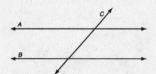

Corresponding angles are
congruent. The corresponding
angles in this figure are

∠1 and ∠5 ∠2 and ∠6
∠3 and ∠7 ∠4 and ∠8

Alternate interior angles are
congruent. The pairs of alternate
interior angles in this figure are
∠ 3 and ∠ 6 m∠ 3 = m∠ 6
∠ 4 and ∠ 5 m∠ 4 = m∠ 5

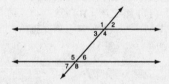

Alternate exterior angles are
congruent. The pairs of alternate
interior angles in this figure are

∠1 and 8 m ∠1 = m ∠8
∠2 and 7 m ∠2 = m ∠7

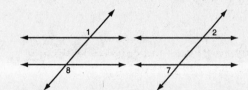

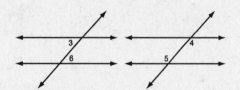

Completed Example

Statement	Reason
$\angle x$ and $\angle z$ are congruent.	Vertical angles are congruent.
$\angle w$ and $\angle y$ are congruent	Corresponding angles are congruent.
$\angle y$ and $\angle x$ are supplementary.	The sum of the angles is 180°.
$\angle v$ and $\angle x$ are complementary.	The large triangle contains a right angle *and* the sum of the other angle is 90°.

Practice Questions

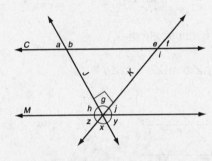

1. If $\overleftrightarrow{C} \parallel \overleftrightarrow{M}$, then which of the following is true?
   (A) m $\angle b$ = m $\angle a$ (B) m $\angle j$ = m $\angle h$
   (C) m $\angle e + \angle f = 90$ (D) m $\angle e$ = m $\angle i$

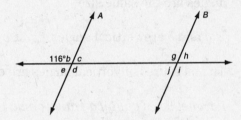

2. If $\overleftrightarrow{A} \parallel \overleftrightarrow{B}$, what is the measure of $\angle j$?
   (A) 116° (B) 64°
   (C) 26° (D) 154°

Answers on page 216.

CLASSIFY SIMPLE PLANE FIGURES ACCORDING TO THEIR PROPERTIES (II B 2)

TEST QUESTION EXAMPLE:

CLAST questions look something like this:

What four-sided figure has opposite sides parallel, all sides the same length, but no right angles?

Polygon—a closed figure made up of line segments; if all sides are the same length, the figure is a regular polygon

Pentagon—Five sides.

Hexagon—Six sides.

Octagon—Eight sides.

Triangle—polygon with three sides and three angles; the sum of the angles is always 180°

Equilateral triangle—all sides are the same length; all angles are the same size, 60°

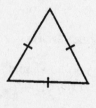

Isosceles triangle—two sides the same length; two angles the same size

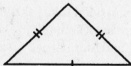

Scalene triangle—all sides different lengths; all angles different sizes

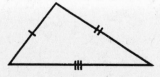

Quadrilateral—polygon with four sides

Square—four sides; opposite sides parallel;
all sides the same length; four right angles

Rhombus—four sides; opposite sides parallel;
all sides the same length

Rectangle—four sides; opposite sides parallel
and same length; four right angles

Parallelogram—four sides; opposite sides parallel
and same length

Trapezoid—four sides; one pair of sides parallel

Completed Example

A four-sided figure is a quadrilateral.
Opposite sides parallel eliminates the trapezoid.
All sides the same length, but no right angles, means it must be the rhombus.

Practice Questions

1. What polygon has equal sides and equal angle measures of 60°?

2. What four-sided figure has equal opposite angles, but not four equal angles, and four sides the same length?

3. What four-sided figure has one pair of sides parallel?

4. A figure has three angles and two of the angle measures are 14° and 87°. What is the third angle measure?

Answers on page 217.

RECOGNIZE SIMILAR TRIANGLES AND THEIR PROPERTIES (II B3)

TEST QUESTION EXAMPLE:

CLAST questions look something like this:

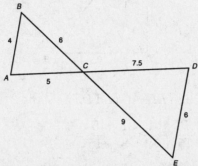

Are triangle *ABC* and triangle *CDE* similar triangles?

Similar Triangles

Corresponding angles are congruent. The ratio of the lengths of corresponding sides are equal. These triangles are similar.

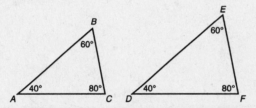

Corresponding angles of the two triangles are congruent.

∠*A* and ∠*D*
∠*B* and ∠*E*
∠*C* and ∠*F*

The measures of congruent angles are equal.

measure of ∠*A* = measure of ∠*D* = 40°
measure of ∠*B* = measure of ∠*E* = 60°
measure of ∠*C* = measure of ∠*F* = 80°

Corresponding sides (Corresponding sides are opposite corresponding angles)

$\overline{BC}$ and $\overline{EF}$

$\overline{AC}$ and $\overline{DF}$

$\overline{AB}$ and $\overline{DE}$

The lengths of corresponding sides are equal.

$$\frac{\overline{BC}}{\overline{EF}} = \frac{\overline{AC}}{\overline{DF}} = \frac{\overline{AB}}{\overline{DE}}$$

Are these triangles similar?

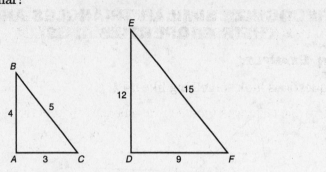

Corresponding sides: $\overline{AB}$ and $\overline{DE}$, $\overline{BC}$ and $\overline{EF}$, $\overline{AC}$ and $\overline{DF}$

Does $\dfrac{AB}{DE} = \dfrac{BC}{EF}$? $\dfrac{AB}{DE} = \dfrac{4}{12}$; $\dfrac{BC}{EF} = \dfrac{5}{15}$; $\dfrac{4}{12} = \dfrac{1}{3}$; $\dfrac{5}{15} = \dfrac{1}{3}$

These triangles are similar. Ratios of corresponding sides of the two triangles are equal.

Completed Example

The ratios of the lengths of corresponding sides are equal.

$\overline{AB}$ and $\overline{DE}$ are corresponding sides.

Does $\dfrac{AC}{CD} = \dfrac{AB}{DE}$? Yes. $\dfrac{5}{7.5} = \dfrac{4}{6}$ $\left(\dfrac{20}{30} = \dfrac{20}{30}\right)$

Practice Questions

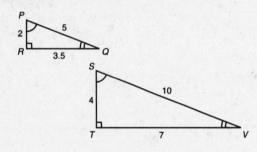

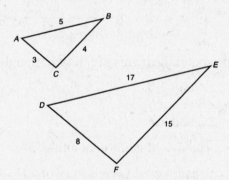

1. Are $\triangle PQR$ and $\triangle SVT$ similar?

3. Which of these statements is true for the triangles above?
   (A) $\angle C$ is congruent to $\angle F$
   (B) $\angle B$ is congruent to $\angle E$

   (C) $\dfrac{AB}{DE} = \dfrac{CB}{FE}$

   (D) $\triangle ABC$ and $\triangle DEF$ are congruent

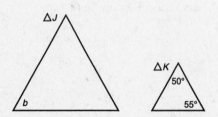

2. The triangles above are similar. What is the measure of $\angle b$?

Answers on page 217.

IDENTIFY APPROPRIATE UNITS OF MEASUREMENT FOR GEOMETRIC OBJECTS (II B4)

TEST QUESTION EXAMPLE:

CLAST questions look something like this:

Should you use degrees, liters, inches, or square meters to describe the height of a building?

Units of measurement	Types of measurement
Length	
centimeters, meters, kilometers	length of a road height of a tower perimeter of a figure
inches, feet, yards, miles	depth of a lake width of a house
Area	
square centimeters, square meters	amount of floor space in a house amount of surface on a cereal box
square inches, square feet, square yards	amount of surface of a basketball amount of fabric needed for a dress amount of lawn to be mowed
Volume/Capacity	
quarts, gallons, liters, fluid ounces, milliliters	amount of liquid in a bottle amount of liquid a bottle can hold
cubic centimeters, cubic meters, cubic inches	amount of dirt in a flower pot amount of space in a room

Completed Example

Height is a length. Use inches, a measure of length.

Practice Questions

1. Which of the following would be appro-
   priate to measure the length of a couch?
   (A) liters
   (B) cubic centimeters
   (C) meters
   (D) square inches

2. Which of the following would be
   appropriate to measure the contents
   of a glass?
   (A) square inches
   (B) fluid ounces
   (C) centimeters
   (D) minutes

3. Which of the following would be
   appropriate to measure the depth
   of a swimming pool?
   (A) yards
   (B) degrees
   (C) square meters
   (D) gallons

4. Which of the following would be
   appropriate to measure the amount
   of garbage in a landfill?
   (A) degrees
   (B) miles
   (C) cubic meters
   (D) hours

Answers on page 217.

INFER FORMULAS FOR MEASURING GEOMETRIC FIGURES (III B1)

TEST QUESTION EXAMPLE:

CLAST questions look something like this:

Look at the pattern below.

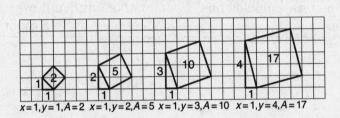

$x=1, y=1, A=2$ $x=1, y=2, A=5$ $x=1, y=3, A=10$ $x=1, y=4, A=17$

Calculate A if $x = 1$ and $y = 6$.

Follow these steps to solve this type of problem.

1. Find the pattern.

2. Write the rule or formula.

3. Predict the result.

Completed Example

1. Find the pattern

x	y	A
1	1	2
1	2	5
1	3	10
1	4	17

The numbers in the A column go up rather rapidly. Notice that each A is one more than a perfect square.

2. The rule is $x^2 + y^2 = A$

3. For $x = 1$ and $y = 6$: $(1)^2 + (6)^2 = A$ $1 + 36 = A$
   $A = 37$

Practice Questions

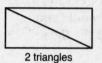 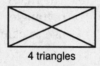

2 triangles
360°

3 triangles
540°

4 triangles
_____

$A = 2$ $A = 5$ $A = 8$ $A = ?$

1. Study the diagram above. What is the sum of the angles when there are four triangles?

2. Study the diagram above. What is the area of the square if the right triangle has sides with lengths of 2 and 3?

Answers on page 217.

SELECT FORMULAS FOR COMPUTING MEASURES OF GEOMETRIC FIGURES (III B2)

TEST QUESTION EXAMPLE:

CLAST questions look something like this:

The figure shows a cube with a cone on top.
Which formula would you use to compute the volume of the figure?

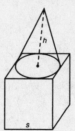

Use the area and volume formulas you know to answer these types of questions.
   Refer to the area and volume formulas on pages 139, 140 and 142.

Completed Example

The figure is a combination of a cube and a cone.

Find the volume of the cube. $(V = s^3)$

Find the volume of the *cone*. $(V = \frac{1}{3} \pi r^2 h)$

Volume of the figure is $V = s^3 + \frac{1}{3} \pi r^2 h$.

Practice Questions

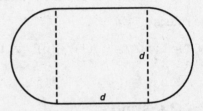

3. The figure above shows a circle and a rectangle. Which formula would you use to calculate the area of the figure?

1. The figure above shows a ball attached to a cube. Which formula would you use to calculate the volume of the figure?

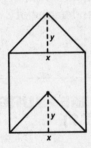

2. Which formula would you use to calculate the area of the figure?

Answers on page 217.

SOLVE REAL-WORLD WORD PROBLEMS ABOUT MEASURES OF GEOMETRIC FIGURES (IV B1)

TEST QUESTION EXAMPLE:

CLAST questions look something like this:

A circular pool with a radius of 10 feet is inscribed inside a square wall. What is the area of the region outside the pool but inside the fence?

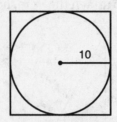

Follow these steps to solve this type of problem.

1. Identify the figure or figures involved.

2. Use the formulas for these figures.

3. Use the results of the formulas to solve the problem.

Completed Example

1. There is a square with $s = 20$ and a circle with $r = 10$. The side of the square is twice the radius of the circle.

2. Find the areas.
   Square: $(A = s^2)$ $(20) \times (20) = 400$
   Circle: $(A = \pi r^2)$ $3.14 \times 10^2 = 3.14 \times 100 = 314$

3. Subtract to find the area inside the square but outside the circle.
   $400 - 314 = 86$

Practice Questions

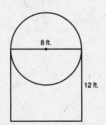

1. The dimensions of part of a basketball court are shown in the diagram above. One pint of paint covers 35 square feet. How much paint would it take to paint the inside region of this part of the court?

2. A roofer uses one bushel of shingles to cover 1200 square feet. How many bushels of shingles are needed to cover these three rectangular roofs?
   Roof 1: 115 ft. by 65 ft.
   Roof 2: 112 ft. by 65 ft.
   Roof 3: 72 ft. by 52 ft.

Answers on page 217.

SOLVE REAL-WORLD WORD PROBLEMS INVOLVING THE PYTHAGOREAN THEOREM (IV B2)

TEST QUESTION EXAMPLE:

CLAST questions look something like this:

A radio tower sticks 40 feet straight up into the air. Engineers attached a wire with no slack from the top of the tower to the ground 30 feet away from the tower. If it costs $90 a foot to attach the wire, how much did the wire cost?

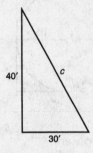

Follow these steps to solve this type of problem.

1. Sketch and label the right triangle.

2. Use the Pythagorean formula.

3. Solve the problem.

Completed Example

1. Sketch and label the right triangle.

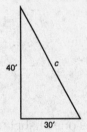

2. Use the Pythagorean formula.
$$a^2 + b^2 = c^2$$
$$(40)^2 + (30)^2 = c^2$$
$$1600 + 900 = c^2$$
$$2500 = c^2$$
$$50 = c \quad \text{The wire is 50 feet long.}$$

3. Solve the problem.
   50 feet at $95 a foot.

   $50 \times 95 = 4740$. The wire costs $4,740 to install.

Practice Questions

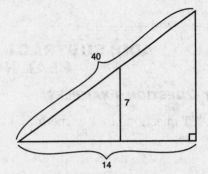

1. A 20-foot ladder is leaning against the side of a tall apartment building. The bottom of the ladder is 15 feet from the wall. At what height on the wall does the top of the ladder touch the building?

3. You are building a staircase. The wall is 14 feet wide and the stairs are 40 feet long. How high is the wall where it touches the top of the stairs?

4. A truck ramp is shaped like a right triangle. The base of the ramp is 300 feet long. The ramp itself is 340 feet long. How high is the third side of the ramp?

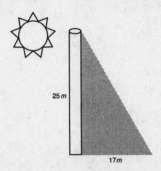

2. A 25-meter telephone pole casts a shadow. The shadow ends 17 meters from the base of the pole. How long is it straight from the top of the pole to the end of the shadow?

Answers on page 218.

ALGEBRA

ADD, SUBTRACT, MULTIPLY, AND DIVIDE REAL NUMBERS (I C1)

TEST QUESTION EXAMPLES:

CLAST questions look something like this:

A. $8\sqrt{3} - 2\sqrt{48}$ B. $\sqrt{12} \times \sqrt{6} =$ C. $\dfrac{\sqrt{90}}{\sqrt{2}} =$ D. $13\pi + 7 + 18\pi =$

Real numbers include rational numbers and irrational numbers. Rational numbers can be represented by fractions (ratios). Irrational numbers cannot be represented by fractions. This objective deals primarily with irrational numbers.

Irrational numbers are usually written as a radical. The radical consists of the radical sign and a *positive* radicand. Some radicals have coefficients.

RADICAL

$$6\sqrt{12}$$

Coefficient   Radicand

Read, "Six times the square root of twelve."

Simplifying Radicals

Use these rules to simplify radicals.

$$\sqrt{a} \times \sqrt{b} = \sqrt{a} \times \sqrt{b} \qquad \frac{\sqrt{a}}{\sqrt{b}} = \sqrt{\frac{a}{b}}$$

$$\sqrt{72} = \sqrt{36} \times \sqrt{2} = \sqrt{36} \times \sqrt{2} = 6 \times \sqrt{2} \qquad \frac{\sqrt{56}}{\sqrt{8}} = \sqrt{\frac{56}{8}} = \sqrt{7}$$

Add and Subtract Irrational Numbers

Subtract

$8\sqrt{7} - \sqrt{63}$

$8\sqrt{7} - 3\sqrt{7} = 5\sqrt{7}$

$\sqrt{63} = \sqrt{9 \times 7} = \sqrt{9}\sqrt{7} = 3\sqrt{7}$

Subtract the coefficients with common radicals.

Form numbers with common radicals.

Add

$2\sqrt{3}+4\sqrt{5}+3\sqrt{48}$

$3\sqrt{48}=3\sqrt{16\times3}$

$=3\times4\sqrt{3}=12\sqrt{3}$

$\left(4\sqrt{5}\text{ cannot be simplified}\right)$

When possible, form numbers with common radicals.

$2\sqrt{3}+12\sqrt{3}+4\sqrt{5}=$

Group the numbers with common radicals.

$14\sqrt{3}+4\sqrt{5}$

Add coefficients with common radicals.

Multiply and Divide Irrational Numbers

Multiply

$\sqrt{8}\times\sqrt{7}$

$\sqrt{8}\times\sqrt{7}=\sqrt{8\times7}$

Rewrite under one radical sign.

$\sqrt{8\times7}=\sqrt{56}$

Multiply.

$\sqrt{56}=\sqrt{4\times14}=2\sqrt{14}$

Simplify.

Divide

The numerator of the answer to a division problem must be a whole number.

$\dfrac{\sqrt{2}}{\sqrt{7}}$

$\sqrt{\dfrac{2}{7}}$

Rewrite under one radical sign.

$\sqrt{\dfrac{2\times(7)}{7\times(7)}}\quad=\quad\sqrt{\dfrac{14}{49}}\quad=\quad\dfrac{\sqrt{14}}{7}$

The numerator does not evenly divide the denominator. Multiply the numerator and denominator by the denominator.

Simplify.

Completed Examples

A. $8\sqrt{3}-2\sqrt{48}\quad=\quad8\sqrt{3}-2\sqrt{16\times3}\quad=\quad8\sqrt{3}-8\sqrt{3}\quad=\quad0$

B. $\sqrt{12}\times\sqrt{6}\quad=\quad\sqrt{72}=\sqrt{9\times8}\quad=\quad3\sqrt{8}$

C. $\dfrac{\sqrt{90}}{\sqrt{2}}\quad=\quad\sqrt{\dfrac{90}{2}}=\sqrt{45}\quad=\quad\sqrt{9\times5}\quad=\quad3\sqrt{5}$

D. $13\pi+7+18\pi\quad=\quad13\pi+18\pi+7\quad=\quad31\pi+7$

Practice Questions

1. $\sqrt{12}+5\sqrt{3}$

2. $\sqrt{8}\times\sqrt{6}$

3. $\dfrac{\sqrt{108}}{\sqrt{36}}$

4. $8\sqrt{28}-3\sqrt{7}$

5. $\dfrac{3\sqrt{144}}{9\sqrt{16}}$

6. $\dfrac{\sqrt{320}}{\sqrt{5}}$

Answers on page 218.

USE THE CORRECT ORDER-OF-OPERATIONS TO COMPUTE (I C2)

TEST QUESTION EXAMPLE:

CLAST questions look something like this:

$$7 + 3 \times 6 + 4^2 - (8 + 4) =$$

Order of Operations

Use this phrase to remember the order in which we do operations:

Please Excuse My Dear Aunt Sally

(1) **P**arentheses (2) **E**xponents (3) **M**ultiplication or **D**ivision (4) **A**ddition or **S**ubtraction
For example,

$$4 + 3 \times 7^2 = 4 + 3 \times 49 = 4 + 147 = 151$$
$$(4 + 3) \times 7^2 = 7 \times 7^2 \qquad = 7 \times 49 \qquad = 343$$
$$(6 - 10 \div 5) + 6 \times 3 = (6 - 2) + 6 \times 3 = 4 + 6 \times 3 = 4 + 18 = 22$$

Completed Example

$$7 + 3 \times 6 + 4^2 - (8 + 4) \qquad = \qquad 7 + 3 \times 6 + 4^2 - \underline{12} \qquad =$$
$$7 + 3 \times 6 + \underline{16} - 12 \qquad = \qquad 7 + \underline{18} + 16 - 12 \qquad = \qquad 29$$

Practice Questions

1. $(12 + 5) \times 3 - 6^2$

2. $100 - 30 \times 5 + 7$

3. $8 \times 5 + 4 - 6 \div 2$

4. $((5 + 2)^2 + 16) \times 8$

Answers on page 218.

USE SCIENTIFIC NOTATION IN CALCULATIONS OF VERY LARGE OR VERY SMALL NUMBERS (I C3)

TEST QUESTION EXAMPLE:

CLAST items based on this objective look something like this:

A. $(2.7 \times 10^{-4}) \times (3.604 \times 10^3) =$ B. $\dfrac{7.45 \times 10^8}{2.5 \times 10^{-10}} =$

Mathematics **161**

Scientific Notation

Scientific notation uses powers of 10. The power shows how many zeros to use.

$$10^0 = 1 \quad 10^1 = 10 \quad 10^2 = 100 \quad 10^3 = 1{,}000 \quad 10^4 = 10{,}000 \quad 10^5 = 100{,}000$$
$$10^{-1} = 0.01 \quad 10^{-2} = 0.001 \quad 10^{-3} = 0.0001 \quad 10^{-4} = 0.00001 \quad 10^{-5} = 0.000001$$

Write whole numbers and decimals in scientific notation. Use a decimal with one numeral to the left of the decimal point.

$2{,}345 \quad = \quad 2.345 \times 10^3$ — The decimal point moved three places to the left. Use 10^3.

$176.8 \quad = \quad 1.768 \times 10^2$ — The decimal point moved two places to the left. Use 10^2.

$0.0034 \quad = \quad 3.4 \times 10^{-3}$ — The decimal point moved three places to the right. Use 10^{-3}.

$2.0735 \quad = \quad 2.0735 \times 10^0$ — The decimal is in the correct form. Use 10^0 to stand for 1.

Rules for Multiplying and Dividing Exponents

$$a^n \times a^m = a^{m+n} \qquad \frac{a^m}{a^n} = a^{m-n}$$

$$10^4 \times 10^7 = 10^{11} \qquad \frac{10^9}{10^{-3}} = 10^{12}$$

$$10^{-4} \times 10^9 = 10^5$$

Multiply $(2.35 \times 10^4) \times (7.6 \times 10^2)$

$$(2.35 \times 7.6) \times (10^4 \times 10^2) \quad = \quad 17.86 \times 10^6 \quad = \quad 1.786 \times 10^5$$

Group the decimals and the exponents. | Multiply. | Write the answer using scientific notation.

Divide $\dfrac{36{,}000}{0.0024}$

$$\frac{3.6 \times 10^4}{2.4 \times 10^{-3}} \quad = \quad \frac{3.6}{2.4} \times \frac{10^4}{10^{-3}} \quad = \quad 1.5 \times 10^7$$

Write the problem with scientific notation. | Group the decimals and the exponents. | Divide the decimals. Divide the exponents.

Completed Examples

A. $(2.7 \times 10^{-4}) \times (3.604 \times 10^3) = (2.7 \times 3.604) \ (10^{-4} \times 10^3) =$
   $9.7308 \times 10^{-1} = 2.5228 \times 10^0$

B. $\dfrac{7.45 \times 10^8}{2.45 \times 10^{-10}} \qquad \dfrac{(7.45) \times (10^8)}{(2.45) \times (10^{-10})} = 2.98 \times 10^{18}$

Practice Questions

> Use scientific notation and find the answer.

1. $(3.4 \times 10^4) \times (4.107 \times 10^5)$

2. $m^k \times m^p$

3. $\dfrac{8.034 \times 10^{12}}{2.06 \times 10^9}$

4. $(3.64 \times 10^{-4}) \times (1.12 \times 10^6)$

5. $\dfrac{6.8565 \times 10^{-3}}{2.1 \times 10^{-4}}$

6. $\dfrac{64000}{0.0032}$

Answers on page 218.

SOLVE LINEAR EQUATIONS AND INEQUALITIES (I C4)

TEST QUESTION EXAMPLES:

CLAST questions look something like this:

A. Solve for x: $6x - 7 = 4 \, (-x + 3)$
B. Solve for n: $7n - 11 > 17$

Equations and Inequalities

The whole idea of solving equations and inequalities is to isolate the variable on one side. The value of the variable is what's on the other side. Substitute your answer in the original equation or inequality to check your solution.

Solving Equations and Inequalities by Adding or Subtracting

$$\text{Solve: } y + 19 = 23$$
$$\text{Subtract 19} \qquad y + 19 - 19 = 23 - 19$$
$$y = 4$$

Check: Does $4 + 19 = 23$? Yes. It checks.

$$\text{Solve: } x - 23 < 51$$
$$\text{Add 23} \qquad x - 23 + 23 < 51 + 23$$
$$x < 74$$

Check: Is $74 - 23 < 51$. Yes. It checks.

Solving Equations and Inequalities by Multiplying or Dividing

$$\text{Solve: } \frac{z}{7} \geq 6$$

Multiply by 7 $\qquad \frac{x}{7} \times 7 \geq 6 \times 7$

$$z \geq 42$$

Check: Is $\frac{42}{7} \geq 6$? Yes. It checks.

$$\text{Solve: } 21 = -3x$$

Divide by –3 $\qquad \frac{21}{-3} = \frac{-3x}{-3}$

$$-7 = x$$

Check: Does $21 = (-3)\,(-7)$?
Yes. It checks.

Solving Two-Step Equations and Inequalities

Add or subtract before you multiply or divide.

$$\text{Solve: } 3x - 6 = 24$$
Add 6 $\qquad 3x - 6 + 6 = 24 + 6$
$$3x = 30$$
Divide by 3 $\qquad \frac{3x}{3} = \frac{30}{3}$
$$3x = 10$$
Check: Does $3 \times \mathbf{10} - 6 = 24$? Yes. It checks.

$$\text{Solve: } \frac{y}{7} + 4 > 32$$

Subtract 4 $\qquad \frac{y}{7} + 4 - 4 > 32 - 4$

$$\frac{y}{7} > 28$$

Multiply by 7 $\qquad \frac{y}{7} \times 7 > (28)(7)$

$$y > 196$$

Check: Is $\frac{\mathbf{196}}{7} + 4 > 32$?

$$28 + 4 = 32. \text{ Yes. It checks.}$$

Special Reminder about Inequalities

Multiplying or dividing by a *negative number* reverses the inequality sign.

$x < -7 \implies -x > 7$

Multiply both sides by (–1).

$5x - 4 \geq 9 \implies -10x + 8 \leq -18$

Multiply both sides by (–2).

$-3x - 12 \leq y \implies x + 4 \geq -\dfrac{y}{3}$

Divide both sides by (–3).

$\dfrac{2}{3}y - 4 > -x + 3 \implies -y + 6 < \dfrac{3}{2}x + 4\dfrac{1}{2}$

Multiply both sides by $\dfrac{(-3)}{(2)}$.

$-9 > -3x - 18 \implies 3 < x < 6$

Divide by (–3).

Completed Examples

A. Expand
    Solve for x:
    Add 7

$$4(-x + 3) = -4x + 12$$
$$6x - 7 = -4x + 12$$
$$\underline{ + 7 + 7}$$

    Add $4x$

$$6x = -4x + 19$$
$$\underline{+ 4x + 4x}$$

    Divide by 10

$$\dfrac{10x}{10} = \dfrac{19}{10}$$

$$x = 1.9$$

B. Solve for n:
    Add 11

$$7n - 11 > 17$$
$$\underline{+ 11 + 11}$$

    Divide by 7

$$\dfrac{7n}{7} > \dfrac{28}{7}$$

$$n > 4$$

Practice Questions

1. Solve for y: $10y + 5 = 15 + 20y$

2. Solve for x: $10x + 3 = -5x + 33$

3. Solve for y: $-6y - 4 = y + 10$

4. Solve for x: $5 + 12x = -4x - 27$

5. Solve for n: $15 - 4n > -21$

6. Solve for k: $7k + 7 < -14$

7. Solve for x: $20 > 2x - 4$

8. Solve for y: $2 > 10 - 14y$

Answers on page 219.

USE NONGEOMETRIC FORMULAS (I C5)

TEST QUESTION EXAMPLE:

CLAST questions look something like this:

Use the interest formula I = PRT.
How much interest is earned on $2,000 invested at 9% for 3 years?

Formulas

Evaluating an Expression or Formula

Evaluate an expression by replacing the variables with values. Remember to use the correct order of operations. For example, evaluate

$$3x - \frac{y}{z} \text{ for } x = 3, y = 8, \text{ and } z = 4$$

$$3(3) - \frac{8}{4} = 9 - 2 = 7$$

Completed Example

Principle (P) is the amount borrowed. Interest (I) is the interest rate. Time (T) is the length of the loan in **years**. (If the loan is for 6 months, T = $\frac{1}{2}$.)

I = PRT
I = (2000) (.09) (3)
I = 180 × 3 I = 540

The investment earns $540 in interest.

Practice Questions

1. Use the interest formula I = PRT. How much interest will be paid on a $12,000 loan at 16% interest for 3 years?

2. Derek puts $5000 down on a $15,000 car and borrows the remainder for 5 years at 12%. How much interest will he pay?

3. What is the interest rate on a 3-year, $5000 loan if the borrower has to pay $900 in interest?

Answers on page 219.

FIND VALUES OF A FUNCTION (I C6)

TEST QUESTION EXAMPLE:

CLAST questions look something like this:

$$f(x) = 2x^3 - 5x^2 + 7 \quad \text{Find } f(-4).$$

Use These Steps to Find Values of a Function

1. Substitute values for variables in the function.

2. Use the correct order of operations to evaluate the function.

Completed Example

$$f(x) = 2x^3 - 5x^2 + 7 \quad \text{Find } f(-4)$$
$$f(-4) = 2(-4)^3 - 5(-4)^2 + 7 = 2(-64) - 5(16) + 7 =$$
$$-128 - 80 + 7 = -201$$
$$f(-4) = -201$$

Practice Questions

Evaluate the function.

1. $f(x) = x^2 + 8$ Find $f(2)$

2. $f(x) = 2x^3 - x^2 - 3$ Find $f(-1)$

3. $f(x) = 4x^3 - 8x^2 + x$ Find $f(3)$

4. $f(x) = 5x^3 - 2x + 6$ Find $f(-4)$

5. $f(x) = 7x^4 - x^2 + 2$ Find $f(-1)$

6. $f(x) = 9x^3 - 3x^2 + 5x + 6$ Find $f(-3)$

Answers on page 219.

FACTOR A QUADRATIC EXPRESSION (I C7)

TEST QUESTION EXAMPLE:

CLAST multiple-choice items look something like this:

Which is the linear factor of $9x^2 - 6x - 8$?

(A) $(9x - 8)$
(B) $(3x + 4)$
(C) $(-3x + 4)$
(D) $(-9x + 8)$

Quadratic Expression

An expression that can be written in the form $ax^2 + bx + c = 0$
(a, b, and c are real numbers, and $a \neq 0$.)

$$12x^2 + 2x - 2 \text{ is a quadratic expression.}$$

Linear Factors

Two expressions whose product is the quadratic equation.

$(4x + 2)$ and $(3x - 1)$ are linear factors of $12x^2 + 2x - 2$

$$(4x + 2) \times (3x - 1) = 12x^2 - 4x + 6x - 2 = 12x^2 + 2x - 2$$

Use these Steps

This type of question always gives you four linear factors as answer choices. One of these is always the correct linear factor for the quadratic equation. ALWAYS work back from the answer choices. Try out each linear factor until you find the correct choice.

Completed Example

Which is the linear factor of $9x^2 - 6x - 8$?

(A) $(9x - 8)$
(B) $(3x + 4)$
(C) $(-3x + 4)$
(D) $(-9x + 8)$

Use a trial and error process.

Try choice (A) $(9x - 8)$

 Think: What would the other linear factor look like?

 The second term would have to be –1. (__ x –1).

 There is no first term that will give $9x^2 - 6x$ for the rest of the quadratic.

 Choice (A) is not correct.

Try choice (B) $(3x + 4)$

 Think: What would the other linear factor look like?

 The second term would have to be 2. (__ x + 2).

 There is no first term that will give $9x^2 - 6x$ for the rest of the quadratic.

 Choice (B) is not correct.

Try choice (C) $(-3x + 4)$

 Think: What would the other linear factor look like?

 The second term would have to be –2. (__ x – 2).

 The first term $-3x$ will give $9x^2 - 6x$ for the rest of the quadratic.

 $(-3x + 4)(-3x - 2) = 9x^2 + 6x - 12x - 4 = 9x^2 - 6x - 4$

 Choice (C) is correct.

 We don't have to try choice (D).

Practice Questions

1. Which is a linear factor of $6x^2 - x - 2$?
 (A) $(2x - 3)$
 (B) $(3x - 2)$
 (C) $(-2x + 3)$
 (D) $(-3x - 2)$

2. Which is a linear factor of $12x^2 - 14x - 6$?
 (A) $(6x - 2)$
 (B) $(6x + 2)$
 (C) $(2x + 1)$
 (D) $(-2x - 1)$

Answers on page 219.

FIND THE ROOTS OF A QUADRATIC EQUATION (I C8)

TEST QUESTION EXAMPLE:

 CLAST questions look something like this:

 Find the solutions to $x^2 - 2x = 1$

Quadratic Formula

The quadratic formula is used to solve a quadratic equation. The solutions, or roots, are values of the variable x. Every quadratic equation has two roots.

$$x = \frac{-b \pm \sqrt{b^2 - 4ac}}{2a}$$ (a, b, and c are the values in the quadratic equation)

Completed Example

Find the solutions to $x^2 - 2x = 1$.

Write the quadratic equation
in standard form. $(ax^2 + bx + c = 0)$

$$
\begin{array}{rcr}
x^2 - 2x & = & 1 \\
-1 & & -1 \\
\hline
x^2 - 2x - 1 & = & 0
\end{array}
$$

Write the values for a, b, and c.

$a = 1, \ b = -2, c = -1$

Substitute the values of a, b, and c into the quadratic formula.

$$\frac{-b \pm \sqrt{b^2 - 4ac}}{2a}$$

$$\frac{-(-2) \pm \sqrt{(-2)^2 - 4(1)(-1)}}{(2)(1)}$$

$$\frac{2 \pm \sqrt{4 + 4}}{2}$$

$$\frac{2}{2} \pm \frac{\sqrt{8}}{2}$$

$$\frac{2}{2} \pm \frac{2\sqrt{2}}{2}$$

$$1 \pm \sqrt{2}$$

The roots (solutions) of the quadratic equation are $1 + \sqrt{2}$ and $1 - \sqrt{2}$.

Practice Questions

1. Find the roots of $2x^2 - 3x = 2$.

2. Find the solutions to $4x^2 = 2x + 5$.

Answers on page 219.

SOLVE A SYSTEM OF TWO LINEAR EQUATIONS IN TWO UNKNOWNS (I C9)

TEST QUESTION EXAMPLES:

CLAST multiple-choice items look something like this:
Choose the correct solution for each system of equations.

A. $3x - 4y - 7 = 0$
$\quad 2x + 8y = -6$

B. $8x - 2y = 4$
$\quad -12x + 3y + 6 = 0$

C. $3x - y = 5$
$\quad -12x + 4y = 7$

(A) (1, –1)

(B) (5, 12)

(C) $\{(x, y) \mid y = 8x\}$

(D) the empty set

(A) (2, 4)

(B) (3, 6)

(C) $\{(x, y) \mid y = 4x - 2\}$

(D) the empty set

(A) (2, 1)

(B) (3, 5)

(C) $\{(x, y) \mid y = \frac{3}{5}x\}$

(D) the empty set

Linear Equation

Any equation in the form $ax + by = c$ ($a \neq 0, \ b \neq 0$)
A linear equation produces a line.

Solving Two Linear Equations

The solution to a linear equation is an ordered pair (x, y).
The solution for two linear equations is a solution for each of the equations.

This type of question always gives you four solutions to choose from.
Exactly one of these choices is correct.
ALWAYS work back from the answer choices.
Try out each solution until you find the correct choice.

There are three answer types.
Try out the answers in this order.

1. *The answer is a single ordered pair.* (The lines meet at one point.)
   Substitute the ordered pair in each equation.
   If the ordered pair works for both equations, that is the correct answer.

2. *The answer looks like* $\{(x, y) \mid y = \frac{5}{8}x\}$. The solution for both equations is $y = \frac{5}{8}x$. (The lines are the same.)
   Solve each equation for y.
   If both solutions match the answer choice, that answer is correct.

3. *The answer states that there is no solution.* The solution is the empty set. (The lines are parallel.)
   Save this choice for last. If the other choices don't work, this is the correct answer.

Completed Examples

A. $3x - 4y - 7 = 0$
   $2x + 8y = -6$

    (A) $(1, -1)$
    (B) $(5, 12)$
    (C) $\{(x, y) \mid y = 8x\}$
    (D) the empty set

Try answer choice (A)

Substitute the ordered pair $(1, 1)$ in the first equation. The expression is correct. $(1, -1)$ is a possible solution.

$3(1) - 4(-1) - 7 \overset{?}{=} 0 \qquad 3 + 4 - 7 = 0$

Try out $(1, -1)$ in the second equation. This expression is correct also.

$2(1) + 8(-1) \overset{?}{=} -6 \qquad 2 + -8 = -6$

The ordered pair $(1, -1)$ worked for both equations.
This is the solution for these equations. Choose answer (A).

B. $8x - 2y = 4$
    $-12x + 3y - 6 = 0$

    (A) $(2, 4)$
    (B) $(3, 6)$
    (C) $\{(x, y) \mid y = 4x - 2\}$
    (D) the empty set

Try answer choice (A)

Substitute the ordered pair $(2, 4)$ in the first equation. The expression is incorrect. Choice (A) is not correct.

$8(2) - 2(4) \overset{?}{=} 4 \qquad 16 - 8 \neq 4$

Try answer choice (B)

Substitute the ordered pair $(3, 6)$ in the first equation. Choice (B) is not correct.

$8(3) - 2(6) \overset{?}{=} 4 \qquad 24 - 12 \neq 4$

Try answer choice (C)

Choice (C) means that the solution is every pair of numbers for which $y = 4x - 2$.

Solve the first equation for y. The solution matches the equation in choice (C).

$8x - 2y = 4 \qquad 8x - 4 = 2y \qquad 4x - 2 = y$

Try it for the second equation. $-12x + 3y + 6 = 0$ $-4x + y + 2 = 0$ $y = 4x - 2$
The solutions for both equations
match the answer choice.

Choice (C) is the correct answer.

C. $3x - y = 5$
    $-12x + 4y = 7$

(A) (2, 1)
(B) (3, 5)
(C) $\{(x, y) \mid y = \frac{3}{5}x\}$
(D) the empty set

Try answer choice (A)
Substitute the ordered pair (2, 1)
in the first equation. $3(2) - (1) \overset{?}{=} 5$ $6 - 1 = 5$
The expression is correct.
(2, 1) is a possible solution.

Try out (2, 1) in the second equation. $-12(2) + 4(1) \overset{?}{=} 5$ $-24 + 4 \neq 5$
(2, 1) does not work. Answer choice
(A) is not correct.

Try answer choice (B)
Try the ordered pair (3, 5) $3(5) - (5) = 5$? $15 - 5 \neq 5$
in the first equation.
Answer choice (B) is not correct.

Try answer choice (C)
Solve the first equation for y. $3x - y = 5$ $3x - 5 = y$
Choice (C) is not correct. $3x - 5 = y$ does not match $y = \frac{3}{4}x$

Choice (D) must be correct.
If one of the choices is the empty set
save that choice for last.

Practice Questions

1. Choose the correct solution for the
   system of equations.
   $-6y + 2x + 12 = 2$
   $4x + 7y = -1$
   (A) (−2, 1)
   (B) (4, 2)
   (C) $\{(x, y) \mid y = 2x\}$
   (D) the empty set

2. Choose the correct solution for the
   system of equations.
   $3y - \frac{1}{2}x = 14$
   $3x + 2y + 5 = 1$
   (A) (−4, 4)
   (B) (−2, 5)
   (C) $\{(x, y) \mid y = x + 1\}$
   (D) the null set

3. Choose the correct solution for the
   system of equations.
   $4x + 2y - 3 = -7$
   $5y - 6x = 6$
   (A) (0, 2)
   (B) (−1, 0)
   (C) $\{(x, y) \mid y = 2x\}$
   (D) the empty set

Answers on page 219.

USE PROPERTIES OF OPERATIONS (II C1)

TEST QUESTION EXAMPLES:

CLAST questions look something like this:

A. Use a property of arithmetic to write an expression equivalent to $8y - 4x$.

B. What property is illustrated by $7^2 + 8^3 = 8^3 + 7^2$?

Properties of the Operations Addition and Multiplication

Commutative $a + b = b + a$ $a \times b = b \times a$

$3 + 5 = 5 + 3$ $3 \times 5 = 5 \times 3$

Associative $(a + b) + c = a + (b + c)$ $(a \times b) \times c = a \times (b \times c)$

$(3 + 4) + 5 = 3 + (4 + 5)$ $(3 \times 4) \times 5 = 3 \times (4 \times 5)$

Identity $a + 0 = a$ $a \times 1 = a$

$5 + 0 = 5$ $5 \times 1 = 5$

Inverse $a + (-a) = 0$ $a \times \dfrac{1}{a} = 1$

$5 + (-5) = 0$ $5 \times \dfrac{1}{5} = 1 \ (a \neq 0)$

Distributive property of $a(b + c) = (a \times b) + (b \times c)$
multiplication over division. $3(4 + 5) = (3 \times 4) + (3 \times 5)$

Completed Examples

A. Use a property of arithmetic to write an expression equivalent to $8y - 4x$.
   These items ask you to identify equivalent statements produced by the properties.
   The distributive property creates the equivalent expressions $4(2y - x)$ or $2(4y - 2x)$.

B. What property is illustrated by $7^2 + 8^3 = 8^3 + 7^2$?
   This statement demonstrates the commutative property.

Practice Questions

1. Use a property to write an expression equivalent to $\frac{6}{8} \times \frac{7}{9}$.

2. What property is illustrated by $(2 + 3) + 4 = 2 + (3 + 4)$?

3. What property is illustrated by $3x(x + 2y) = 3x^2 + 6xy$?

4. Write an expression equivalent to $a(6) + a(3)$.

5. What property is illustrated by $3a + 3b = 3b + 3a$?

6. Choose a statement that is *not* true for all real numbers.
   (A) $A(1/A) = 0$ for $A \neq 0$.
   (B) $x^2(y^2) = (x^2 y)^2$
   (C) $(3x + y)(x - y) = (x - y)(3x + y)$
   (D) $10^2 + 12 = 12 + 10^2$

Answers on page 219.

DETERMINE IF A NUMBER IS A SOLUTION TO AN EQUATION OR INEQUALITY (II C2)

TEST QUESTION EXAMPLE:

CLAST questions look something like this:

For each of the statements below, determine whether $x = -3$ is a solution.

i. $3x^2 - 2 = 2x + 3$
ii. $(x - 2)(x - 3) > -12$
iii. $|x - 5| = 8$

To Answer this Type of Question

Try out the given solution in each of the equations or inequalities.
The solution may work for some, all, or none of them.

Completed Example

Substitute -3 for x in statement i.

$$3(-3)^2 - 2 \overset{?}{=} 2(-3) + 3$$
$$3(9) -2 \qquad -6 \quad + 3$$
$$25 \quad \neq \quad -3$$

-3 is **not a solution** for equation i.

Substitute -3 for x in statement ii.

$$(-3 -2)(-3 - 3) \overset{?}{>} -12$$
$$-5 \times -6 \qquad -12$$
$$30 \qquad > -12$$

-3 **is a solution** for statement ii.

Substitute -3 for x in statement iii.

$$|-3 - 5| \overset{?}{=} 8$$
$$|-8| \qquad 8$$
$$8 \quad = 8$$

-3 **is a solution** for statement iii.

$x = -3$ is a solution for statements ii and iii.

Practice Questions

1. Which statement(s) below have $x = -2$ as a solution?

   (A) $2x^2 - 5 = 9 + 3x$
   (B) $(x - 2)(x + 1) < 1$
   (C) $|x - 4| = 2$

2. In which statement(s) below is $x = 3$ a solution?

   (A) $3x + x^2 = 4x - 2$
   (B) $(x - 2)(x + 2) < 5$
   (C) $|-4 - x| = 7$

3. For which statement(s) is $y = -1$ a solution?

   (A) $4y^2 + 2y = 5y - 10$
   (B) $(5y)(6 - y) > 27$
   (C) $|5 - y| = 6$

Answers on page 219.

RECOGNIZE STATEMENTS AND CONDITIONS OF PROPORTIONALITY AND VARIATION (II C3)

TEST QUESTION EXAMPLE:

CLAST questions look something like this:

The baker makes 3 loaves of whole wheat bread for every 7 loaves of rye bread. If the baker makes 51 loaves of whole wheat bread, how many loaves of rye bread will be made? Write a statement for the given condition.

The test asks you to identify the correct proportion.

Ratio, Proportion, and Percent

Ratio

A ratio is a way of comparing two numbers with division. It conveys the same meaning as a fraction. There are three ways to write a ratio.

Using words 3 to 4   As a fraction $\frac{3}{4}$ Using a colon 3 : 4

Proportion

A proportion shows two ratios that have the same value; that is, the fractions representing the ratios are equivalent. Use cross multiplication. If the cross products are equal, then the two ratios form a proportion.

$\frac{3}{8}$ and $\frac{27}{72}$ form a proportion. The cross products are equal. $(3 \times 72 = 8 \times 27)$

$\frac{3}{8}$ and $\frac{24}{56}$ do not form a proportion. The cross products are not equal.

Writing a Proportion: You may have to write a proportion to solve a problem. For example, the mason mixes cement and sand using a ratio of 2 : 5. Twelve bags of cement will be used. How much sand is needed? To solve, use the numerator to stand for cement. The denominator will stand for sand.

$$\frac{2}{5} = \frac{12}{S}$$

$$2 \times S = 5 \times 12$$
$$2S = 60$$
$$S = 30$$

Cross multiply to solve.

Thirty bags of sand are needed.

Completed Example

The problem compares loaves of whole wheat bread with loaves of rye bread. Let the numerators stand for loaves of whole wheat bread. The denominators stand for loaves of rye bread.

Ratio of whole wheat to rye. $-\dfrac{3}{7}$ Ratio of whole wheat to rye for $\dfrac{51}{R}$
51 loaves of whole wheat.

Write a proportion. $-\dfrac{3}{7} = \dfrac{51}{R}$

Solution $3R = 357$ $R = 119$

Practice Questions

1. A salesperson sells 7 vacuum cleaners for every 140 potential buyers. If there are 280 potential buyers, how many vacuums are sold?

2. There is one teacher for every 8 preschool students. How many teachers are needed if there are 32 preschool students?

3. There are 3 rest stops for every 20 miles of highway. How many rest stops would there be on 140 miles of highway?

Answers on page 219.

MATCH REGIONS OF THE COORDINATE PLANE WITH EQUATIONS AND INEQUALITIES (II C4)

TEST QUESTION EXAMPLES:

CLAST questions look something like this:

A. Shade the coordinate plane to show the inequality. $2x + y \leq 8$

B. Write the equation for the shaded region of the coordinate plane.

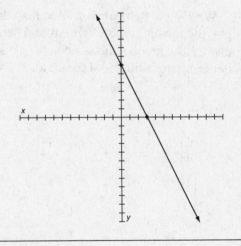

Coordinate Grid

You can plot ordered pairs of numbers on a coordinate grid.

The x axis goes horizontally from left to right. The first number in the pair tells how far to move left or right from the origin. A minus sign means move left. A plus sign means move right.

The y axis goes vertically up and down. The second number in the pair tells how far to move up or down from the origin. A minus sign means move down. A plus sign means move up.

Pairs of numbers show the x coordinate first and the y coordinate second (x, y). The origin is point $(0, 0)$ where the x axis and the y axis meet.

Plot these pairs of numbers on the grid.

A $(^+3, ^-7)$ **B** $(^+5, ^+3)$ **C** $(^-6, ^+2)$ **D** $(^-3, ^-6)$

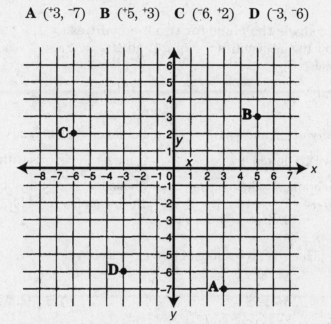

Shading Regions on a Coordinate Plane

A region on the plane will always be bounded by a line.

A solid line means the inequality is $\leq$ or $\geq$. A dotted line means the inequality is $<$ or $>$.

Follow these steps to shade the plane for one inequality:

Shade the plane to show the inequality $x + 2y < 6$.

1. Sketch the boundary line. (Think: $x + 2y = 6$)

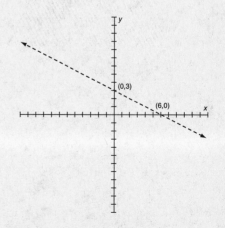

Substitute 0 for x and solve.
$0 + 2y = 6$; $y = 3$.
One point on the boundary line is $(0, 3)$.

Substitute 0 for y and solve.
$x + 0 = 6$; $x = 6$.
One point on the boundary line is $(6, 0)$.

Plot the points. Connect them with a line.
Draw a dotted line to show that the inequality is $<$.

2. Shade the side of the boundary that satisfies
   the inequality $x + 2y < 6$.

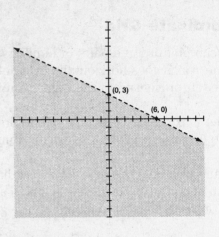

Follow these steps to shade the plane for two inequalities:

Shade the plane to show the inequalities $x + 2y < 4$ and $4x + 2y \geq 8$.

Sketch the boundary lines.

$x + 2y < 4$	$4x + 2y \geq 8.$
– Points on the boundary: $(0, 2)$ and $(4, 0)$	– Points on the boundary: $(0, 4)$ and $(2, 0)$
– Connect the points with a dotted line.	– Connect the points with a solid line.
– Shade the side of the boundary that shows the inequality $x + 2y < 4$	– Shade the side of the boundary that shows the inequality $4x + 2y > 8$.

Shade the parts of the plane shared by both of the regions above.

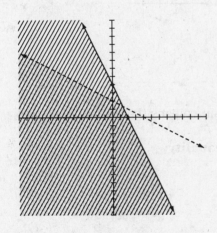

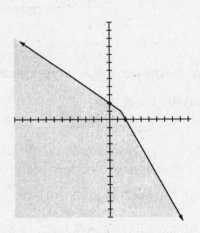

Completed Examples

A. The shaded portion of the plane for $2x + y \leq 8$.

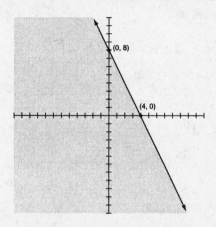

(0, 8)

(4, 0)

B. The equation for the shaded portion of the plane is $3x + y = 6$.

Practice Questions

Shade the plane to show these inequalities.

1. $3x + 6y < 12$

3. $2x + 3y \geq 6$ and $4x + y < 12$.

2. $x + 4y \geq 8$

Answers on page 219.

IDENTIFY EQUIVALENT EQUATIONS AND INEQUALITIES (III C2)

Test Question Example:

CLAST questions look something like this:

Write an inequality that is equivalent to $-x > 3y - 7$

Identify Equivalent Expressions

Two equations or two inequalities are equivalent if they mean the same thing.

That is two equations or two inequalities are equivalent if they have the same solution.

To form equivalent expressions, add or subtract the same number on each side of the equation or inequality. Multiply or divide the same nonzero number on each side of the equation or inequality.

Equivalent Equations

$3x + 7 = y \Rightarrow 3x = y - 7$
Subtract 7 from both sides.

$4x - 8 = 3y \Rightarrow 4x = 3y + 8$
Add 8 to both sides.

$-\frac{1}{2}x = 2y - 4 \Rightarrow x = -4y + 16$
Multiply both sides by (–2).

$-9x = -y + 6 \Rightarrow x = \frac{y}{9} - \frac{2}{3}$
Divide both sides by (–9).

Equivalent Inequalities

Important reminder about inequalities.
Multiplying or dividing by a *negative number* reverses the inequality sign.

$x < -5 \Rightarrow -x > 5$
Multiply both sides by (–1).

$4x - 6 \geq 9 \Rightarrow -8x + 12 \leq -18$
Multiply both sides by (–2).

$-3x - 12 \leq y \Rightarrow x + 4 \geq -\frac{y}{3}$
Divide both sides by (–3).

$\frac{2}{3}y - 4 > -x + 3 \Rightarrow -y + 6 < \frac{3x}{2} + 4\frac{1}{2}$
Multiply both sides by $\frac{(-3)}{(2)}$.

$$-9 > -3x > -18 \Rightarrow 3 < x < 6$$
Divide each term by (–3).

Completed Example

Some of the inequalities that are equivalent to $-x > 3y - 7$ are shown below.

$-x > 3y - 7 \Rightarrow 0 > x + 3y - 7$
Add x to both sides.

$-x > 3y - 7 \Rightarrow -x - 3y > 7$
Subtract $3y$ from both sides.

$-x > 3y - 7 \Rightarrow x < -3y + 7$
Multiply both sides by (–1).

$-x > 3y - 7 \Rightarrow 1 < \frac{3y - 7}{-x}$
Divide both sides by (–x).

Practice Questions

1. Write an inequality equivalent to:
   $-x > 8 + 2y$

2. Write an inequality equivalent to:
   $2y < 4x - 10$

3. Write an equation equivalent to:
   $-x = 12y - 10$

Answers on page 220.

SOLVE NONGEOMETRIC WORD PROBLEMS INVOLVING VARIABLES (IV C1)

TEST QUESTION EXAMPLES:

CLAST items based on this objective look something like this:

A. A mechanic uses this formula to estimate the displacement (P) of an engine. $P = 0.8(d^2)(s)(n)$ where *d* is the diameter, *s* is the stroke length of each cylinder, and *n* is the number of cylinders. Estimate the displacement of a 6-cylinder car whose cylinders have a diameter of 2 inches and a stroke length of 4 inches.

B. The accountant calculates that it takes $3 in sales to generate $0.42 in profit. How much cost does it take to generate a profit of $5.46?

Two Questions Types

You will see a formula to solve the problem. Some of the formulas may appear complex. Ignore the complexity of the formula and concentrate on substituting values for variables.
  If you see a problem to be solved with a proportion, set up the proportion and solve.

Completed Examples

A. 1. Write the formula. $\qquad$ $P = 0.8(d^2)(s)(n)$

2. Write the values of the variables. $\qquad$ $d = 2, s = 4, n = 6$

3. Substitute the values for the variables. $\qquad$ $P = 0.8(2^2)(4)(6)$

4. Solve. $\qquad$ $P = 0.8(4)(24) = (3.2)(24)$
$P = 76.8$

The displacement of the engine is about 76.8 cubic inches.

B. 1. Write a proportion.
   Use *s* for sales. $\qquad$ $\dfrac{3}{.42} = \dfrac{s}{5.46}$

2. Cross multiply. $\qquad$ $.42s = 16.38$

3. Solve. $\qquad$ $s = \dfrac{16.38}{0.42}$

$s = 39$

It will take $39 in sales to generate $5.46 in profits.

Practice Questions

1. A retail store makes a profit of $3.75 for each $10 of goods sold. How much profit would the store make on a $45 purchase?

2. The formula for calculating average speed is $d/T_2 - T_1$. If T_1 (start time) is 5:00 PM and T_2 (end time) is midnight the same day, and 287 miles were traveled, what was the average speed?

3. A car purchased for $12,000 (**O**) depreciates 10% (**P**) a year (**Y**). If the car is sold in 3 years, what is its depreciated value if V = O − POY?

4. There is a square grid of dots. A figure is made of line segments that connect the dots. The formula for the area of a figure on the grid is $\dfrac{T-2}{2} + I$.

   T is the number of dots touching the figure, and I is the number of dots inside. What is the area of a figure with 14 dots touching and 5 dots inside?

   Answers on page 220.

SOLVE PROBLEMS THAT INVOLVE THE STRUCTURE AND LOGIC OF ALGEBRA (IV C2)

TEST QUESTION EXAMPLE:

CLAST questions look something like this:

The sum of the digits of a two-digit number is one more than the product of the two digits. What equation shows this relationship?

From Words to Symbols

Items associated with this objective ask you translate words into symbols.
You are not asked to solve the equation.

3 more than x	$x + 3$	The product of 3 and x	$3x$
x increased by 3	$x + 3$	Three times x	$3x$
x more than 3	$x + 3$	The reciprocal of x	$\dfrac{1}{x}$
3 less than x	$x - 3$		
x decreased by 3	$x - 3$	The opposite of x	$-x$
3 decreased by x	$3 - x$	x cubed	x^3
Two consecutive integers	$x + (x + 1)$		
Three consecutive integers	$x + (x + 1) + (x + 2)$		

Completed Example

Write out the sentence in words. Then write the symbols and the equation.

The *sum of the digits of a two-digit number* is *1 more than the product of the two digits.*

$$t + o \;=\; (t \times o) + 1$$

(t is the tens digit; o is the ones digit)

Practice Questions

1. The product of two consecutive numbers is 10 more than the sum of the numbers. What equation shows this relationship?

2. The sum of three consecutive numbers is three times the largest number. What equation shows this relationship?

3. Five times a number is equal to that number plus half of the sum of the next two consecutive numbers. What equation shows this relationship?

4. The product of four consecutive numbers is 10 times the first number. What equation shows this relationship?

Answers on page 220.

STATISTICS AND PROBABILITY

IDENTIFY INFORMATION CONTAINED IN BAR, LINE, AND CIRCLE GRAPHS (I D1)

TEST QUESTION EXAMPLE:

CLAST questions look something like this:

The Bar Graph

The bar graph represents information by the length of a bar.

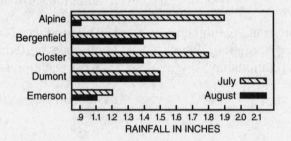

Rainfall in July and August for Five Towns

How much more rain fell in Alpine in July than in Closter during August?

The Line Graph

The line graph plots information against two axes.

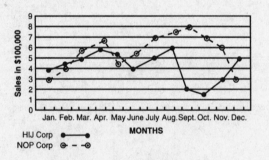

Sales During the Year

Read up from June and across from Sales in $100,000 to see that the HIJ Corp had $400,000 in sales during June.

The Circle Graph

The circle represents an entire amount. Each wedge-shaped piece of the graph represents some percent of that whole.

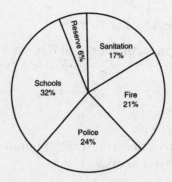

Percent of Tax Money Spent for Town Services

Use the circle graph to answer this question.
If the town collects $400,000 in tax money, how much does the town spend on schools?

$$32\% \times \$400,000 \qquad 0.32 \times \$400,000 \ = \ \$128,000$$

The town spends $128,000 on schools.

Completed Example

About 1.9 inches fell in Alpine during July.
About 1.4 inches fell in Closter during August.

$$1.9 - 1.4 = 0.5$$

About 0.5 more inches of rain fell in Alpine during July than in Closter during August.

Practice Questions

1. The greatest drop in sales occurred during which months? (Use the line graph on page 184.)

2. How many inches of rain fell in Bergenfield during July and August? (Use the bar graph on page 184.)

3. Use the circle graph above. The town decreased its expenditures for Sanitation by 2% from the amount shown in the graph. If the amount of taxes collected by the town was $2,200,000, how much is now spent on sanitation?

Answers on page 220.

DETERMINE THE MEAN, MEDIAN, AND MODE OF A SET OF NUMBERS (I D2)

TEST QUESTION EXAMPLE:

CLAST questions look something like this:

What is the mean (median, mode) of this set of data?
7, 13, 18, 4, 14, 22

Statistics

Descriptive statistics are used to explain or describe a set of numbers. Most often we use the mean, median, or mode to describe these numbers.

Mean (Average)

The mean is a position midway between two extremes. To find the mean:

1. Add the items or scores.

2. Divide by the number of items.

For example, find the mean of 23, 17, 42, 51, 36.

$$23 + 17 + 42 + 51 + 36 = 170 \quad 170 \div 5 = 34$$

The mean or average is 34.

Median

The median is the middle number. To find the median:

1. Arrange the numbers from least to greatest.

2. If there are an odd number of scores, then find the middle score.

3. If there is an even number of scores, average the two middle scores.

For example, find the median of these numbers.

6, 9, 11, <u>17</u>, <u>21</u>, 33, 45, 71

There are an even number of scores.

$$17 + 21 = 38 \quad 38 \div 2 = 19$$

The median is 19.

Don't forget to arrange the scores in order before finding the middle score!

Mode

The mode is the number that occurs most often. For example, find the mode of these numbers.

6, 3, 7, 6, 9, 3, 6, 1, 2, 6, 7, 3

The number 6 occurs most often, so 6 is the mode.

Not all sets of numbers have a mode. Some sets of numbers may have more than one mode.

Completed Example

Mean   Add the scores and divide by the number of scores.
$7 + 13 + 18 + 4 + 14 + 22 = 78 \div 6 = 13$ The mean is 13.

Median   Arrange the scores in order. Find the middle score.
4, 7, 13, 14, 18, 22 $13 + 14 = 27 \div 2 = 13.5$ The median is 13.5.

Mode   Find the score that occurs most often.
Each score occurs only once.   There is no mode.

Practice Questions

1. A group of fourth graders received the following scores on a science test.

   80 87 94 100 75 80 98 85 80 95 92

   Which score represents the mode?

2. What is the mean of the following set of data?

   44, 13, 84, 42, 12, 18

3. What is the median of the following set of data?

   8, 9, 10, 10, 8, 10, 7, 6, 9

4. What measure of central tendency does the number 16 represent in the following data?

   14, 15, 17, 16, 19, 20, 16, 14, 16

5. What is the mean of the following set of scores?

   100, 98, 95, 70, 85, 90, 94, 78, 80, 100

6. What is the mode of the following data?

   25, 30, 25, 15, 40, 45, 30, 20, 30

Answers on page 220.

USE THE FUNDAMENTAL COUNTING PRINCIPLE (I D3)

TEST QUESTION EXAMPLE:

CLAST questions look something like this:

An ice cream stand has a sundae with choices of 28 flavors of ice cream, 8 types of syrups, and 5 types of toppings. How many different sundae combinations are available?

Permutations

A permutation is the way a set of things can be arranged in order. There are 6 permutations of the letters A, B, and C.

A B C   **A C B**   **B A C**   **B C A**   **C A B**   **C B A**

Permutation Formula

The formula for the number of permutations of n things is **n! (n factorial)**.

$$6! = 6 \times 5 \times 4 \times 3 \times 2 \times 1 \qquad 4! = 4 \times 3 \times 2 \times 1 \qquad 2! = 2 \times 1$$

There are 120 permutations of 5 things.

$$n! = 5! = 5 \times 4 \times 3 \times 2 \times 1 = 120$$

Combinations

A combination is the number of ways of choosing a given number of elements from a set. The order of the elements does not matter. There are 3 ways of choosing 2 letters from the letters A, B, and C.

AB AC BC

Combination Formula

The formula for combinations is $\dfrac{n!}{r!\,(n-r)!}$ **n** is the number of elements in the set.
    r is the number of elements being chosen.

There are 15 ways of choosing 4 elements from a set of 6.

Write the formula. $\dfrac{n!}{r!\,(n-r)!}$

Write the values and substitute. $n = 6$ $r = 4$ $\dfrac{6!}{4!\,(6-4)!} = \dfrac{6!}{4! \times 2!} = \dfrac{6 \times 5 \times 4 \times 3 \times 2 \times 1}{4 \times 3 \times 2 \times 1 \times 2 \times 1}$

Solve. $\dfrac{6 \times 5 \times \cancel{4} \times \cancel{3} \times \cancel{2} \times \cancel{1}}{\cancel{4} \times \cancel{3} \times \cancel{2} \times \cancel{1} \times 2 \times 1} = \dfrac{6 \times 5}{2 \times 1} = \dfrac{30}{2} = 15$

Fundamental Counting Principle

The fundamental counting principle is used to find the total number of possibilities. Multiply the number of possibilities from each category.

Completed Example

$$28 \quad \times \quad 8 \quad \times \quad 5 \quad = \quad 1{,}120$$
$$\text{flavors} \qquad \text{syrups} \quad \text{toppings} \quad \text{sundaes}$$

There are 1,120 possible sundaes.

Practice Questions

1. There are 5 chairs left in the auditorium, but 10 people are without seats. In how many ways could 5 people be chosen to sit in the chairs?

2. The books *Little Women, Crime & Punishment, Trinity, The Great Santini, Pygmalion, The Scarlet Letter,* and *War and Peace* are on a shelf. In how many different ways can they be arranged?

3. A license plate consists of 2 letters and 3 numerals. How many different license plates can be formed?

Answers on page 220.

RECOGNIZE RELATIONSHIPS AMONG THE MEAN, MEDIAN, AND MODE (II D1)

TEST QUESTION EXAMPLE:

CLAST questions look something like this:

A class of twenty students received their test scores. All but three received an 85. The remaining students received 88, 79, and 76. Describe the relationship among the mean, median, and mode of these scores.

Recognizing Relationships

Questions associated with this objective ask you to think about the mean, median, and mode and to decide when they are the same, or when one is more or less than another. You may see a bar graph of data or read about the data in a short paragraph.

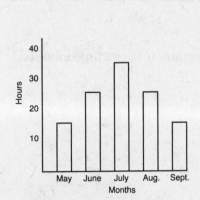

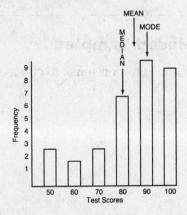

Overtime Hours

The mean, median, and mode are the same.

Test Scores

The mode is the tallest bar. The median is in the center. The mean is "pulled" toward the higher scores.

Completed Example

More than half the students received an 85.   The mode is 85.
The midmost score must also be 85.   The median is 85.
The other scores are close to 85.   The mean must be 85.

The mean, median, and mode are all the same.

Practice Questions

1. Thirty part-time workers make $6 an
   hour. The three part-time supervisors
   make $7, $8, and $9 an hour. Describe
   the relationship among the mean,
   median, and mode for this set of data.

2. What is the relationship among the
   mean, median, and mode of the data
   shown in the opposite graph?

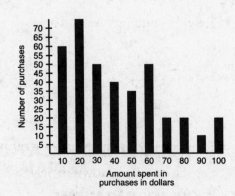

Answers on page 220.

CHOOSE THE MOST APPROPRIATE PROCEDURE FOR SELECTING AN UNBIASED SAMPLE (II D2)

TEST QUESTION EXAMPLE:

CLAST questions look something like this:

The college cafeteria manager wants to find out which new selections students
want added to the menu. What procedure would be appropriate for selecting an
unbiased sample?

Selecting Unbiased Samples

Use these guidelines and common sense to choose the best procedure for selecting unbiased
samples.

Choose a Process That Involves Random Selection

Random selection means that the sample is picked by chance. Every person in the larger population has an equal chance of being picked.

Examples of random sampling:

Pick a sample of names by chance out of a container with all the names.

Have a computer use a random selection program to choose the sample.

Partition a group into a male group and a female group, and then choose names at random from each group.

Examples of nonrandom sampling:

Sample the first 100 people you meet.

Choose every sixth person from a list of names.

Rely on voluntary responses.

Choose Your Sample From The Correct Population

The random selection must be from the group you want to study.

Examples of sampling from the wrong population:

Sample college alumni to determine current reactions to the cafeteria.

Sample from one town to determine statewide views.

Sample from 18–22-year-old military recruits to determine the views of college students.

Completed Example

You could gather the names of all the students who ate in the cafeteria during the week and then draw a random sample from those names. You should not draw a sample from all the students in the school. You should not interview every fifth student entering the cafeteria during the week.

Practice Questions

1. A group is taking a poll to determine working parents' day-care needs. They interview parents at work. Give examples of good and poor sampling techniques.

2. The town architect wants to find out about senior community members' ideas for the new senior center. Give examples of good and poor sampling techniques.

Answers on page 220.

IDENTIFY THE PROBABILITY OF AN OUTCOME (II D3)

TEST QUESTION EXAMPLE:

CLAST questions look something like this:

In one high school, 40 % of the students go on to college. Two graduates of the high school are chosen at random. What is the probability that they both went to college?

Probability

The probability of an occurrence is the likelihood that it will happen. Most often, we write probability as a fraction.

Flip a fair coin and the probability that it will come up heads is $\frac{1}{2}$. The same is true for tails. Write the probability this way.

$$P(H) = \frac{1}{2} \qquad P(T) = \frac{1}{2}$$

If something will never occur the probability is 0. If something will always occur, the probability is 1. Therefore, if you flip a fair coin,

$$P(7) = 0 \qquad P(H \text{ or } T) = 1$$

Write the letters A, B, C, D, and E on pieces of paper. Pick them randomly without looking. The probability of picking any letter is $\frac{1}{5}$.

A   B   C   D   E

$$P(\text{vowel}) = \frac{2}{5} \qquad P(\text{consonant}) = \frac{3}{5}$$

Rules for Computing Probability

$$P(A \text{ or } B) = P(A) + P(B) = \frac{1}{5} + \frac{1}{5} = \frac{2}{5}$$

$$P(A \text{ and } B) = P(A) \times P(B) = \frac{1}{5} \times \frac{1}{5} = \frac{1}{25}$$

$$P(\text{not } C) = 1 - P(C) = 1 - \frac{1}{5} = \frac{4}{5}$$

Completed Example

In one high school, 40% of the students go on to college. Two graduates of the high school are chosen at random. What is the probability that they both went to college?

Write the probabilities you know.

$P \text{ (college)} = {}^{40}/_{100} = {}^{2}/_{5}$

Solve the problem.

P *(A and B)* probability the two students went to college.

$P(A \text{ and } B) = P(A) \times P(B) = {}^{2}/_{5} \times {}^{2}/_{5} = {}^{4}/_{25}$

The probability that they both went to college is ${}^{4}/_{25}$.

Practice Questions

1. There are 3 black, 2 white, 2 gray, and 3 blue socks in a drawer. What is the probability of drawing a sock that is not black?

2. Six goldfish are in a tank; 4 are female and 2 are male. What is the probability of scooping out a male?

3. A regular deck of playing cards is spread face down on a table. What is the probability of choosing a card that is a king or a queen?

4. Six names are written on pieces of paper. The names are Aaron, Ben, Carl, Edith, Elizabeth, and Phyllis. One name is picked and replaced. Then another name is picked. What is the probability that the names were Carl and Phyllis?

Answers on page 221.

INFER RELATIONS AND MAKE PREDICTIONS FROM STATISTICAL DATA (III D1)

TEST QUESTION EXAMPLE:

CLAST questions look something like this:

Year	Hourly Salary
1991	$ 3.00
1992	$ 3.30
1993	$ 3.65
1994	$ 4.00
1995	$ 4.40

Write a statement that describes the pattern in the table shown above.

Question Types

You will be asked to interpret a table, a bar graph, or a scattergraph.

Scattergraph

Scattergraphs suggest the relationship that exists between two sets of data.
Scattergraphs do **not** show a cause-effect relationship.

A scatter from upper right to lower left shows a positive relationship between *P* and *Q*.
A scatter from upper left to lower right shows a negative relationship between *P* and *Q*.
A diffused scatter shows no relationship between *P* and *Q*.

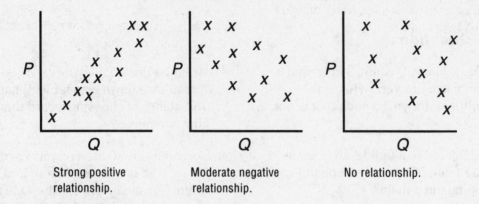

Strong positive relationship.

Moderate negative relationship.

No relationship.

Completed Example

The hourly wage increases every year by about 10%.

Practice Questions

Month	Field Goal Percentage
Nov.	83%
Dec.	85%
Jan.	88%
Feb.	90%
March	92%
April	94%

1. Write a statement that illustrates the relationship between the month and the field goal percentage.

Price of a car (P)	Year Y
$	
9,000	1990
11,000	1991
13,000	1992
15,000	1993
17,000	1994
19,000	1995
21,000	1996

2. Which scattergram best represents the data shown in the table above?

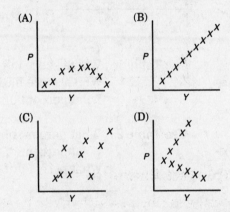

Answers on page 221.

INTERPRET REAL-WORLD DATA FROM FREQUENCY TABLES (IV D1)

TEST QUESTION EXAMPLES:

CLAST questions look something like this:

Table 1	
Scores	**Percent of Students**
0 – 59	2
60 – 69	8
70 – 79	39
80 – 89	38
90 – 100	13

Table 2	
Standardized Score	**Percentile Rank**
80	99
70	93
60	68
50	39
40	22
30	13
20	2

Use Table 1. Which score interval contains the mode?
Which score interval contains the median?
What percent of the students scored above 79?

Use Table 2. What percent of the scores are below 50?
What percent of the scores are between 30 and 70?
What percent of the scores are above 60?

Question Types

Items based on this objective will give tables similar to the ones above. You will be asked to interpret data from the tables.

Percent

Percent tables show the percent or proportion of a particular score or characteristic. We can see from Table 1 that 13% of the students got a score from 90 through 100.

Completed Example

Table 1

Which score interval contains the mode?

The largest percentage is 39% for 70–79. The interval 70–79 contains the mode.

Which score interval contains the median?

The cumulative percentage of 0–79 is 49%.
The median is in the interval in which the cumulative percentage of 50% occurs. The score interval 80–89 contains the median.

What percent of the students scored above 79?

>Add the percentiles of the intervals above 79. $38 + 13 = 51$
>51% of the students scored above 79.

Percentile Rank

The percentile rank shows the percent of scores below a given value. We can see from Table 2 that 68% of the scores fell below 60.

Completed Example

Table 2

What percent of the scores are below 50?

>The percentile rank next to 50 is 39. That means 39% of the scores are below 50.

What percent of the scores are between 30 and 70?

>Subtract the percentile rank for 30 from the percentile rank for 70.
>93% − 13% = 80%. 80% of the scores are between 30 and 70.

What percent of the scores are at or above 60?

>Subtract the percentile rank for 60 from 100%.
>100% − 68% = 32%. 32% of the scores are at or above 60.

Practice Questions

Use Table 1 and Table 2 on page 196.

Table 1

1. What percent of the scores are below 70?

2. In which score interval is the median?

3. What percent of the scores are from 80 to 100?

Table 2

4. The lowest passing score is 50. What percent of the scores are passing?

5. What percent of the scores are from 20 to 50?

Answers on page 221.

SOLVE REAL-WORLD WORD PROBLEMS INVOLVING PROBABILITY (IV D2)

TEST QUESTION EXAMPLE:

CLAST questions look something like this:

Table 1

	Air Express	Rail	Truck
5 pounds and over	0.07	0.34	0.18
Under 5 pounds	0.23	0.02	0.16

The table shows the method used to ship packages in two weight classes.

What is the probability that a package picked at random was sent Air Express?
What is the probability that a package picked at random weighed under five pounds?
What is the probability that a package picked at random weighing under five pounds was sent by rail?

Follow these steps:

1. Identify the probability in the chart.

2. Add when necessary to find the total probability.

Completed Example

What is the probability that a package picked at random was sent Air Express?

> Add the two proportions for Air Express.
> 0.07 + 0.23 = 0.30
> The probability that a randomly picked package was sent Air Express is 0.3.

What is the probability that a package picked at random weighed under five pounds?

> Add the three proportions for under five pounds.
> 0.23 + 0.02 + 0.16 = 0.42
> The probability that a randomly chosen package weighed under five pounds is 0.42.

What is the probability that a package picked at random weighing under five pounds was sent by rail?

> Look at the cell in the table where *under five pounds* and *rail* intersect.
> That proportion is 0.02.
> The probability that a randomly chosen package under five pounds was sent by rail is 0.02.

Practice Questions

> Use Table 1 on page 198.

1. What is the probability that a package was sent by truck?

2. What is the probability of a 10-pound package being randomly chosen?

3. What is the probability that a 10-pound package picked at random was sent by Air Express?

4. What is the probability of randomly choosing a 3-pound package that was sent other than by rail?

Answers on page 221.

LOGIC

DEDUCE FACTS OF SET INCLUSION LOGIC OR SET NONINCLUSION FROM A DIAGRAM (I E1)

TEST QUESTION EXAMPLES:

CLAST questions look something like this.

None of the regions are empty.
What statements can be made about this diagram?

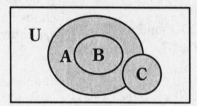

All, Some, and None

Diagrams can show the logical connectives all, some, and none. View the following diagrams for an explanation.

All—
All vowels are letters.

Some—
Some prime numbers are even.

None—
No odd numbers are divisible by two.

Completed Example

The statements include:

Any element of A is an element of U.
No element of B is an element of C.
Some of the elements of C are elements of A.

Practice Questions

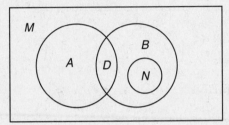

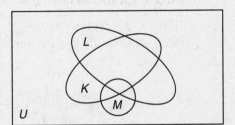

1. Which of the following is true for the diagram above, assuming that none of the regions are empty?

    (A) Any element of B is an element of D.
    (B) No element is a member of all three sets, A, D, B.
    (C) Any element of D is an element of A.
    (D) None of the above statements are true.

2. Which of the following statements is true about the diagram above, assuming none of the regions are empty?

    (A) Every element of M is a member of K and L.
    (B) Some elements of K are also elements of L.
    (C) Any element of U is an element of M.
    (D) None of the above statements are true.

Answers on page 221.

IDENTIFY NEGATIONS OF SIMPLE AND COMPOUND STATEMENTS (II E1)

TEST QUESTION EXAMPLE:

CLAST questions look something like this:

Write the negation of the statement: "If it is raining, then the ground is wet."

Examples of Negations

English Form

Statement	Negation
I am happy.	I am **not** happy.
I am not happy.	I am happy.
I am happy **and** I am tired.	I am **not** happy **or** I am **not** tired.
I am happy **or** I am tired.	I am **not** happy **and** I am **not** tired.
If I am happy, **then** I am tired.	I am happy **and** I am **not** tired.

Symbolic Form

Statement	Negation
p	not p
not p	p
p and q	not p or q
p or q	not p and q
If p, then q	p and not q

Negation of Some and All

Use the square of opposition to determine the negation of some and all.

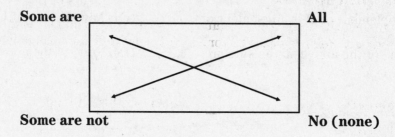

Some are　　　　　　　　　　　　　**All**

Some are not　　　　　　　　　　**No (none)**

English Form

Statement	Negation
Some are happy.	**None** are happy.
None are happy.	**Some are** happy.
All are happy.	**Some are not** happy.
Some are not happy.	**All** are happy.

Symbolic Form

Statement	Negation
Some are p	**None** are p
None are p	**Some are** p
All are p	**Some are not** p
Some are not p	**All** are p

Practice Questions

> Write the negations for the following statements.

1. All dogs wear collars.

2. None of the students are girls.

Answers on page 222.

3. If Ann eats spinach, then she drinks water.

4. Liz is a teacher and she works in Hillsdale.

DETERMINE THE EQUIVALENCE OR NONEQUIVALENCE OF STATEMENTS (II E2)

TEST QUESTION EXAMPLE:

CLAST questions look something like this:

Write a statement that is logically equivalent to:

If there is a lot of traffic, then it takes longer to get to the airport.

Equivalent Statements

Equivalent statements have the same meaning. Here are some symbolic examples and their English counterparts. Refer to page 202 for a list of equivalent statements that involve negations.

Statement	Equivalent Statement
if p, then q	if not q, then not p
If it is raining, then you are wet.	If you are not wet, then it is not raining.
if p, then q	not p or q
If it is raining, then you are wet.	It is not raining, or you are not wet.

"Mistaken" Equivalent Statements

These two examples show the two statements most often mistaken as equivalent statements. If the question asks you to identify a statement that is not equivalent, then look for these:

If p then q	**not equivalent to:**	If q then p
If it is raining, then you are wet	**not equivalent to:**	If you are wet, then it is raining.

If p then q	**not equivalent to:**	If not p then not q.
If it is raining, then you are wet	**not equivalent to:**	If it is not raining, then you are not wet.

Completed Example

There are several possibilities for equivalent statements.

If it does not take longer to get to the airport then there is not a lot of traffic.
There is not a lot of traffic or it does not take longer to get to the airport.

Practice Questions

> Write a logically equivalent statement for
> each of the following.

1. If it rains, Max will stay at home.

2. If Grace is not at the office, then they call her at the gym.

Answers on page 222.

3. If the children like peanut butter, they don't get jam for a snack.

4. It is not true that if Jo-Ann wants a puppy, then her father will buy one for her.

DRAW LOGICAL CONCLUSIONS FROM DATA (II E3)

TEST QUESTION EXAMPLE:

CLAST questions look something like this:

Which conclusion can be logically deduced from these two statements?

i. Take the CLAST now or take it later.
ii. I'm not going to take it now.

The logical conclusions will follow one of these forms:

Premises	If a, then b	If it rains, then you get wet.
	a	It rains.
Conclusion	b	You get wet.
Premises	If a, then b	If it rains, you get wet.
	not b	You did not get wet.
Conclusion	not a	It did not rain.
Premises	If a, then b	If it rains, then you get wet.
	If b, then c	If you get wet, then you dry off.
Conclusion	If a, then c	If it rains, you will dry off.
Premises	a or b	It will rain, or it will snow.
	not a	It did not rain.
Conclusion	b	It snowed.

Completed Example

The premises follow this form:

$$\frac{\begin{array}{l} \text{a or b} \\ \text{not } \underline{a} \end{array}}{\text{b}}$$

Conclusion: Take it later.

Practice Questions

1. What can be deduced from these two statements?
    i. If I finish my work I will go biking.
    ii. I finished my work.

2. What can be deduced from these two statements?
    i. If your team wins, they will go to New York.
    ii. The team did not go to New York.

3. What can be deduced from these two statements?
    i. If the whistle is blown, the dog will come.
    ii. The dog did not come.

4. Which conclusion can be logically deduced from these statements?
    i. If the cat is hungry, she will meow.
    ii. If the cat meows, the dog comes running.

Answers on page 222.

RECOGNIZE INVALID ARGUMENTS WITH TRUE CONCLUSIONS (II E4)

TEST QUESTION EXAMPLE:

CLAST questions look something like this:

All of the following arguments have true conclusions. Select the one argument that is valid.

(A) All vowels are letters and no vowels are consonants; therefore, all consonants are letters.
(B) Some letters are consonants. All vowels are letters and none are consonants; therefore, some letters are not vowels.
(C) All consonants are not vowels. Some letters are consonants; therefore, all vowels are letters.
(D) Some letters are not vowels. Some letters are not consonants. therefore, all vowels are letters.

Use the diagrams for Objective I E1 on page 200.

Completed Example

Draw the diagram for the statements. If that diagram clearly shows the conclusion, then the argument is valid. You may not need to draw the diagrams. If you are able to identify valid conclusions from the statements alone, then rely on that approach.

A. This diagram shows the statements:
All vowels are letters.
No vowels are consonants.

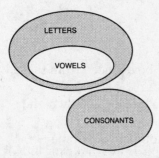

It does not show the conclusion:
All consonants are letters.
The argument is invalid.

B. This diagram shows the statements:
Some letters are consonants.
All vowels are letters and none are consonants.

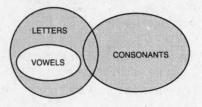

It does show the conclusion:
Some letters are not vowels.
The argument is valid.

C. This diagram shows the statements:
All consonants are not vowels.
Some letters are consonants.

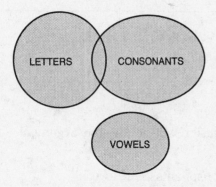

It does not show the conclusion:
All vowels are letters.
The argument is invalid.

D. This diagram shows the statements:
Some letters are not vowels.
Some letters are not consonants.

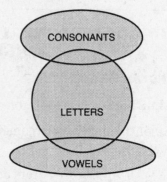

It does not show the conclusion:
All vowels are letters.
The argument is invalid.

Practice Question

1. All of the following arguments have true conclusions. Draw a diagram for each argument. Select the argument that is not valid.

   (A) All Persians have whiskers, and all cats have whiskers. Therefore, all Persians are cats.

   (B) All dogs have four legs and all huskies have four legs. Therefore, all huskies are dogs.

   (C) Every town in Florida is in the United States. Lake Placid is a city in Florida. Therefore, Lake Placid is in the United States.

   (D) All birds live in nests, and all sparrows live in nests. Therefore, all sparrows are birds.

Answer on page 222.

RECOGNIZE VALID REASONING PATTERNS IN EVERYDAY LANGUAGE (III E1)

TEST QUESTION EXAMPLE:

CLAST questions look something like this:

Write a conclusion that makes the following argument valid.

If I drive over the speed limit, I get a traffic ticket.
I did not get a traffic ticket.

Rely on these reasoning patterns:

Premises	If a, then b	If it rains, then you get wet.
	a	It rains.
Conclusion	b	You get wet.
Premises	If a, then b	If it rains, you get wet.
	not b	You did not get wet.
Conclusion	not a	It did not rain.
Premises	If a, then b	If it rains, then you get wet.
	If b, then c	If you get wet, then you dry off.
Conclusion	If a, then c	If it rains, you will dry off.
Premises	a or b	It will rain, or it will snow.
	not a	It did not rain.
Conclusion	b	It snowed.

Completed Example

If I drive over the speed limit, I get a traffic ticket.
I did not get a traffic ticket.

These premises follow the form:

Premises	If a, then b
	not b
Conclusion	not a

The correct conclusion is: I did not drive over the speed limit.

Practice Questions

> Write a valid conclusion for each of the following statements.

1. If it is windy, my hat will fly off my head. My hat did not fly off.

2. If the Yankees win the pennant, they can beat the Marlins. The Yankees won the pennant.

3. On my thirtieth birthday, I will throw a big party. I will not throw a big party.

4. All the stores are closed or it is not a holiday. It is a holiday.

Answers on page 222.

SELECT RULES USED TO TRANSFORM STATEMENTS (III E2)

TEST QUESTION EXAMPLE:

CLAST questions look something like this:

Select the logical rule used to transform statement i to statement ii.
i. If you pass the CLAST, then we'll throw a party.
ii. If we don't throw a party, then you didn't pass the CLAST.

Refer to page 202 for a list of equivalent statements that involve negations.

Statement	Equivalent Statement
If p, then q	if not q, then not p
If it is raining, then you are wet.	If you are not wet, then it is not raining.
If p, then q	not p or q
If it is raining, then you are wet.	It is not raining or you are not wet.

Mistaken Equivalent Statements

These two examples show the two statements most often mistaken as equivalent statements. If the question asks you to identify a statement that is not equivalent, then look for these.

If p then q	**not equivalent to:**	If q then p.
If it is raining, then you are wet	**not equivalent to:**	If you are wet then it is raining.
If p then q	**not equivalent to:**	If not p then not q.
If it is raining then you are wet	**not equivalent to:**	If it is not raining then you are not wet.

Completed Example

i. If you pass the CLAST, then we'll throw a party.
ii. If we don't throw a party, then you didn't pass the CLAST.

Statement i. has the form If a, then b.
Statement ii. has the form If not b, then not a.

The logical rule *If p, then q* is equivalent to *If not q, then not p.*

Practice Questions

1. Write a logical rule to transform statement i to statement ii.
   i. If you want to be successful, you must work hard.
   ii. If you don't work hard, you won't succeed.

2. Write a logical rule to transform statement i to statement ii.
   i. If there is not enough food then you go to the store.
   ii. There is enough food or you go to the store.

3. Write a logical rule to transform statement i to statement ii.
   i. It is false that there is candy on the table or the kids want it.
   ii. There is no candy on the table and the kids don't want it.

4. Write a logical rule used to transform statement i to statement ii.
   i. Not all television sets have remote controls.
   ii. Some television sets do not have remote control.

Answers on page 223.

DRAW LOGICAL CONCLUSIONS WHEN FACTS WARRANT (IV E1)

TEST QUESTION EXAMPLE:

CLAST questions look something like this:

Study the information below. Write a logical conclusion or state that there is no conclusion.

If I exercise every day, I will be more relaxed.
If I am more relaxed, then I will perform better on the CLAST.
I performed better on the CLAST.

Use combinations of these forms to identify conclusions:

Premises	If a, then b	If it rains, then you get wet.
	a	It rains.
Conclusion	b	You get wet.
Premises	If a, then b	If it rains, you get wet.
	not b	You did not get wet.
Conclusion	not a	It did not rain.
Premises	If a, then b	If it rains, then you get wet.
	If b then c	If you get wet, then you dry off.
Conclusion	If a, then c	If it rains, you will dry off.
Premises	a or b	It will rain, or it will snow.
	not a	It did not rain.
Conclusion	b	It snowed.

Completed Example

Statement	Form
If I exercise every day, I will be more relaxed.	If a, then b
If I am more relaxed, then I will perform better on the CLAST.	If b, then c
I performed better on the CLAST.	c

The premises do not follow one of the patterns above.
The form of the premises does not lead to a conclusion.

Practice Questions

> Write a logical conclusion for each set of
> statements.

1. If I send out 100 resumes, I will get
   some interviews. If I get some
   interviews, I can get a better job.
   I got a better job.

2. If I miss the 7:30 train, I will be late for
   work. I am not late for work.

3. The game will be postponed if it rains. If
   the game is postponed, it will be played
   on Monday. The game will be on
   Monday.

Answers on page 223.

MATHEMATICS PRACTICE EXPLAINED ANSWERS

Arithmetic

I A1 a page 112

1. $\frac{1}{4} = \frac{3}{12}$
    $+\frac{1}{6} = \frac{2}{12}$
    $\overline{\quad\quad \frac{5}{12}}$

2. $\frac{1}{3} = \frac{2}{6}$
    $-\frac{1}{6} = -\frac{1}{6}$
    $\overline{\quad\quad \frac{1}{6}}$

3. $\frac{6}{7} = \frac{30}{35}$
    $+\frac{1}{5} = +\frac{7}{35}$
    $\overline{\quad\quad \frac{37}{35} = 1\frac{2}{35}}$

4. $\frac{1}{8} = \frac{3}{24}$
    $+\frac{5}{6} = \frac{20}{24}$
    $\overline{\quad\quad \frac{23}{24}}$

5. $6 = 5\frac{5}{5}$
    $-\frac{3}{5} = -\frac{3}{5}$
    $\overline{\quad\quad 5\frac{2}{5}}$

6. $6\frac{1}{2} = 6\frac{2}{4} = 5\frac{6}{4}$
    $-4\frac{3}{4} = -4\frac{3}{4} = -4\frac{3}{4}$
    $\overline{\quad\quad\quad\quad\quad\quad 1\frac{3}{4}}$

7. $3\frac{1}{3} = 3\frac{5}{15}$
    $+2\frac{4}{5} = +2\frac{12}{15}$
    $\overline{\quad\quad\quad 6\frac{2}{15}}$

8. $5\frac{1}{6} = 5\frac{5}{30}$
    $+\frac{4}{5} = +\frac{24}{30}$
    $\overline{\quad\quad 5\frac{29}{30}}$

9. $6\frac{7}{12}$
    -4
    $\overline{\quad 2\frac{7}{12}}$

10. $5\frac{2}{5} = 5\frac{8}{20}$
    $-2\frac{1}{4} = -2\frac{5}{20}$
    $\overline{\quad\quad\quad 3\frac{3}{20}}$

11. $\frac{7}{12} = \frac{14}{24}$
    $2\frac{5}{8} = +2\frac{15}{24}$
    $\overline{\quad\quad\quad 2\frac{29}{24} = 3\frac{5}{24}}$

12. $3\frac{3}{4} = 2\frac{35}{20}$
    $-2\frac{4}{5} = -2\frac{16}{20}$
    $\overline{\quad\quad\quad\quad \frac{19}{20}}$

I A1 a page 112

1. $^{+}9$
    $+\ ^{+}6$
    $\overline{\quad 15}$

2. $^{+}10$
    $+\ ^{-}7$
    $\overline{\quad 3}$

3. $^{-}17$
    $-\ ^{+}12$
    $\overline{\quad ^{-}29}$

4. $^{-}25$
    $-\ ^{-}9$
    $\overline{\quad ^{-}16}$

5. $^{+}37$
    $-\ ^{+}19$
    $\overline{\quad ^{+}18}$

6. $^{-}124$
    $+\ ^{+}48$
    $\overline{\quad ^{-}76}$

7. $^{+}\frac{1}{2}$
    $+\ ^{-}\frac{1}{4}$
    $\overline{\quad ^{+}\frac{1}{4}}$

8. $^{-}\frac{3}{8}$
    $+\ ^{-}\frac{1}{4}$
    $\overline{\quad ^{-}\frac{5}{8}}$

9. $^{+}\frac{7}{10}$
    $-\ ^{-}\frac{2}{5}$
    $\overline{\quad ^{+}\frac{9}{10}}$

10. $^{-}2\frac{1}{2}$
    $-\ ^{+}5\frac{1}{4}$
    $\overline{\quad ^{-}7\frac{3}{4}}$

11. $^{+}4\frac{1}{5}$
    $-\ ^{+}3\frac{1}{4}$
    $\overline{\quad \frac{19}{20}}$

12. $-4\,^6/_7$

$\underline{-\,-5\,^2/_5}$

$^{19}/_{35}$

I A1 b page 115

1. $^3/_4 \times ^3/_4 = ^9/_{16}$
2. $^2/_5 \times 3 = ^6/_5 = 1\,^1/_5$
3. $^4/_5 \times ^{10}/_{16} = ^{40}/_{80} = ^1/_2$
4. $^5/_{12} \times ^4/_7 = ^{20}/_{84} = ^5/_{21}$
5. $4\,^1/_4 \times 2\,^2/_5 = ^{17}/_4 \times ^{12}/_5 = 10\,^1/_5$
6. $2\,^4/_5 \times 1\,^3/_7 = ^{14}/_5\,x\,^{10}/_7 = 4$
7. $^5/_7 \div ^1/_2 = ^5/_7 \times 2 = ^{10}/_7 = 1\,^3/_7$
8. $^6/_8 \div ^{16}/_{20} = ^6/_8 \times 20/16 = ^3/_4 \times ^5/_4 = ^{15}/_{16}$
9. $^5/_{10} \div 1\,^1/_2 = ^1/_2 \times ^2/_3 = ^1/_3$
10. $^7/_8 \div ^5/_6 = ^7/_8 \times ^6/_5 = ^{21}/_{20} = 1\,^1/_{20}$
11. $5\,^3/_5 \div 3\,^3/_5 = ^{28}/_5 \times ^5/_{18} = ^{28}/_{18} = ^{14}/_9 = 1\,^5/_9$
12. $10 \div ^4/_6 = ^{10}/_1 \times ^6/_4 = ^{60}/_4 = 15$

I A1 b page 115

1. $+10$
2. -30
3. $+120$
4. 180
5. $-^{15}/_{24} = -^5/_8$
6. $^{50}/_{14} = 3\,^4/_7$
7. $+6$
8. -10
9. -52
10. $-^{60}/_{48} = -1\,^1/_4$
11. $^{19}/_{10} = 1\,^9/_{10}$
12. $-^{48}/_3 = -16$

I A2 page 117

1. 32.6
2. -7.45
3. $4.02\ (4\ R2)$
4. 16.45
5. -330.2
6. -0.04308

I A2 page 117

1. -1.8
2. 2.4
3. 2.75
4. 50.70
5. -26.34
6. -477.88
7. 314.65
8. 1.269
9. -7.6
10. 79.9
11. 5.34
12. -11.93

II A3 page 119

	decimal	percent	fraction
1. 20%	0.2		$^1/_5$
2. .16		16%	$^4/_{25}$
3. $^6/_{20}$	0.3	30%	
4. 0.035		3.5%	$^7/_{200}$
5. 40%	0.40		$^2/_5$
6. $^4/_{25}$	0.16	16%	
7. $^6/_{50}$	0.12	12%	
8. 70%	0.7		$^7/_{10}$
9. $^3/_{10}$	0.3	30%	
10. 35%	0.35		$^7/_{20}$
11. 0.45		45%	$^9/_{20}$
12. 0.80		80%	$^4/_5$

I A3 page 121

1. Amount of increase $\$35 - 25 = \$10$

   $\dfrac{10}{25} = 0.4 = 40\%$

   Percent of increase $= 40\%$

2. Discount: $\$100 \times .25 = \$25$

   $\$100 - \$25 = \$75$

   Sale price $= \$75$

3. Discount $\$80 \times 15\% = \$12$

   $\$80 - \$12 = \$68$

   New price $= \$68$

4. Amount of increase $\$150 - \$120 = \$30$

   $\dfrac{30}{120} = \dfrac{1}{4} = 25\%$

   Percent of increase $= 25\%$

5. Discount $75 \times 10\% = \$7.50$
$75 - \$7.50 = \$67.50$
Sale price = $67.50

6. Amount of decrease $18 - \$6 = \$12$

$$\frac{12}{18} = \frac{2}{3} = 66\frac{2}{3}\%$$

Percent of decrease = $66\frac{2}{3}\%$

7. Amount of decrease $225 - \$180 = \$45$

$$\frac{45}{225} = 0.2 = 20\%$$

Percent of decrease = 20%

8. Discount $150 = x - 0.25x$
$150 = 0.75x$
$x = \$220$
Original price: $200

I A4 page 122

1. $\square \times 240 = 120$
$\square = {}^{120}/_{240}$
$\square = .5 = 50\%$

2. $.15 \times 70 = \square$
$.15 \times 70 = 10.5$
$\square = 10.5$

3. $.6 \times 300 = \square$
$.6 \times 300 = 180$
$\square = 180$

4. $\square \times 60 = 42$
$\square = {}^{42}/_{60}$
$\square = 70\%$

5. $\square\% \times 25 = 2.5$
$\square\% = {}^{2.5}/_{25}$
$\square = 10\%$

6. $40\% \times \square = 22$
$\square = {}^{22}/_{.4}$
$\square = 55$

7. $.7 \times \square = 85$
$\square = {}^{85}/_{.7}$
$\square = 121\frac{3}{7}$

8. $25\% \times 38 = \square$
$.25 \times 38 = 9.5$
$\square = 9.5$

9. $.35 \square = 24$
$\square = {}^{24}/_{.35}$
$\square = 68\frac{4}{7}$

II A1 page 124

1. 241
2. 81
3. 8
4. 900
5. 35
6. 51
7. $4^6 = 4{,}096$
8. $2^5 = 32$
9. 44
10. 1,000
11. $4^4 = 256$
12. 72

II A2 page 125

1. tenths
2. 450
3. tens
4. 68,400.03
5. ten-thousandths
6. 0.0781
7. thousandths
8. 0.3050709

II A4 page 126

1. $89.753 \leq 89.755$
2. $\sqrt{81} \leq 9.5$
3. $|-7| \geq |-3|$
4. $10^3 = 1000$
5. $7\frac{3}{4} = 7.75$
6. $-56.7 \geq -56.9$
7. $-604 \geq -610$
8. $|-25.5| \geq -25.5$

II A5 page 129

1. Round all the scores and add the round scores.
   $$90 + 100 + 90 + 90 + 100 + 90 = 560$$

   Divide by the number of scores.
   $$560 \div 6 = 93.3$$
   93 is a reasonable estimate of the average.

2. Round the lengths and add the rounded lengths.
   $$10 + 20 + 20 + 20 = 70$$

   70 is a reasonable estimate of the amount of wood needed.

3. Round the number of dozens to the nearest 10.

   Divide the rounded numbers.
   $$170/10 = 17$$

   17 is a reasonable estimate of the number of batches needed.

4. Round the number of minutes and number of days to the nearest 10.

   Multiply the rounded numbers
   $$50 \times 30 = 1{,}500$$
   Divide to find hours.
   $$1{,}500 \div 60 = 25$$
   25 is a reasonable estimate of the number of hours.

III A1 page 130

1. **−6** is the missing term. Subtract 2 from each term.
2. **14** is the missing term. Add 2.5 to each term.
3. **7.5** is the missing term. Divide each term by 2 to get the next term.
4. **720** is the missing term. The sequence follows the pattern (1×1) (1×2) $(1 \times 2 \times 3)$ $(1 \times 2 \times 3 \times 4)$...
5. **$\frac{1}{65}$** is the missing term. Multiply the previous denominator by 2 and subtract.
6. **21** is the missing term. Add 4 to find the next term.
7. (22, **30**) is the missing term. Add 8 to the first term to find the second term.
8. (30, **4**) is the missing term. Divide the first term by 10 and add 1 to find the second term.

9. (5, **25**) is the missing term. Square the first term to get the second term.
10. (1/9, **1/3**) is the missing term. Multiply the first term by 3 to get the second term.
11. ($\sqrt{5}$, **10**) is the missing term. Square the first term and then multiply by 2 to find the second term.

IV A1 page 132

1. Multiply to find the cost of printing the extra pamphlets.
   $$20 \times \$2.50 = \$50$$
   Add to find the cost of 100 pamphlets.
   $$\$115.00 + \$50 = \underline{\$165}$$

2. 7 warm months − 5 winter months. Multiply to find the costs.
   $$7 \times \$37 = \$259$$
   $$5 \times \$55 = \$275$$
   Find the average. $\$534/_{12} = \underline{\$44.50}$
   Do not use the number of apartments to solve the problem.

3. Multiply to find the amount of coffee used in one day.
   $$4 \times 1.5 = 6 \text{ teaspoons per day}$$
   Divide to find how many days of coffee are in the jar.
   $$^{135}\!/_6 = 22.5 \text{ days} \left(22 \text{ full days}\right)$$

4. Add to find the number of flights. Intercontinental: 21,600 Continental: 3,450 Total: 25,050
   Subtract to find the extra miles flown.
   $$25{,}050 - 20{,}000 = 5{,}050$$

   Divide to find the number of bonuses.
   $$5{,}050 \div 50 = 101$$

   Multiply to find the bonus money.
   $$\mathbf{101} \times \$25 = \$2{,}525$$

IV A2 page 133

1. 40% of the budget is left.
   $$0.4 \times \$3{,}200 = \$1{,}280.$$
   There is $1,280 left over.

2. The 2 players account for 85 goals.
   $$340 - 85 = 255 \text{ goals made by others}$$
   $$255 \div 340 = .75$$
   Others made 75% of the goals.

3. ____ $\times 200 = 65$
____ $= {}^{65}\!/_{200} = 0.325$
32.5% are lobster dinners.

4. $100,000 + 5\%$ of $100,000 = $105,000$ (year 1)
$105,000 + 5\%$ of $105,000 = $110,250$ (year 2)
The total amount is $110,250.

5. 15% of $249 = $37.25
$249 - 37.25 = 211.75$ (Zoom's)
$225 - $211.75 = $13.35
The difference is $13.35.

IV A3 page 134
1. 1, 5, 25
2. 1, 2, 4, 8, 16, 32
3. 3, 6, 9, 12, 15
4. 7, 14, 21, 28, 35
5. 1, 3, 9
6. 1

Geometry and Measurement

I B1 page 136
1. 102 pounds
2. 684.4 meters
3. 10,100 yards
4. 7 cm
5. 1:00 AM
6. 408 km

I B2 page 139
1. πr^2
$3.14 \times (9)^2 =$
$3.14 \times 81 = 254.34 \text{m}^2$
2. b = 3h = 2.6
$(1/2)(3)(2.6) = 3.9$
$4 \times 3.9 = 15.6 \text{ in}^2 + 9 \text{ in}^2 = 24.6 \text{ in}^2$
3. Hexagon is 6-sided
$6 \times 5 \text{ ft} = 30 \text{ ft perimeter}$

4.

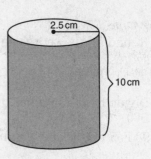

$2 \quad \pi \quad r \quad h$
$2(3.14)(1.25)(10)$
$= 78.5 \text{ cm}^2$

5. $(x + 5) + (x + 5) + x + x = 90$
$4x + 10 = 90$
$4x = 80 \quad x = 20$
length $= x + 5$
length $= 25 \text{ ft.}$

6. Area of each side $= 25 \text{ cm}^2$
Cube is 6-sided.
$6 \times 25 = 150 \text{ cm}^2$

I B2 page 139
1. Volume of a brick $= l\,w\,h$
$V = 2 \times 4 \times 8 = 64 \text{ in}^3$
$8 \times 64 \text{ in}^3 = 512 \text{ in}^3$

2. Volume of a cone $= 1/3\ \pi\ r^2\ h$
$134 = \frac{1}{3}(3.14)(4)^2 h$
$134 = 16.7\ h$
$h = 8 \text{ cm}$

3. Volume of a sphere $= 4/3\ \pi\ r^3$
$V = \frac{4}{3}(3.14)(274.6)$
$V = 1149.66 \text{ in}^3$

4. Volume of a rectangular solid $= l\,w\,h$
$1920 = (16)(12)w$
$1920 = 192w \quad w = 10$
Shaded area $= 12 \times 10 = 120\,m^2.$

II B1 page 143
1. D $\angle$e and $\angle$i are vertical angles
2. B $\angle$g measures 116 ($\angle$b and $\angle$g are congruent. $\angle$j and $\angle$g are supplementary angles.)

II B2 page 147

1. Equilateral triangle
2. Rhombus
3. Trapezoid
4. Triangles have 180°.
   $14° + 87° = 101°$. $180° − 101° = 79°$

II B3 page 149

1. Yes, the ratios of the lengths of corresponding sides are equal.
   $$\frac{PR}{ST} = \frac{2}{4}; \frac{PQ}{SV} = \frac{5}{10}; \frac{2}{4} = \frac{5}{10}$$
2. The measures of corresponding angles are equal.
   Find the measure of the angle in K.
   Angle b in triangle J is the same size.
   $180 − (50 + 55) = 75$.

   The measure of angle b is 75°.
3. A. True. Both are right angles.
   B. False
   C. False
   D. False
   The triangles are not similar.

II B4 page 151

1. C   meters
2. B   fluid ounces
3. A   yards
4. C   cubic meters

III B1 page 152

1.

# of triangles (n)	Sum of angles
2	360°
3	540°
4	(720)°

Sum of angles = $n \times 180$

2. **Length of sides of triangle**

a	b	Area of square (A)
1	1	2
1	2	5
2	2	8
2	3	(13)

$A = a^2 + b^2$

III B2 page 153

1. V of sphere $= 4/3\pi r^3$
   V of cube $= s^3$
   V cube and V sphere =
   $\frac{4}{3}\pi\, r^3 + s^3$
2. A triangle + A trapezoid =
   A. triangle $= \frac{1}{2}xy$
   A. figure $= 5\left(\frac{1}{2}xy\right) =$
   $2.5xy$
3. A. circle $= \pi\left(\frac{d}{2}\right)$
   A. square $= d^2$
   A. figure =
   $\pi\dfrac{d^2}{4} + d^2 =$
   $\pi\left(1\frac{1}{4}\,d^2\right)$ or
   $\pi\left(\dfrac{5}{4}\,d^2\right)$

IV B1 page 155

1. Area of half the circle ($r = 4$)
   $1/2\ (3.14)(16) = (3.14)(8)$ is approximately 25.12 sq. ft.

   Area of the rectangle
   $12 \times 8 = 96$ sq. ft.

   Area of the entire figure
   $25.12 + 96 = 121.12$ sq. ft.

   $121.12 \div 35$ is approximately 3.5 pints
   Round up. You need 4 pints of paint.
2. Find the area of the roofs.
   Roof 1: $115 \times 65 = 7{,}475$ sq. ft.
   Roof 2: $112 \times 65 = 7{,}280$ sq. ft.
   Roof 3: $72 \times 52 = \underline{2{,}744}$ sq. ft.
   TOTAL 18,499 sq. ft.
   $18{,}499 \div 1{,}200 = 15.4$
   Round up. You need 16 bushels.

IV B2 page 156

1.

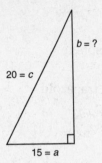

$a^2 + b^2 = c^2$

$(15)^2 + b^2 = (20)^2$

$225 + b^2 = 400$

$b^2 = 400 - 225 = 175$

b = approximately 13.2 ft.

2.

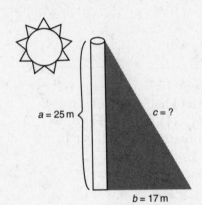

$a^2 + b^2 = c^2$

$(25)^2 + (17)^2 = c^2$

$625 + 289 = c^2$

$c^2 = 914, c$ = approximately 30.2 m.

3.

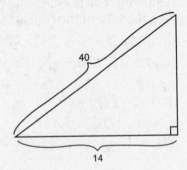

$a^2 + b^2 = c^2$

$(14)^2 + b^2 = (40)^2$

$196 + b^2 = 1,600$

$b^2 = 1,404$

b = approximately 37.5

The height is about 37.5 feet.

4.

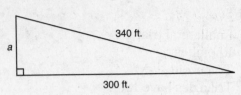

$a^2 + b^2 = c^2$

$a^2 + (300)^2 = (340)^2$

$a^2 = 115,600 - 90,000 = 25,600$

$a = 160$ ft

The ramp is 160 feet high.

Algebra

I C1 page 158

1. $\sqrt{12} + 5\sqrt{3} = \sqrt{4 \times 3} + 5\sqrt{3} =$
   $2\sqrt{3} + 5\sqrt{3} = 7\sqrt{3}$

2. $\sqrt{8} \times \sqrt{6} = \sqrt{48} = \sqrt{4 \times 12^2} = 2\sqrt{12} = 4\sqrt{3}$

3. $\dfrac{\sqrt{108}}{\sqrt{36}} = \dfrac{\sqrt{36 \times 3}}{6} = \dfrac{6\sqrt{3}}{6} = \sqrt{3}$

4. $8\sqrt{28} - 3\sqrt{7} = 16\sqrt{7} - 3\sqrt{7} = 13\sqrt{7}$

5. $\dfrac{3\sqrt{144}}{9\sqrt{16}} = \dfrac{36}{36} = 1$

6. $\dfrac{\sqrt{320}}{\sqrt{5}} = \dfrac{\sqrt{64 \times 5}}{\sqrt{5}} = \dfrac{8\sqrt{5}}{\sqrt{5}} = 8$

I C2 page 160

1. $16 \times 3 - 35 = 15$
2. $-50 + 7 = -43$
3. $40 + 4 - 3 = 41$
4. $(49 + 16) \times 8 = 520$

I C3 page 160

1. $(3.4 \times 4.107) \times (10^4 \times 10^5) =$
   1.39638×10^9

2. $m^k \times m^p = m^{k+p}$

3. $\dfrac{8.034}{2.06} \times \dfrac{10^{12}}{10^9} = 3.9 \times 10^3$

4. 4.0768×10^2

5. $\dfrac{6.8565}{2.11} \times \dfrac{10^{-3}}{10^{-4}} = 3.27 \times 10$

6. $\dfrac{6.40}{3.2} \times \dfrac{10^4}{10^{-3}} = 2 \times 10^7$

I C4 page 162
1. $y = -1$
2. $x = 2$
3. $y = -2$
4. $x = -2$
5. $n < 9$
6. $k < -3$
7. $x < 12$
8. $y > \frac{4}{7}$

I C5 page 165
1. I = $5,760.00
2. I = $6,000
3. R = 6%

I C6 page 166
1. $f(-4) = 12$
2. $f(-1) = -6$
3. $f(3) = 39$
4. $f(-4) = -306$
5. $f(-1) = 8$
6. $f(-3) = -279$

I C7 page 167
1. B $3x - 2$
2. B $(6x + 2)$

I C8 page 168
1. The roots of the quadratic equation are $(2, -\frac{1}{2})$.
2. The roots of the quadratic equation are
$$\frac{1 - \sqrt{21}}{4} \text{ and } \frac{1 + \sqrt{21}}{4}$$

I C9 page 170
1. (A) is the correct answer. The ordered pair $(-2, 1)$ works in both equations.
2. (A) is the correct answer. The ordered pair $(-4, 4)$ works in both equations.
3. (B) is the correct answer. The ordered pair $(-1, 0)$ works in both equations.

II C1 page 173
1. Commutative Property $\frac{6}{8} \times \frac{7}{9} = \frac{7}{9} \times \frac{6}{8}$
2. Associative Property
$(2 + 3) + 4 = 2 + (3 + 4)$
3. The equation represents the distributive property.
4. Distributive property creates the expression $a(6 + 3)$.
5. The commutative property creates the expression.
6. (A) is not true for all real numbers. In fact the answer to A × (1/A) is always 1.

II C2 page 174
1. $x = -2$ is a solution for A.
2. $x = 3$ is a solution for C.
3. $y = -1$ is a solution for C.

II C3 page 175
1. 14 vacuum cleaners for 280 houses
2. 4 teachers for 32 children
3. 21 rest stops for 140 miles

II C4 page 176
1.

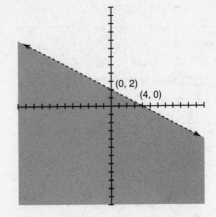

2.

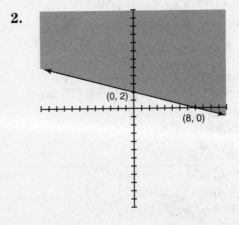

3.

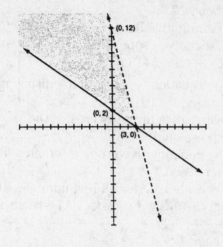

III C2 page 179
For example:
1. $-x > 8 + 2y$ is equivalent to:
   $-x + 3 > 11 + 2y$ and $\frac{1}{2} \times < -4 \ -y$
2. $2y < 4x - 10$ is equivalent to:
   $y < 2x - 5$ and $10 + 2y < 4x$
3. $-x = 12y -10$ is equivalent to:
   $10 - x = 12 \ y$

Other answers are possible.

IV C1 page 181
1. P = about $16.88
2. $s = 41$ mph
3. v = $8,400
4. A = 11

IV C2 page 182
1. $(x)(x + 1) = (x) + (x + 1) + 10$
2. $(x) + (x + 1) + (x + 2) = 3\,(x + 2)$
3. $5(x) = x + \dfrac{(x + 1) + (x + 2)}{2}$
4. $x(x + 1)(x + 2)(x + 3) = 10x$

Statistics and Probability

I D1 page 184
1. August to September ($600,000 to $200,000)
2. 3 inches
3. $330,000

I D2 page 186
1. mode 80
2. mean (average) 35.5
3. median 9 (Remember to arrange the numbers in order.)
4. 16 is the median, the mode, and very close to the mean.
5. mean 89
6. mode 30

I D3 page 187
1. There are 252 combinations of 5 people to sit in the chairs.
2. There are 5,040 possible arrangements of the 7 books on the shelf.
3. 67,600 ($26 \times 26 \times 10 \times 10$)

II D1 page 189
1. mean 6.2, median 6, mode 6
   The mean, median, and mode are about the same.
2. median 30.5, mode 20, mean about 47

II D2 page 190
1. Good Sampling Techniques

   Randomly ask people at work about their child care needs.
   Randomly sample working parents of children ages 1–5.
   Randomly sample parents who have their children in day care.

   Poor Sampling Techniques

   Randomly sample women with children.
   Randomly sample people outside a supermarket.
   Randomly sample people who have no children.

2. Good Sampling Techniques

> Randomly sample seniors at the present centers.
> Randomly sample seniors at banks during business hours.
> Randomly sample people 65 and older.

Poor Sampling Techniques

> Conduct a mail-in survey of people 65 and older.
> Speak to the first 50 people who show up at the current senior center.

II D3 page 192

1. There are 10 socks in the drawer. 7 of the 10 are not black.
P (not black) = 7/10

2. There are 6 goldfish; 2 of the 6 are male.
P (male) = 2/6 = 1/3

3. There are 52 cards in a deck. There are 4 kings and 4 queens.
P (king or queen) = P (king) + P (queen) =
4/52 + 4/52 = 8/52 = 2/13

4. There are 6 different names.
P (Carl and Phyllis) =
P (Carl) × P (Phyllis) =
1/6 × 1/6 = 1/36

III D1 page 193

1. This table shows a positive relationship between the length of the season and the field-goal percentage. The field-goal percentage goes up steadily as the season progresses.

2. Choice B reflects the strong positive relationship between P and Y shown in the table.

IV D1 page 196

1. Add the percentiles of the intervals below 70.
2 + 8 = 10 10% of the students scored below 70.

2. The median score would be in the interval 80–89.

3. The percent of scores from 80 to 100 is
38 + 13 = 51
51% of the students scored from 80 to 100.

4. The question is asking for the number of scores that are above 50. The percentile rank next to 50 is 39. So 39% of the scores are below 50, 39% failed.
100 − 39 = 61. 61% passed.

5. The percent of the scores from 20 to 50 is the percentile rank for 50, less the percentile rank for 20.
39 − 2 = 37
37% of the scores are from 20 to 50.

IV D2 page 198

1. Add two proportions for truck.
0.18 + 0.16 = 0.34
The probability that a package picked at random was sent by truck is 0.34.

2. Add the three proportions for 5 pounds and over.
0.07 + 0.34 + 0.18 = 0.59
The probability of choosing a 10-pound package is .59.

3. The proportion for Air Express over 5 pounds is .07.

4. Add proportions for under 5 pounds by Air Express and under 5 pounds by truck.
0.23 + 0.16 = 0.39
The probability of choosing a 3-pound package not sent by rail is 0.39.

Logic

I E1 page 200

1. C   Set D is where Set A and Set B overlap. So every element of Set D is an element of Set A.

2. B   Some, but not all, parts of Set K and Set L have common elements.

II E1 page 201

The negations are:
1. Some dogs don't wear collars.
2. Some of the students are girls.
3. Ann eats spinach and she does not drink water.
4. Liz is not a teacher or she works in Hillsdale.

II E2 page 203

The equivalent statements are:
1. If it does not rain or Max will stay home.

or

If Max does not stay home, then it did not rain.
2. If they do not call her at the gym, Grace is at the office.

or

Grace is at the office or they call her at the gym.
3. If they get jam for a snack, the children don't like peanut butter.

or

The children don't like peanut butter or they don't get jam for a snack.
4. Jo-Ann wants a puppy and her father will not buy one for her.

II E3 page 204

1. Premise: If a then b | If I finish my work, I will go biking.

_____ a | I finished my work.

Conclusion b | I will go biking.
2. Premise If a then b | If your team wins, they will go to New York.

_____ not b | The team will not go to New York.

Conclusion not a | Your team did not win.
3. Premise: If a then b | If the whistle is blown, the dog will come.

_____ not b | The dog didn't come.

Conclusion not a | The whistle was not blown.

4. Premise: If a then b | If the cat is hungry, she will meow.

_____ If b then c | If the cat meows, the dog comes running.

Conclusion If a then c | If the cat is hungry, the dog comes running.

II E4 page 205

The diagrams for each argument are shown below. Only diagram C confirms the conclusion.

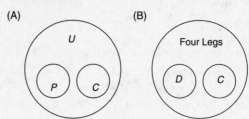

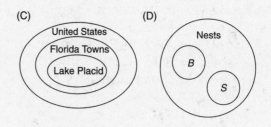

III E1 page 207

1. Premises If a then b
_____ not b
Conclusion a | It is not windy.
2. Premises If a then b
_____ a
Conclusion b | The Yankees can beat the Marlins.

3. Premises If a then b
_____ not b
Conclusion not a | It is not my thirtieth birthday.

4. Premises a or not b
_____ not b
Conclusion a | The stores are closed.

III E2 page 209

The logical rule is:

1. *If p then q* is equivalent to *If not q then not p.*
2. *If not p then q* is equivalent to *p or q.*
3. *Not (p or q)* is equivalent to *(not p) and (not q).*
4. *Not (all are p)* is equivalent to *some are not p.*

IV E1 page 210

1.	If a then b	If I send resumes, I will get interviews.
	If b then c	If I get interviews, I can get a better job.
	Conclusion: If a then c	If I send resumes, I will get a better job.
2.	If a then b	If I miss the 7:30 train, I will be late for work.
	not b	I am not late for work.
	Conclusion: If not b then not a	I was not late for work so I did not miss the 7:30 train.
3.	If b then a	The game will be postponed to Friday, if it rains.
	If a then c	If the game is postponed, it will be played Monday.
	Conclusion: If b then c	If it rains the game will be played on Monday.

STRATEGIES FOR PASSING THE MATHEMATICS TEST

Remember to use the general test strategies discussed in the Introduction.

Write in the Test Booklet

It is particularly important to write in the test booklet while taking the mathematics portion of the test. Use these hints for writing in the test booklet.

Do Your Calculations in the Test Booklet.

Do all your calculations in the test booklet to the right of the question. This makes it easy to refer to the calculations as you choose the correct answer.

This example should make you feel comfortable about writing in the test booklet.

What number times 0.00708 is equal to 70.8

(A) 100,000 × 0 . 0 0 7 0 8 = 708

(B) 10,000 × 0 . 0 0 7 0 8 = 70.8

(C) 1,000

(D) 0.01

(E) 0.0001

The correct answer is (B) 10,000.

Draw Diagrams and Figures in the Test Booklet.

When you come across a geometry problem or related problem, draw a diagram in the test booklet to help.

All sides of a rectangle are shrunk in half. What happens to the area?
(A) Divided by two
(B) Divided by four
(C) Multiplied by two
(D) Multiplied by six
(E) Does not change

Answer (B), divided by 4, is the correct answer. The original area is evenly divided into four parts.

Circle Important Information and Key Words. Cross Out Information You Don't Need.

This approach will draw your attention to the information needed to answer the question. A common mistake is to use information from the question that has nothing to do with the solution.

Example:

> In the morning, a train travels at a constant speed over an 800 kilometer distance. In the afternoon the train travels back over this same route. There is less traffic and the train travels four times as fast as it did that morning. However, there are more people on the train during the afternoon. Which of the following do you know about the train's afternoon trip?

(A) The time is divided by four
(B) The time is multiplied by four
(C) The rate and time are divided by four
(D) The rate is divided by four
(E) The distance is the same so the rate is the same

To solve the problem you just need to know that the speed is constant, four times as fast, and the same route was covered. Circle this information you need to solve the problem.

The distance traveled or that there were more people in the afternoon is extra information. Cross off this extra information, which may interfere with your ability to solve the problem.

> In the morning, a train travels at a constant speed over an 800 kilometer distance. In the afternoon the train travels back over this same route. There is less traffic and the train travels four times as fast as it did that morning. However, there are more people on the train during the afternoon. Which of the following do you know about the train's afternoon trip?

The correct answer is (A), the time is divided by four. The route is the same, but the train travels four times as fast. Therefore, the time to make the trip is divided by four. Rate means the same thing as speed, and we know that the speed has been multiplied by four.

Estimate to Be Sure Your Answer Is Reasonable

You can use estimation and common sense to be sure that the answer is reasonable. You may make a multiplication error or misalign decimal points. You may be so engrossed in a problem that you miss the big picture because of the details. These difficulties can be headed off by making sure your answer is reasonable. A few examples follow.

A question involves dividing or multiplying. Multiply: 28×72.

Estimate first: $30 \times 70 = 2,100$. Your answer should be close to 2,100. If not, then your answer is not reasonable. A mistake was probably made in multiplication.

A question involves subtracting or adding. Add: $12.9 + 0.63 + 10.29 + 4.3$.

Estimate first: $13 + 1 + 10 + 4 = 28$. Your answer should be close to 28. If not, then your answer is not reasonable. The decimal points may not have been aligned.

A question asks you to compare fractions to $^{11}/_{10}$.

Think $^{11}/_{10}$ is more than 1. Any number 1 or less will be less than $^{11}/_{10}$. Any number $1\frac{1}{8}$ or larger will be more than $^{11}/_{10}$. You have to look closely only at numbers between 1 and $1\frac{1}{8}$.

A question asks you to multiply two fractions or decimals.

The fractions or decimals are less than 1. The product of two fractions or decimals less than one is less than either of the two fractions or decimals. If not, you know that your answer is not reasonable.

Stand back for a second after you answer each question and ask, "Is this reasonable? Is this at least approximately correct? Does this make sense?"

Check answers to computation, particularly division and subtraction. When you have completed a division or subtraction example, do a quick, approximate check. Your check should confirm your answer. If not, your answer is probably not reasonable.

Work from the Answers.

If you don't know how to solve a formula or relation try out each answer choice until you get the correct answer. Look at this example.

What percent times $^{1}/_{4}$ is $^{1}/_{5}$?
(A) 25%
(B) 40%
(C) 80%
(D) 120%
(E) None of the above

Just take each answer in turn and try it out.

$$0.25 \times \frac{1}{4} = \frac{1}{4} \times \frac{1}{4} = \frac{1}{16} \qquad \text{That's not it.}$$

$$0.40 \times \frac{1}{4} = \frac{4}{10} \times \frac{1}{4} = \frac{4}{40} = \frac{1}{10} \qquad \text{That's not it either.}$$

$$0.8 \times \frac{1}{4} = \frac{4}{5} \times \frac{1}{4} = \frac{4}{20} = \frac{1}{5}$$

You know that 0.8 is the correct answer, and so choice (C) is correct.

Try Out Numbers.

Look at the preceding question.

Work with fractions at first. Ask: What number times $^{1}/_{4}$ equals $^{1}/_{5}$?

Through trial and error you find out that $^{4}/_{5} \times ^{1}/_{4} = ^{1}/_{5}$.

The answer in fractions is $\frac{4}{5}$.

$$\frac{4}{5} = 0.8 = 80\%.$$

The correct choice is (C).

In this example, we found the answer without ever solving an equation. We just tried out numbers until we found the one that works.

Eliminate and Guess.

Use this approach when all else has failed. Begin by eliminating the answers you know are wrong. Sometimes you know with certainty that an answer is incorrect. Other times, an answer looks so unreasonable that you can be fairly sure that it is not correct.

Once you have eliminated incorrect answers, a few will probably be left. Just guess among these choices. There is no method that will increase your chances of guessing correctly, although some experts report that there may be more correct (B) and (C) choices.

6 PRACTICE TEST 1

Take each of these subtests after you have finished the appropriate subject review.

SCORE TRACKING CHART

Use this chart to track your scores.

Essay

☐ × 2 = ☐ (A total score of 6 or more is passing.)
Rating   Total
       Score

English Language Skills

☐ – 5 = ☐ (A raw score of 26 to 28 or higher is usually passing.)
Number   Raw
Correct   Score

Reading

☐ – 5 = ☐ (A raw score of 24 to 26 or higher is usually passing.)
Number   Raw
Correct   Score

Mathematics

☐ – 5 = ☐ (A raw score of 33 to 35 or higher is usually passing.)
Number   Raw
Correct   Score

ESSAY

60 minutes

Take this practice subtest in a realistic, timed setting. Do not take this practice subtest until you have reviewed Chapter 3, English Language Skills, and Chapter 4, Essay.

The test rules allow you exactly one hour to write your essay. Write your outline below and write your essay on the following lined pages. Remember, your outline is not read and it is not graded. Do not try to copy your essay.

Write an essay on one of these two topics.

1. A sports figure who influences school children.

2. A societal issue that affects people.

You may write your initial thoughts below. Only the essay is scored.

_____
_____
_____
_____
_____
_____
_____
_____
_____
_____
_____
_____
_____
_____
_____
_____
_____
_____
_____
_____
_____
_____
_____
_____
_____
_____
_____
_____

(Show your completed essay to an English professor or an English teacher. Ask them to rate your essay using the rating scale and criteria on page 97.)

ENGLISH LANGUAGE SKILLS / READING

80 minutes

Take this practice subtest in a realistic, timed setting. Do not take this subtest until you have reviewed Chapter 2, Reading, and Chapter 3, English Language Skills.

The test rules allow you exactly 80 minutes to complete both the English Language Skills and Reading subtests. It is recommended that you spend about 25 minutes on the English Language Skills subtest and about 55 minutes on the Reading subtest.

Use the answer sheet that follows.

ENGLISH LANGUAGE SKILLS / READING

English Language Skills

1 Ⓐ Ⓑ Ⓒ Ⓓ Ⓔ	9 Ⓐ Ⓑ Ⓒ Ⓓ Ⓔ	17 Ⓐ Ⓑ Ⓒ Ⓓ Ⓔ	25 Ⓐ Ⓑ Ⓒ Ⓓ Ⓔ	33 Ⓐ Ⓑ Ⓒ Ⓓ Ⓔ
2 Ⓐ Ⓑ Ⓒ Ⓓ Ⓔ	10 Ⓐ Ⓑ Ⓒ Ⓓ Ⓔ	18 Ⓐ Ⓑ Ⓒ Ⓓ Ⓔ	26 Ⓐ Ⓑ Ⓒ Ⓓ Ⓔ	34 Ⓐ Ⓑ Ⓒ Ⓓ Ⓔ
3 Ⓐ Ⓑ Ⓒ Ⓓ Ⓔ	11 Ⓐ Ⓑ Ⓒ Ⓓ Ⓔ	19 Ⓐ Ⓑ Ⓒ Ⓓ Ⓔ	27 Ⓐ Ⓑ Ⓒ Ⓓ Ⓔ	35 Ⓐ Ⓑ Ⓒ Ⓓ Ⓔ
4 Ⓐ Ⓑ Ⓒ Ⓓ Ⓔ	12 Ⓐ Ⓑ Ⓒ Ⓓ Ⓔ	20 Ⓐ Ⓑ Ⓒ Ⓓ Ⓔ	28 Ⓐ Ⓑ Ⓒ Ⓓ Ⓔ	36 Ⓐ Ⓑ Ⓒ Ⓓ Ⓔ
5 Ⓐ Ⓑ Ⓒ Ⓓ Ⓔ	13 Ⓐ Ⓑ Ⓒ Ⓓ Ⓔ	21 Ⓐ Ⓑ Ⓒ Ⓓ Ⓔ	29 Ⓐ Ⓑ Ⓒ Ⓓ Ⓔ	37 Ⓐ Ⓑ Ⓒ Ⓓ Ⓔ
6 Ⓐ Ⓑ Ⓒ Ⓓ Ⓔ	14 Ⓐ Ⓑ Ⓒ Ⓓ Ⓔ	22 Ⓐ Ⓑ Ⓒ Ⓓ Ⓔ	30 Ⓐ Ⓑ Ⓒ Ⓓ Ⓔ	38 Ⓐ Ⓑ Ⓒ Ⓓ Ⓔ
7 Ⓐ Ⓑ Ⓒ Ⓓ Ⓔ	15 Ⓐ Ⓑ Ⓒ Ⓓ Ⓔ	23 Ⓐ Ⓑ Ⓒ Ⓓ Ⓔ	31 Ⓐ Ⓑ Ⓒ Ⓓ Ⓔ	39 Ⓐ Ⓑ Ⓒ Ⓓ Ⓔ
8 Ⓐ Ⓑ Ⓒ Ⓓ Ⓔ	16 Ⓐ Ⓑ Ⓒ Ⓓ Ⓔ	24 Ⓐ Ⓑ Ⓒ Ⓓ Ⓔ	32 Ⓐ Ⓑ Ⓒ Ⓓ Ⓔ	40 Ⓐ Ⓑ Ⓒ Ⓓ Ⓔ

Check the answers and explanations on page 260.

Reading

1 Ⓐ Ⓑ Ⓒ Ⓓ Ⓔ	10 Ⓐ Ⓑ Ⓒ Ⓓ Ⓔ	19 Ⓐ Ⓑ Ⓒ Ⓓ Ⓔ	28 Ⓐ Ⓑ Ⓒ Ⓓ Ⓔ	37 Ⓐ Ⓑ Ⓒ Ⓓ Ⓔ
2 Ⓐ Ⓑ Ⓒ Ⓓ Ⓔ	11 Ⓐ Ⓑ Ⓒ Ⓓ Ⓔ	20 Ⓐ Ⓑ Ⓒ Ⓓ Ⓔ	29 Ⓐ Ⓑ Ⓒ Ⓓ Ⓔ	38 Ⓐ Ⓑ Ⓒ Ⓓ Ⓔ
3 Ⓐ Ⓑ Ⓒ Ⓓ Ⓔ	12 Ⓐ Ⓑ Ⓒ Ⓓ Ⓔ	21 Ⓐ Ⓑ Ⓒ Ⓓ Ⓔ	30 Ⓐ Ⓑ Ⓒ Ⓓ Ⓔ	39 Ⓐ Ⓑ Ⓒ Ⓓ Ⓔ
4 Ⓐ Ⓑ Ⓒ Ⓓ Ⓔ	13 Ⓐ Ⓑ Ⓒ Ⓓ Ⓔ	22 Ⓐ Ⓑ Ⓒ Ⓓ Ⓔ	31 Ⓐ Ⓑ Ⓒ Ⓓ Ⓔ	40 Ⓐ Ⓑ Ⓒ Ⓓ Ⓔ
5 Ⓐ Ⓑ Ⓒ Ⓓ Ⓔ	14 Ⓐ Ⓑ Ⓒ Ⓓ Ⓔ	23 Ⓐ Ⓑ Ⓒ Ⓓ Ⓔ	32 Ⓐ Ⓑ Ⓒ Ⓓ Ⓔ	41 Ⓐ Ⓑ Ⓒ Ⓓ Ⓔ
6 Ⓐ Ⓑ Ⓒ Ⓓ Ⓔ	15 Ⓐ Ⓑ Ⓒ Ⓓ Ⓔ	24 Ⓐ Ⓑ Ⓒ Ⓓ Ⓔ	33 Ⓐ Ⓑ Ⓒ Ⓓ Ⓔ	
7 Ⓐ Ⓑ Ⓒ Ⓓ Ⓔ	16 Ⓐ Ⓑ Ⓒ Ⓓ Ⓔ	25 Ⓐ Ⓑ Ⓒ Ⓓ Ⓔ	34 Ⓐ Ⓑ Ⓒ Ⓓ Ⓔ	
8 Ⓐ Ⓑ Ⓒ Ⓓ Ⓔ	17 Ⓐ Ⓑ Ⓒ Ⓓ Ⓔ	26 Ⓐ Ⓑ Ⓒ Ⓓ Ⓔ	35 Ⓐ Ⓑ Ⓒ Ⓓ Ⓔ	
9 Ⓐ Ⓑ Ⓒ Ⓓ Ⓔ	18 Ⓐ Ⓑ Ⓒ Ⓓ Ⓔ	27 Ⓐ Ⓑ Ⓒ Ⓓ Ⓔ	36 Ⓐ Ⓑ Ⓒ Ⓓ Ⓔ	

Check the answers and explanations on page 261.

Remove answer sheet by cutting on dotted line.

ENGLISH LANGUAGE SKILLS

> The selections that follow contain some errors, which appear in the underlined part of the test questions. Read the passage. Then answer each question by selecting the answer choice that corrects the error. Choose *No change is necessary* if there is no error. Each item contains no more than one error.

First Passage

Europeans had started to devote significant resources to medicine, when Louis Pasteur was born December 7, 1822. By the time he died in the fall of 1895, he made enormous significant contributions to science and had founded microbiology. At 32 he was named professor and dean at a French university dedicated to supporting the production of alcoholic beverages. Pasteur immediated began work on yeast and fermentation. He found that he could kill harmful bacteria in the initial brewing process, by subjecting the liquid to high temperature. This finding was extended to milk in the process called pasteurization. This work led him to the conclusion that human disease could be causes of germs. In Pasteur's time, there was a wide held belief that germs were spontaneously generated. Pasteur conducted experiments that proved germs were always introduced initially and never appeared spontaneously. These results was questioned by other scientists for over a decade. He proved his theory of vaccination and his theory of disease during his work with anthrax, a fatally animal disease. He vaccinated some sheep with weakened anthrax germs and left other sheep without vaccine. Then he ingected all the sheep with a potentially fatal dose of anthrax bacteria. The unvaccinated sheep died while the other vaccinated sheep lived. He developped vaccines for many diseases. Pasteur is best known for his vaccine for rabies. The rabies vaccine was first tried on a human when a young boy arrived at Pasteurs' lab. The treatment of the boy is successful.

> Choose the correct replacement for the underlined portion.

1. Europeans <u>had started</u> to devote
           A

   significant resources to <u>medicine, when</u>
                           B

   Louis Pasteur was born

   <u>December 7, 1822</u> .
          C

   (A) have started
   (B) medicine when
   (C) December 7 1822
   (D) No change is necessary.

2. By the time he died in the <u>fall</u> of 1895, he
                           A

   made <u>enormous</u> significant
          B

   contributions to <u>science and</u> had
                C

   founded microbiology.

   (A) Fall
   (B) enormously
   (C) science, and
   (D) No change is necessary.

3. <u>At 32 he was</u> named professor and <u>dean</u>
    A   B
at a French <u>university</u> dedicated
            C
to supporting the production of
alcoholic beverages.

(A) At 32, he was
(B) Dean
(C) University
(D) No change is necessary.

4. Pasteur <u>immediated</u> <u>began</u> <u>work</u> on
           A   B   C
yeast and fermentation.

(A) immediately
(B) had begun
(C) working
(D) No change is necessary.

5. He found that <u>he could kill</u> harmful
                   A
bacteria in the <u>initial</u> brewing
               B
<u>process, by</u> subjecting the liquid to high
      C
temperature.

(A) he killed
(B) inicial
(C) process by
(D) No change is necessary.

6. <u>This finding</u> <u>was extended</u> to milk in the
      A   B
process called <u>pasteurization</u>.
             C

(A) This, finding
(B) extended
(C) Pasteurization
(D) No change is necessary.

7. This work led him to the <u>conclusion that</u>
                      A
human <u>disease</u> could be <u>causes of germs</u>.
      B   C

(A) conclusion, that
(B) diseased
(C) caused by germs
(D) No change is necessary.

8. In Pasteur's <u>time, there</u> was a <u>wide</u> held
            A   B
belief that germs were

<u>spontaneously generated</u>.
        C

(A) time there
(B) widely
(C) spontaneous generation
(D) No change is necessary.

9. Pasteur conducted <u>experiments that</u>
                   A
proved germs <u>were always introduced</u>
              B
initially and never appeared
<u>spontaneously</u>.
   C

(A) experiments, that
(B) was always introduced
(C) spontaneous
(D) No change is necessary.

10. <u>These results</u> was <u>questioned</u> by other
     A   B
<u>scientists for</u> over a decade.
    C

(A) This result
(B) questioning
(C) scientiists, for
(D) No change is necessary.

11. He proved his theory of <u>vaccination and</u>
                      A
his theory of disease during his work

with <u>anthrax, a</u> <u>fatally</u> animal disease.
     B   C

(A) vaccination, and
(B) anthrax a
(C) fatal
(D) No change is necessary.

12. He vaccinated <u>some sheep with</u>
                         A

   <u>weakened anthrax</u> germs
          B

   and left other sheep <u>without vaccine</u>.
                             C

   (A) some, with
   (B) weak anthrax
   (C) unvaccinated
   (D) No change is necessary.

13. Then he <u>ingected</u> all the sheep with
              A

   a <u>potentially fatal</u> dose of anthrax
             B

   <u>bacteria</u>.
    C

   (A) injected
   (B) a potential fatality
   (C) bakteria
   (D) No change is necessary.

14. The unvaccinated <u>sheep died</u> while
                 A

   <u>the other</u> vaccinated <u>sheep lived</u>.
     B   C

   (A) sheep died;
   (B) the
   (C) sheep, lived
   (D) No change is necessary.

15. He <u>developped</u> <u>vaccines</u> for many
       A   B

   <u>diseases</u>.
    C

   (A) developed
   (B) vaccines
   (C) diseases
   (D) No change is necessary.

16. <u>Pasteur</u> is best known for his
     A

   <u>vaccine</u> for <u>rabies</u>.
    B   C

   (A) Pasteur, is
   (B) vacine
   (C) rabid
   (D) No change is necessary.

17. The <u>rabies</u> <u>vaccine</u> was first tried on a
       A   B

   human when a young boy arrived at
   <u>Pasteurs'</u> lab.
     C

   (A) rabies'
   (B) vacine
   (C) Pasteur's
   (D) No change is necessary.

18. The <u>treatment</u> of the boy <u>is</u> <u>successful</u>.
       A   B   C

   (A) treatments
   (B) was
   (C) succesful
   (D) No change is necessary.

Second Passage

It is striking how uninformed todays youth are about Acquired Immune Deficiency Syndrome. Because of their immaturity and ignorance. Many young people engage in high-risk behavior. Many of these young adults do not realize that this disease can be contacted through almost any contact with an infected person's blood and bodily fluids. Some do not realized that symptoms of the disease may not appear for 10 years or more. Others may not realize the dangers involved in shared intravenous needles. The problem of sharing needles is that a small amount of blood remains in a used needle and is then injected into the next user's body. A masive education campaign is needed to fully inform today's youth about AIDS.

19. It is striking how uninformed todays
          A   B
     youth are about Acquired Immune
     C
     Deficiency Syndrome.

    (A) striking, how
    (B) today's
    (C) youths
    (D) No change is necessary.

20. Because of their immaturity and
                    A
     ignorance. Many young people
              B
     engage in high-risk behavior.
     C

    (A) immaturity
    (B) ignorance, many
    (C) engaged
    (D) No change is necessary.

21. Many of these young adults do not
                        A
     realize that this disease can be
     contacted through almost any contact
     B
     with an infected person's blood and
                       C
     bodily fluids.

    (A) adults, do
    (B) contracted
    (C) persons blood
    (D) No change is necessary.

22. Some do not realized that symptoms of
              A   B
     the disease may not appear for 10 years
            C
     or more.

    (A) realize
    (B) simptoms
    (C) disease, may
    (D) No change is necessary.

23. Others may not realize the dangers
                       A
     involved in shared intravenous needles.
            B   C

    (A) dangerous
    (B) in sharing
    (C) intrevenous
    (D) No change is necessary.

24. The problem of sharing needles is that a
         A   B
     small amount of blood remains
                       C
     in a used needle and is then injected
     into the next user's body.

    (A) problem with
    (B) was
    (C) remained
    (D) No change is necessary.

25. A <u>masive</u> <u>education campaign</u> <u>is needed</u>
     A   B   C
to fully inform today's youth about AIDS.

   (A) massive
   (B) educational campaign
   (C) needs
   (D) No change is necessary.

Select the best answer choice.

---

26. Which sentence does not represent a parallel structure?
   (A) Cathy will get a raise either by putting in longer hours or by volunteering in her spare time.
   (B) The basketball player was famous for his aggressiveness on the court and good nature off the court.
   (C) When the marathon runners cross the Brooklyn Bridge, they are halfway between the boroughs of Brooklyn and Manhattan.
   (D) No change is necessary.

For the underlined sentence, choose the option that expresses the meaning with the most fluency and the most logic.

---

27. The English language emerged 1500 years ago. <u>It evolved from the Germanic languages on the European continents and developed primarily in England</u>.
   (A) Developed primarily in England, it evolved from Germanic languages on the European continent.
   (B) Germanic languages on the European continent were developed primarily in England.
   (C) It developed primarily in England but evolved from the Germanic languages of the European continent.
   (D) It evolved on the European continent from Germanic languages that developed primarily in England.

28. Teachers are authority figures. <u>Those teachers who are good classroom managers understand their dual role as an authority figure and as someone who helps children adapt to school and to life</u>.
   (A) Those teachers who are good classroom managers understand their dual role as an authority figure and as someone who helps children adapt to school and to life.
   (B) Their dual role as someone who helps children adapt to school and to life and as an authority figure is understood by teachers who are good classroom managers.
   (C) Helping children adapt to school and life and serving as an authority figure constitute a dual role, which is understood by teachers who are good classroom managers.
   (D) As good classroom managers, those teachers who help children adapt to school and to life and being an authority figure, understand their dual roles.

Choose the underlined portion that is not necessary in the context of the sentence.

---

29. <u>Following a concert</u>, <u>a fan</u> asked a
           A   B
popular singer why <u>the</u> songs sounded
                  C
<u>so</u> different live, <u>in person</u>, than on the
 D   E
recording.

   (A) Following a concert
   (B) a fan
   (C) the
   (D) so
   (E) in person,

30. People <u>who set fires</u> are <u>frequently</u>
            A   B
   captured <u>commonly</u> at the scene
              C
   <u>of the crime</u> <u>when the ashes settle</u>.
        D   E

   (A) who set fires
   (B) frequently
   (C) commonly
   (D) of the crime
   (E) when the ashes settle

Identify the error. Choose the correct replacement for the underlined portion.

---

31. Amanda <u>wanted to write</u> a letter about her <u>faulty</u> sunglasses but she knew not to <u>who</u> to send it.

   (A) wrote
   (B) falty
   (C) whom
   (D) no change necessary

Choose the most effective word or phrase within the context suggested by the sentence.

---

32. The archaeologist was ___ an ancient limestone tablet when the earthquake hit and destroyed the dig site.

   (A) integrating
   (B) inscribing
   (C) investigating

33. President Hoover's ___ to combat the Depression could best be described as a slow establishment of loan programs for the unemployed.

   (A) appeal
   (B) approach
   (C) reproach

34. The English soldiers who fired on colonial ___, killing five, during the Boston Massacre were defended by John Adams and other patriots.

   (A) protestors
   (B) projectors
   (C) programmers

Choose the sentence that clearly and effectively expresses the thought with no structural errors.

---

35. (A) In the debate during the late 1700s over a stronger versus a weaker federal government, the Federalists wanted a strong federal body.
   (B) The Federalists, in the debate during the late 1700s over a stronger versus a weaker federal government wanted a strong federal body.
   (C) During the late 1700s, in the debate over a stronger versus a weaker federal government, the Federalists wanted a strong Federal body.

36. (A) Jazz music, developed by African American musicians about 100 years ago, is characterized by improvisation.
   (B) Developed by African American musicians about 100 years ago and characterized by improvisation is jazz music.
   (C) About 100 years ago, jazz music developed by African American musicians was characterized by improvisation.

37. (A) All American cars have a reputation for being inferior in design and dependability to their Japanese counterparts.
   (B) Having a reputation for being inferior in design and dependability to their Japanese counterparts, all American cars have a reputation.
   (C) Being inferior in design and dependability, all American cars have a reputation as opposed to their Japanese counterparts.

Choose the sentence that logically expresses the comparison.

38. (A) Louise is the fast runner at the trischool meet.
    (B) Louise is the faster runner at the trischool meet.
    (C) Louise is the fastest runner at the trischool meet.

39. (A) The more convenient store for groceries is Food Lion not A & P.
    (B) The most convenient store for groceries is Food Lion rather than A & P.
    (C) The convenient store for groceries is Food Lion rather than A & P.

Choose the sentence that clearly and logically expresses the thought with no structural errors.

40. (A) Unfortunately, the five-car accident caused several people to be hurt in a tragedy.
    (B) The five-car accident was a tragedy; unfortunately, several people were hurt.
    (C) Several people were hurt in the five-car accident that was a tragedy, unfortunately.

READING

Computer graphing programs are capable of graphing almost any equations, including advanced equations from
Line calculus. The student just types in the
(5) equation and the graph appears on the computer screen. The graphing program can also show the numerical solution for any entered equation. I like having a com-
(10) puter program that performs the mechanical aspects of these difficult calculations. However, these programs do not teach about graphing or mathematics because the computer does not
(15) "explain" what is going on. A person could type in an equation, get an answer, and have not the slightest idea what either meant.

Relying on this mindless kind of graph-
(20) ing and calculation, students will be completely unfamiliar with the meaning of the equations they write or the results they get. They will not be able to understand how to create a graph from an
(25) equation or to understand the basis for the more complicated calculations.

It may be true that a strictly mechanical approach is used by some teachers. There certainly is a place for students
(30) who already understand equations and graphing to have a computer program that relieves the drudgery. But these computer programs should never and can never replace the teacher. Mathe-
(35) matical competence assumes that understanding precedes rote calculation.

1. What is the main idea of this passage?

   (A) Graphing programs are not effective for initially teaching mathematics.
   (B) Students should use this graphing program as one part of instruction.
   (C) Teachers should use graphing programs as one part of instruction.
   (D) Graphing programs rely too heavily on the student's knowledge of computers.

2. What does the word *competence* on line 35 mean?

   (A) willingness
   (B) excellence
   (C) ability
   (D) acuteness

3. The author's statement on lines 23–26 that "They will not be able to understand how to create a graph from an equation or to understand the basis for the more complicated calculations" is a statement of

   (A) fact
   (B) opinion

4. What is the relationship between the sentence beginning on line 9 (*I like having a computer...*) and the sentence beginning on line 12 (*However, these programs...*)?

   (A) addition
   (B) compare and contrast
   (C) generalization and example
   (D) definition

In response to my opponent's question about my record on environmental issues, I want to say that the real problem in this election is not my record. Rather the problem is the influence of my opponent's rich friends in the record industry. I hope you will turn your back on his rich supporters and vote for me.

5. What type of fallacious reasoning is found in the passage?

   (A) nonsequitur
   (B) false analogy
   (C) red herring
   (D) begging the question

6. Which of the following statements best illustrates the author's primary purpose?

   (A) clearing the author's name
   (B) describing the problems of running for office
   (C) informing the public of wrong doing
   (D) convincing the voting populous

   Using percentages to report growth patterns can be deceptive. If there are 100 new users for a cereal currently used
   Line by 100 other people, the growth rate is
   (5) 100 percent. _____ if there are 50,000 new users for a cereal currently used by 5,000,000 people, the growth rate is 1 percent. It seems obvious that the growth rate of 1 percent is preferable
   (10) to the growth rate of 100 percent.

   _____ percentages do provide a useful way to report growth patterns, we must know the initial number the growth percentage is based on before we make
   (15) any conclusions.

7. What is the missing word(s) in line 5?

   (A) so while
   (B) however
   (C) therefore
   (D) although

8. What is (are) the missing word(s) in line 11?

   (A) So while
   (B) Therefore
   (C) However
   (D) Although

9. What occupation would most likely be concerned with a study such as the one in the passage?

   (A) marketing specialist
   (B) sociologist
   (C) nutritionist
   (D) retail grocer

   Advances in astronomy and space exploration during the past twenty-five years have been significant, and we now know
   Line more answers to questions about the uni-
   (5) verse than ever before, _____ we still cannot answer the ultimate question, "How did our universe originate?"

10. The author's primary purpose is to

    (A) clarify how much money is spent on space exploration.
    (B) narrate the history of space exploration.
    (C) present a key question about space that is not yet answered.
    (D) list answers to questions about space.

11. The missing word in line 5 is

    (A) but
    (B) while
    (C) since
    (D) therefore

    The Board of Adjustment can exempt a person from the requirements of a particular land use ordinance. Several cases
    Line have come before the Board concerning
    (5) three ordinances. One ordinance states that religious and other organizations cannot build places of worship or meeting halls in residential zones. A second ordinance states that any garage must be
    (10) less than 25 percent of the size of a house on the same lot, while a third ordinance restricts a peron's right to convert a one-family house to a two-family house.
    It is interesting to note how a person
    (15) can be in favor of an exemption in one case but opposed to exemption in another. For example, one homeowner applied to build a garage 45 percent of the size of her house but was opposed to a
    (20) neighbor converting his house from a one-family to a two-family house. This second homeowner was opposed to a church being built in his neighborhood. The woman opposed to his proposal was
    (25) all for the church construction project.
    The pressure on Board of Adjustment

members who also live in the community is tremendous. It must sometimes seem to them that any decision is the wrong
(30) one. But that is what Board of Adjustments are for, and we can only hope that this example of America in action will best serve the community and those who live there.

12. The word *residential* in line 8 means

    (A) urban
    (B) rural
    (C) where businesses are
    (D) where people live

13. In which of the following publications would you expect this passage to appear?

    (A) a local newspaper
    (B) a national newspaper
    (C) a news magazine
    (D) an economics textbook

14. The author's organizational pattern in the second paragraph (lines 14–25) could best be described as

    (A) generalization/example
    (B) classification
    (C) definition
    (D) spatial order

15. What is the meaning of the word *converting* in line 20?

    (A) switching
    (B) constructing
    (C) evolving
    (D) changing

16. What is the relationship between the sentences *Several cases have come...* (lines 3–4), *One ordinance states...* (line 5), and *A second ordinance states...* (lines 8–9)?

    (A) time order
    (B) addition
    (C) listing
    (D) comparison

Researchers were not sure at first what caused AIDS nor how it was transmitted. They did know early on that eve-
Line ryone who developed AIDS died.
(5) _____ researchers began to understand that the disease is caused by the HIV virus, which could be transmitted through blood and blood products. Even after knowing this, some blood compa-
(10) nies resisted testing blood for the HIV virus. Today we know that the HIV virus is transmitted through blood and other bodily fluids. Women may be more *susceptible* than men, and the prognosis
(15) hasn't changed.

17. The word *susceptible* in line 14 means

    (A) accessible
    (B) subject to infection
    (C) experiencing
    (D) infected

18. The statement *They did know early on that everyone who developed AIDS died* represents

    (A) fact
    (B) opinion

19. The author's purpose in writing this passage is

    (A) to show that blood companies can't be trusted
    (B) to give a detailed history of AIDS
    (C) to warn women about the danger of AIDS
    (D) to raise awareness about AIDS

20. The word missing from line 5 is most likely

    (A) Then
    (B) While
    (C) When
    (D) However

The computers in the college dormitories are actually more sophisticated than the computers in the college computer labs, and they cost less. It seems that the person who bought the dormitory computers looked around until she found powerful computers at a low price. The person who runs the labs just got the computers offered by the regular supplier.

21. The best statement of the main idea of this paragraph is

    (A) it is better to use the computers in the dorms.
    (B) the computers in the dorms are always in use so, for most purposes, it is better to use the computers in the labs.
    (C) it is better to shop around before you buy.
    (D) wholesale prices are usually better than retail prices.

An analysis of models of potential space vehicles prepared by engineers revealed that the parts of the hull of the vehicles that were strongest were the ones that had the most potential for being weak.

22. What conclusion can be drawn from the statement above?

    (A) The parts of the hull that are potentially strongest do not receive as much attention from engineers as those that are potentially weakest.
    (B) The potentially weaker parts of the hull appear stronger in models than the potentially stronger parts of the hull.
    (C) Being potentially weaker, these parts of the hull appear relatively stronger in a model.
    (D) Potentially weaker parts of the hull have the most potential for being stronger.

23. The word *potential* in line 1 means

    (A) stored energy
    (B) capable
    (C) possible
    (D) actual

Cellular telephones, once used by the very rich, are now available to almost everyone. Drug pushers and drug runners have begun using this method of communication because calls can be made from just about anywhere to just about anywhere. Law enforcement officials will be forced to lobby for new legislation, which can help them monitor usage of cellular service. It is getting harder and harder to fight crime every day.

Line (5)
(10)

24. What is the author's tone?

    (A) desperate
    (B) frightened
    (C) indifferent
    (D) concerned

25. What does the word *monitor* on line 9 mean?

    (A) to look after
    (B) a computer screen
    (C) a cathode ray tube
    (D) to keep track of

26. In this passage, the author shows bias against

    (A) drug dealers
    (B) legislators
    (C) law enforcement officials
    (D) cellular service sales representatives

27. The central idea of this passage could best be described as

    (A) Long time cellular phone use causes cancer.
    (B) There are many difficulties in monitoring cellular phones.
    (C) Cellular phones are becoming a driving hazard.
    (D) Cellular phones often end up in the wrong hands.

I think women are discriminated against; however, I think men are discriminated against just as much as
Line women. It's just a different type of dis-
(5) crimination. Consider these two facts: Men die about 6 years earlier than women, and men are the only people who can be drafted into the armed forces. That's discrimination!

28. What is the author's purpose in writing this passage?

   (A) anger
   (B) indifference
   (C) persuasiveness
   (D) entertainment

29. What is the author's main point in writing this passage?

   (A) Men are discriminated against more than women are.
   (B) Both sexes are discriminated against.
   (C) On average, men die earlier than women.
   (D) Men are not discriminated against.

30. The author's organizational pattern can best be described as

   (A) classification
   (B) generalization/example
   (C) compare/contrast
   (D) summary

31. When the author says, *It's just a different type of discrimination*, this conclusion is logically

   (A) valid
   (B) invalid

The War of 1812 is one of the least understood conflicts in American history. However, many events associated with
Line the war are among the best remembered
(5) from American History. The war began when the United States invaded British colonies in Canada. The invasion failed, and the United States was quickly put on the defensive. Most Americans are not
(10) aware of how the conflict began. During the war, the *USS Constitution* (Old Ironsides) was active against British ships in the Atlantic. Captain William Perry, sailing on Lake Erie, was famous for his yell-
(15) ing to his shipmates, "Don't give up the ship." Most Americans remember Perry, and his famous plea but not where, or in which war, he was engaged.

Most notably, British troops sacked
(20) and burned Washington, D.C., during this conflict. Subsequent British attacks on Fort McHenry near Baltimore were repulsed by American forces. It was during this battle that Francis Scott Key wrote
(25) the "Star Spangled Banner" while a prisoner on a British ship. The "rockets red glare, bombs bursting in air" referred to ordinance used by the British to attack the fort. Many Americans mistakenly be-
(30) lieve that the "Star Spangled Banner" was written during or shortly after the Revolutionary War.

32. What is the central idea of this passage?

   (A) The Americans fought the British in the War of 1812.
   (B) Many Americans are unaware of events associated with the War of 1812.
   (C) The British were cruel to American composers during this war.
   (D) Captain Perry is most famous for saying, "Don't give up the ship."

33. The line that states, *It was during this battle that Francis Scott Key wrote the "Star Spangled Banner" while a prisoner on a British ship* could be considered a statement of

    (A) fact
    (B) opinion

34. Which detail is not illustrated in this passage?

    (A) Foreign armies burned Washington.
    (B) The "Star Spangled Banner" was written during the Revolutionary War.
    (C) The *USS Constitution* was active against the British Navy.
    (D) The War of 1812 began when British colonies were invaded in Canada.

35. What pattern did the author use to organize the information presented in this passage?

    (A) summary
    (B) classification
    (C) statement/explanation
    (D) order of importance

36. What can be inferred about Francis Scott Key from lines 23–26 of this passage?

    (A) He did not survive the battle.
    (B) While a prisoner on the British ship, he became a British spy.
    (C) He was released by or escaped from the British.
    (D) He returned to Britain where he lived out his days.

37. Which of the following would be a synonym for *sacked* in line 19?

    (A) fortified
    (B) looted
    (C) enclosed
    (D) ravaged

Computer-based word processing programs have spelling checkers and even a thesaurus to find synonyms and anto-
Line nyms for highlighted words. To use the
(5) thesaurus, the student just types in the word, and a series of synonyms and antonyms appears on the computer screen. The program can also show recommended spellings for misspelled words. I
(10) like having a computer program that performs these mechanical aspects of writing. _____ these programs do not teach about spelling or word meanings. A person could type in a word, get a
(15) synonym and have not the slightest idea what either meant.

Relying on this mindless way of checking spelling and finding synonyms, students will be completely unfamiliar with
(20) the meanings of the words they use. _____ one of the most common misuses is to include a word that is spelled correctly but used incorrectly in the sentence.
(25) It may be true that a strictly mechanical approach to spelling is used by some teachers. There certainly is a place for students who already understand word meanings to use a computer program
(30) that relieves the drudgery of checking spelling and finding synonyms. But these computer programs should never and can never replace the teacher. Understanding words—their uses and
(35) meanings—should precede this more mechanistic approach.

38. Which word best fits in line 12?

    (A) Although
    (B) While
    (C) And
    (D) However

39. Which word or phrase best fits in line 21?

    (A) In fact
    (B) For example
    (C) While
    (D) Therefore

40. Which aspect of spell-checking and thesaurus programs does the author like?

    (A) Synonyms and alternate spellings are done very quickly.
    (B) The difficult mechanical aspects are performed.
    (C) They can't replace teachers.
    (D) You don't have to know how to spell to use them.

When Lyndon Johnson succeeded John F. Kennedy, he was able to gain congressional approval for programs suggested by Kennedy but never implemented. These programs, called Great Society programs, included low-income housing and project Head Start. To some, this made Johnson a better president.

41. The author's purpose is to explain how

    (A) Johnson was a better president than Kennedy
    (B) Johnson gained approval for Kennedy's proposed programs
    (C) Johnson was a member of the great society
    (D) Johnson was president before Kennedy

MATHEMATICS

90 minutes

Take this practice subtest in a realistic, timed setting. Do not take this practice subtest until you have reviewed Chapter 5, Mathematics.

The test rules allow you exactly 90 minutes to complete this practice subtest. You have a little over one and one-half minutes to answer each question. Answer the easier questions right away and leave the more difficult questions until the end of the test.

Use the answer sheet that follows.

Mathematics
90 minutes

1 Ⓐ Ⓑ Ⓒ Ⓓ Ⓔ	12 Ⓐ Ⓑ Ⓒ Ⓓ Ⓔ	23 Ⓐ Ⓑ Ⓒ Ⓓ Ⓔ	34 Ⓐ Ⓑ Ⓒ Ⓓ Ⓔ	45 Ⓐ Ⓑ Ⓒ Ⓓ Ⓔ
2 Ⓐ Ⓑ Ⓒ Ⓓ Ⓔ	13 Ⓐ Ⓑ Ⓒ Ⓓ Ⓔ	24 Ⓐ Ⓑ Ⓒ Ⓓ Ⓔ	35 Ⓐ Ⓑ Ⓒ Ⓓ Ⓔ	46 Ⓐ Ⓑ Ⓒ Ⓓ Ⓔ
3 Ⓐ Ⓑ Ⓒ Ⓓ Ⓔ	14 Ⓐ Ⓑ Ⓒ Ⓓ Ⓔ	25 Ⓐ Ⓑ Ⓒ Ⓓ Ⓔ	36 Ⓐ Ⓑ Ⓒ Ⓓ Ⓔ	47 Ⓐ Ⓑ Ⓒ Ⓓ Ⓔ
4 Ⓐ Ⓑ Ⓒ Ⓓ Ⓔ	15 Ⓐ Ⓑ Ⓒ Ⓓ Ⓔ	26 Ⓐ Ⓑ Ⓒ Ⓓ Ⓔ	37 Ⓐ Ⓑ Ⓒ Ⓓ Ⓔ	48 Ⓐ Ⓑ Ⓒ Ⓓ Ⓔ
5 Ⓐ Ⓑ Ⓒ Ⓓ Ⓔ	16 Ⓐ Ⓑ Ⓒ Ⓓ Ⓔ	27 Ⓐ Ⓑ Ⓒ Ⓓ Ⓔ	38 Ⓐ Ⓑ Ⓒ Ⓓ Ⓔ	49 Ⓐ Ⓑ Ⓒ Ⓓ Ⓔ
6 Ⓐ Ⓑ Ⓒ Ⓓ Ⓔ	17 Ⓐ Ⓑ Ⓒ Ⓓ Ⓔ	28 Ⓐ Ⓑ Ⓒ Ⓓ Ⓔ	39 Ⓐ Ⓑ Ⓒ Ⓓ Ⓔ	50 Ⓐ Ⓑ Ⓒ Ⓓ Ⓔ
7 Ⓐ Ⓑ Ⓒ Ⓓ Ⓔ	18 Ⓐ Ⓑ Ⓒ Ⓓ Ⓔ	29 Ⓐ Ⓑ Ⓒ Ⓓ Ⓔ	40 Ⓐ Ⓑ Ⓒ Ⓓ Ⓔ	51 Ⓐ Ⓑ Ⓒ Ⓓ Ⓔ
8 Ⓐ Ⓑ Ⓒ Ⓓ Ⓔ	19 Ⓐ Ⓑ Ⓒ Ⓓ Ⓔ	30 Ⓐ Ⓑ Ⓒ Ⓓ Ⓔ	41 Ⓐ Ⓑ Ⓒ Ⓓ Ⓔ	52 Ⓐ Ⓑ Ⓒ Ⓓ Ⓔ
9 Ⓐ Ⓑ Ⓒ Ⓓ Ⓔ	20 Ⓐ Ⓑ Ⓒ Ⓓ Ⓔ	31 Ⓐ Ⓑ Ⓒ Ⓓ Ⓔ	42 Ⓐ Ⓑ Ⓒ Ⓓ Ⓔ	53 Ⓐ Ⓑ Ⓒ Ⓓ Ⓔ
10 Ⓐ Ⓑ Ⓒ Ⓓ Ⓔ	21 Ⓐ Ⓑ Ⓒ Ⓓ Ⓔ	32 Ⓐ Ⓑ Ⓒ Ⓓ Ⓔ	43 Ⓐ Ⓑ Ⓒ Ⓓ Ⓔ	54 Ⓐ Ⓑ Ⓒ Ⓓ Ⓔ
11 Ⓐ Ⓑ Ⓒ Ⓓ Ⓔ	22 Ⓐ Ⓑ Ⓒ Ⓓ Ⓔ	33 Ⓐ Ⓑ Ⓒ Ⓓ Ⓔ	44 Ⓐ Ⓑ Ⓒ Ⓓ Ⓔ	55 Ⓐ Ⓑ Ⓒ Ⓓ Ⓔ

Check the answers and explanations on page 262.

Remove answer sheet by cutting on dotted line.

1. $-\frac{3}{4} + (-2\frac{1}{3}) =$

    (A) $-3\frac{1}{12}$
    (B) $-1\frac{7}{12}$
    (C) $-4\frac{1}{12}$
    (D) $1\frac{1}{12}$

2. $6 \div 2\frac{1}{4} =$

    (A) $13\frac{1}{2}$
    (B) $12\frac{1}{4}$
    (C) $2\frac{2}{3}$
    (D) $3\frac{2}{3}$

3. $-0.058 - (-2.56) =$

    (A) -5.202
    (B) -2.618
    (C) $+2.058$
    (D) $+2.502$

4. $-0.377 \times (-2.16) =$

    (A) -2.537
    (B) -1.7832
    (C) $+0.81432$
    (D) $+5.73432$

5. If the original price is $83.00, what would be the sale price if the sale took off 35%?

    (A) $136.25
    (B) $ 53.25
    (C) $ 53.95
    (D) $ 41.50

6. What percent of 125 is 105?

    (A) 84%
    (B) 0.84%
    (C) 119%
    (D) 1.19%

7. $(5^3)^4 =$

    (A) 125^7
    (B) 5^{12}
    (C) 5^7
    (D) 5^1

8. $\frac{8}{25} =$

    (A) 0.32%
    (B) 8%
    (C) 32%
    (D) 3.25%

9. Which symbol would make this a true statement?

    $$2.97 \;\square\; 2.970$$

    (A) $=$
    (B) $<$
    (C) $\leq$
    (D) $>$

10. What is the missing term?
    $(15, 3) (14, 2.8) (10, 2) (5, \underline{\quad})$

    (A) 1.8
    (B) 1
    (C) 8
    (D) 5

11. Miss Stendel's class is forming groups. When they form groups of 2, 3, or 4 students, there is never anyone left over. How many are in the class?

    (A) 24
    (B) 25
    (C) 21
    (D) 30

12. The length of a caterpillar would best be measured by

    (A) cubic centimeters
    (B) ounces
    (C) square inches
    (D) millimeters

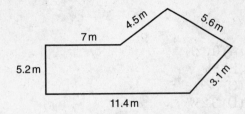

13. What is the best estimate of the perimeter of this polygon?

   (A) 39 m
   (B) 40 m
   (C) 73 m
   (D) 37 m

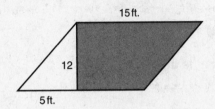

14. What is the area of the shaded portion?

   (A) 45 square feet
   (B) 270 square feet
   (C) 150 square feet
   (D) 180 square feet

15. $\sqrt{12} - \sqrt{3} =$

   (A) $\sqrt{36}$
   (B) $\sqrt{9}$
   (C) $\sqrt{3}$
   (D) $2\sqrt{3}$

16. $9/\sqrt{10} =$

   (A) $9/10\sqrt{10}$
   (B) $9\sqrt{10}$
   (C) $10\sqrt{9}$
   (D) $5/9\sqrt{10}$

17. $2n + 3n^2 - 5n \times 3 - 6n^2 =$

   (A) $-12n$
   (B) $-13n - 3n^2$
   (C) $13n + 3n^2$
   (D) $-6n^2$

18. $(2.4 \times 10^8)(1.3 \times 10^{-5}) =$

   (A) 312×10^4
   (B) 31.2×10^3
   (C) 3.12×10^3
   (D) 3.12×10^{13}

19. Solve for x: $11x - 5 = -6 + 6x$

   (A) $x = 5$
   (B) $x = -5$
   (C) $x = \frac{1}{5}$
   (D) $x = -\frac{1}{5}$

20. The formula for converting a kilogram weight (K) to a pound weight (P) is $P = 2.2\,K$. If a dog weighs 15.6 pounds, how many kilograms does the dog weigh?

   (A) 3.43 kg
   (B) 34.32 kg
   (C) 7.09 kg
   (D) 70.9 kg

21. Given the following function, find $f(-1)$.
$$f(x) = -4x^3 - 5x^2 + x - 10$$

   (A) $f(-1) = -12$
   (B) $f(-1) = -18$
   (C) $f(-1) = 0$
   (D) $f(-1) = 10$

22. Which is a linear factor of the following expression?
$$6x^2 - x - 2$$

   (A) $(3x - 2)$
   (B) $(3x + 3)$
   (C) $(2x + 3)$
   (D) $(x + 2)$

23. What are the real roots of this equation?
$$2x^2 - x = 3$$

   (A) $(2, 3)$
   (B) $(-1\frac{1}{2}, 1)$
   (C) $(2, 1)$
   (D) $(-1, 1\frac{1}{2})$

24. Choose the correct solution set for the system of linear equations.

$$4x - 2y = -10$$
$$2x - 4y = 10$$

(A) $(\frac{1}{2}, -\frac{1}{2})$
(B) $\{(x,y):y = x + 3\}$
(C) $(5, -5)$
(D) the empty set

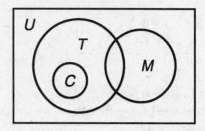

August

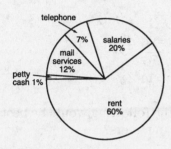

25. The pie chart above represents the monthly expenses of a small business for August. In what area is the most money spent?

(A) mail services, telephone, and salaries
(B) salaries, telephone, and petty cash
(C) petty cash and salaries
(D) rent

26. What number represents the median of the following set of data?

4, 10, 8, 7, 7, 6, 5, 0, 2

(A) 10
(B) 5.2
(C) 6
(D) 7

27. There are five parking spots in the lot in which eight cars have permits. How many combinations of five cars can park in the lot?

(A) 56
(B) 7,200
(C) 14,200
(D) 120

28. Which of the following statements is true about sets C, T, M, and U, assuming that no region is empty?

(A) An element that is a member of set C is a member of set M.
(B) An element of set T is a member of set M.
(C) An element is a member of C, T, and M.
(D) An element of set C is a member of set T.

29. $a(4 + 3) =$

(A) $(4)(4)(4) \times (3)(3)(3) \times (a) =$
(B) $a\,(4) + a\,(3)$
(C) $a(4) \times a(3) =$
(D) $a(4 \times 3) + a(4 \times 3) =$

30. Select the correct numeral for the following expanded notation.

$$(5 \times 10^2) + (2 \times 10^0) + (3 \times 10^{-1}) + (6 \times 10^{-2})$$

(A) 52.36
(B) 50,236
(C) 5,236
(D) 502.36

31. $0.63 =$

(A) $^{63}/_{100}$
(B) $^{100}/_{63}$
(C) $^{11}/_{40}$
(D) $^{36}/_{63}$

32. Which equation represents a true statement when $x = -2$?

    (A) $3x - 1 \geq 6$
    (B) $-4x - x = -3$
    (C) $2x + 1 \leq -1$
    (D) $x - 5 \geq 1$

33. What is the best estimate of the average of 38 and 104?

    (A) 71
    (B) 70
    (C) 140
    (D) 142

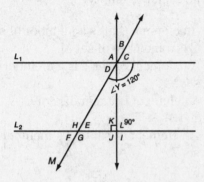

34. Which of the following statements is true about the diagram above?

    (A) Since m $\angle Y$ = 120 degrees, m $\angle H$ = 120 degrees
    (B) Since m $\angle L$ = 90 degrees, m $\angle D$ = 45 degrees
    (C) m $\angle C$ = m $\angle B$
    (D) None of the above statements is true.

35. Which diagram shows a pair of congruent triangles?

    (A) 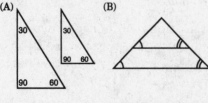   (B)

    (C) 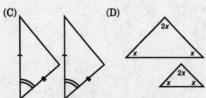   (D)

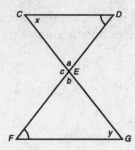

36. Which of the statements is true for the diagram above?

    (A) $\overline{CE} = \overline{EG}$
    (B) m $\angle a$ = m $\angle b$
    (C) $\overline{CD} \perp \overline{FG}$
    (D) m $\angle x$ = m $\angle y$

37. Which of the following would be best measured in meters?

    (A) the amount of carpet in a room
    (B) the amount of water in a fish tank
    (C) the depth of a swimming pool
    (D) the weight of a television set

38. Which of the following properties is illustrated by $3 \times 4 = 4 \times 3$?

    (A) distributive property
    (B) associative property
    (C) inverse property of multiplication
    (D) commutative property

39. For each of the statements below, determine whether $x = 5$ is a possible solution.

    i $\frac{1}{x} - \frac{1}{2} < = 0$
    ii $(2x - 12)(-x + 3) = 4$
    iii $-3x - 4 = -12x$

    (A) i only
    (B) ii only
    (C) i and ii only
    (D) ii and iii only

40. Find the volume of a right circular cone that is 12 cm high and has a diameter of 6 cm.

    (A) $432\ \pi\ cm^3$
    (B) $108\ \pi\ cm^3$
    (C) $72\ \pi\ cm^3$
    (D) $36\ \pi\ cm^3$

41. Elijah needs to buy enough fencing to enclose a 3 foot by 4 foot garden and to build a diagonal fence from one corner to the opposite corner. How much fencing is needed?

    (A) 12 square feet
    (B) 19 square feet
    (C) 14 square feet
    (D) 17 square feet

42. What expression is equivalent to $(x^2)^3$ $(y^3)\,(y^2)$

    (A) $x^5\,y^6$
    (B) $x^6\,y^6$
    (C) $x^5\,y^5$
    (D) $x^6\,y^5$

43. Which expression is equivalent to $-5 > 10p > 45$.

    (A) $1 > -2p > -9$
    (B) $10 > -20p > -90$
    (C) $1 < -2p < -9$
    (D) $-10 < 20p < 90$

44. According to the National Weather Council, each inch of snowfall equals 0.175 inches of rain. If it snows five inches, what proportion best represents the amount of rain (r)?

    (A) $1/.175 = r/5$
    (B) $r/.175 =. 1/5$
    (C) $1/.175 = 5/r$
    (D) $r/1.75 = 5/1$

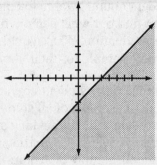

45. Identify the conditions that correspond to the shaded region of the plane shown above.

    (A) $x \geq 0$ and $y \geq 2$
    (B) $y = -x$
    (C) $x < 4, y > -2, y > x$
    (D) $x \geq y + 3$

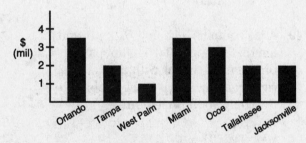

Federal Funding in 1994

46. The graph above represents the distribution of federal funding to Florida public schools in 1994. Which statement about the data is true?

    (A) West Palm represents the median amount.
    (B) Miami represents the mean.
    (C) Orlando represents the mean.
    (D) Jacksonville represents the mode.

47. The student council wants to conduct a survey to find out what seniors intend to do after graduation. What would be an appropriate sample for their survey?

    (A) seniors on the student council
    (B) a random sample of all students
    (C) all student athletes seeking scholar-ships
    (D) a random sample of seniors

48. Select the negation for this statement:

    If I pass this test, I will apply to law school.

    (A) I pass this test, and I do not apply to law school.
    (B) If I do not pass this test, I will apply to law school.
    (C) If I do not pass this test, I will not apply to law school.
    (D) I passed this test and I do apply to law school.

49. A jar contains 3 cherry, 5 grape, and 4 lemon lollipops. Two lollipops are drawn from the jar without replacement. What is the probability that they are both lemon?

    (A) $^4/_{12} \times ^3/_{11}$
    (B) $^4/_{12} \times ^3/_{12}$
    (C) $^7/_{12}$
    (D) $^8/_{12} \times ^7/_{11}$

50. Select the statement that is logically equivalent to:

    If Kerry does not wear a hat, he will get sunburned.

    (A) If Kerry wears a hat, he will not get sunburned.
    (B) If Kerry does not get sunburned, then he wore a hat.
    (C) If Kerry wears a hat, he will get sun-burned.
    (D) Kerry wears a hat and Kerry gets sunburned.

51. Given that:

    i. If a person believes in UFOs, they are gullible.
    ii. Max is not gullible.

    What can logically be deduced from these statements?

    (A) UFOs may still exist.
    (B) Max does not believe in UFOs.
    (C) Max may believe in UFOs.
    (D) Max will have to see a UFO before he believes.

52. Choose the logical rule used to transform statement i to statement ii.

    i. If the road is wet, the car will skid.
    ii. It is not wet or the car will skid.

    (A) If p then q $\leftrightarrow$ p or not q
    (B) If p then q $\leftrightarrow$ p and q
    (C) If p then q $\leftrightarrow$ not p or q
    (D) If p then q $\leftrightarrow$ p and not q

53. Identify the missing term in the following geometric progression.

    $$15, \ -5, \ 1^2/_3, \ -^5/_9, \ \underline{\hspace{1cm}}$$

    (A) $^5/_{27}$
    (B) $-^5/_{27}$
    (C) $^1/_3$
    (D) $-1^4/_9$

54. Which of the following inequalities means the same as $9 < x + 4 < 10$?

    (A) $9 < x < 10$
    (B) $4 > x > 5$
    (C) $5 < x < 6$
    (D) $16 > x > 18$

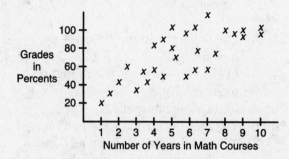

Grades in Percents

Number of Years in Math Courses

55. The graph shows the grade distribution on a standardized mathematics test. Which of the following best describes the relationships between test score and number of years in mathematics courses?

(A) People who took fewer years of math scored highest.
(B) People who took more math courses scored lower.
(C) There is a negative relationship.
(D) There is a positive relationship.

PRACTICE TEST 1 — ANSWERS AND EXPLANATIONS

English Language Skills

1. **B** When the main clause is followed by a dependent clause, no comma is necessary.
2. **B** *Enormously* is an adverb that modifies the adjective *significant.*
3. **A** Choice B *dean* and Choice C *university* would only be capitalized if in the form Dean Robert Kerek and University of Florida.
4. **A** *Immediately* modifies the verb *began.*
5. **C** The comma is not necessary.
6. **D** The only other possible answer might be B, but the verb *extended* does not make sense in the sentence.
7. **C** The verb tense of *causes* is incorrect.
8. **B** *Widely* modifies the verb *held.*
9. **D** The original sentence is correct.
10. **A** *This result* agrees with the singular verb *was.*
11. **C** *Fatal* is an adjective that modifies the noun *disease.*
12. **C** *Unvaccinated* is a better word choice than *without vaccine.*
13. **A** *Injected* is misspelled.
14. **B** The *other* is not essential to the sense of the statement.
15. **A** The word *developed* is spelled incorrectly.
16. **D** All the words are spelled correctly.
17. **C** *Pasteur's* is the correct possessive form.
18. **B** Use the verb *was* to show past tense.
19. **B** *Today's* is possessive and therefore needs an apostrophe.
20. **B** *Because of their immaturity and ignorance* cannot stand alone as a sentence; it is a phrase.
21. **B** *Contracted* is a better substitution for *contacted.*
22. **A** The present tense is kept constant throughout the passage.

23. **B** The danger is in the action—in *sharing.*
24. **A** Choice A expresses the thought most clearly.
25. **A** *Massive* is misspelled.
26. **B** The parallel structure would be, "The basketball player was famous for his aggressiveness on the court and *his* good nature off the court."
27. **C** Choice C is the only choice that maintains the logic of the text.
28. **A** The other choices are constructed awkwardly.
29. **E** *In person* means *live*, which is extraneous.
30. **C** *Commonly* is extraneous.
31. **C** *Amanda* is the subject of the sentence, while the person she wants to send a letter to is the object. *Whom* is the objective pronoun.
32. **C** *Investigating* makes sense in this context.
33. **B** *Approach* best describes the actions Hoover used to combat the Depression.
34. **A** *Protesters* makes the most sense.
35. **B** The term *Federalists* appeared early in the sentence.
36. **A** Jazz music is mentioned first in this sentence.
37. **A** The structure and word order of choice A is the most logical.
38. **C** The superlative is the best choice because Louise is being compared to more than one runner.
39. **A** Use the comparative form. The words *rather than* suggest a comparison of two items.
40. **B** The word order in choices A and C is clearly unorganized. The thought is expressed most clearly in choice B.

Reading

1. **A** Main Idea. Choice A is the best answer because the passage is based on the concern that students need to learn the manual way first.

2. **C** Words in Context. The word *competence* in the given context means having skills enough to perform mathematical computations.

3. **A** Fact or Opinion. The statement can be objectively proven right or wrong by conducting a study. The statement represents fact.

4. **B** Organizational Pattern. The first quote shows one side of an argument while the second shows the opposite side.

5. **D** Valid or Invalid. Begging the question assumes that part of an argument is true without providing proof.

6. **D** Author's Purpose. The author is denying one accusation and making another. Choice D is the best answer because the author is trying to convince others.

7. **A** Relationship Between Sentences. The word *However* highlights the relationship between sentences.

8. **A** Relationship Within Sentences. The words *so while* are a logical choice for the structure of the sentence.

9. **A** Logical Inference. The passage is referring to research on use of a cereal. Therefore, a person involved with market research would work with such a study.

10. **C** Author's Purpose. The author's clear intent is to present the last question in the passage.

11. **A** Relationship Within Sentences. The sentence is written to contrast its two parts. The word *but* suggests contrast.

12. **D** Words in Context. A residential area is one in which there are mostly houses. Therefore, choice D is the best answer.

13. **A** Logical Inference. The passage discusses zoning regulations for a specific locality.

14. **A** Organizational Pattern. The clue is the phrase *for example* in line 15.

15. **D** Words in Context. The sentence means changing an already existing structure.

16. **C** Relationship Between Sentences. The key words are the sequence words *one, second,* and *third*.

17. **A** Words in Context. *Susceptible,* in this context, means *may be more likely* to [get] AIDS.

18. **A** Fact or Opinion. The statement is fact. The historial accuracy can be verified.

19. **D** Author's Purpose. The other choices are too specific to be the main idea of such a general passage.

20. **A** Relationship Between Sentences. *Then* indicates the pattern time order.

21. **C** Main Idea. Shopping around got better quality for a lower price.

22. **A** Logical Inference. The other choices attempt to restate the given information. Choice A is the only inferential option.

23. **C** Words in Context. A *potential* space vehicle might possibly become a space vehicle.

24. **D** Author's Tone. The author shows concern for the growing use of cell phones by criminals. Choices A and B are too strong to be correct.

25. **D** Words in Context. *Monitor* means to keep track of the usage, and screen cellular calls to deter criminal activity.

26. **A** Bias. The focus of the passage is to express concern about drug dealers using cellular phones. Therefore, the bias would be against drug dealers.

27. **D** Main Idea. Cellular phones are being used by criminals and therefore ending up in the wrong hands.

28. **A** Author's Tone. The final statement, *That's discrimination*, is evidence of anger.

29. **B** Main Idea. The author says and gives an example of how both men and women are discriminated against.

30. **B** Organizational Pattern. A general statement is made in sentence one; then support is given with examples in sentence three.

31. **A** Valid or Invalid. The supporting details of the passage make this statement valid.

32. **B** Main Idea. A and D are true but they do not represent the main idea. Choice C is not true.

33. **A** Fact or Opinion. This historical fact can be checked.

34. **B** Details. Choice B is the only detail not listed in the passage. In fact, it is refuted.

35. **C** Organizational Pattern. The statement is made in the initial sentence and the explanation follows.

36. **C** Logical Inference. He must have survived and lived in America because his song is our national anthem. All other choices are not likely.

37. **D** Word in Context. *Sacked* means to attack and damage. *Ravaged* has the most similar meaning.

38. **D** Relationship Between Sentences. *However* is the only logical choice. It provides an explanation for a conditional detail.

39. **A** Relationship Between Sentences. *In fact* works best because it precedes an example.

40. **B** Details. The fourth sentence in the first paragraph explains that the author likes having a program to perform the mechanical aspects.

41. **B** Author's Purpose. Johnson's achievements were a result of Kennedy's ideas, therefore choice B is the purpose.

Mathematics

1. **A** $-\frac{3}{4} + (-2\frac{1}{3}) = -\frac{3}{4} - 2\frac{1}{3} =$
   $-\frac{9}{12} - 2\frac{4}{12} = -2\frac{13}{12} = -3\frac{1}{12}$
   To add fractions of the same sign, combine the fractions and keep the sign.

2. **C** To divide two fractions, invert the second fraction (the divisor) and multiply. Leave answer in lowest terms.
   6 divided by $2\frac{1}{4} = \frac{6}{1} \times \frac{4}{9} = \frac{24}{9} =$
   $2\frac{6}{9} = 2\frac{2}{3}$

3. **D** When combining decimals, line up the decimals and subtract. Keep sign of larger number.

   $+2.560$
   $\underline{-0.058}$
   $+2.502$

4. **C** When multiplying decimals, multiply and then count the total number of decimal places.

   $-.377$ (3 decimal places)
   $\underline{\times -2.16}$ (2 decimal places)
   $.81432$ (5 decimal places)

5. **C** Use formula $a\%$ of b is c.
   $35\% \times \$83.00 = ?$
   $.35 \times \$83 = \$29.05$
   $\$83 - \$29.05 = \$53.95$

6. **A** $84\% = 0.84$ $0.84 \times 125 = 105$

7. **B** $(5^3)^4 = (5^{3 \times 4}) = 5^{12}$

8. **C** $\frac{8}{25} = \frac{32}{100} = 0.32 = 32\%$

9. **A** Drop the trailing 0 from 2.970.

10. **B** To find the second term, divide the first term by 5.

11. **A** This is the only number in the answer choice divisible by 2, 3, and 4.

12. **D** Choice D is the only measurement of length.

13. **D** Perimeter is calculated by adding measures of all sides. Round the measures and add, to get the best estimate.

14. **C** To find the area of a triangle use the formula $A = \frac{1}{2}\, bh = 30$.
To find the area of a parallelogram use the formula $A = (bh) = 180$.
Subtract: Area (parallelogram) – Area (triangle) = Area (shaded portion)
$180 - 30 = 150$

15. **C** Simplify the radical, then subtract.
$\sqrt{12} - \sqrt{3} = \sqrt{4 \times 3} - \sqrt{3} = 2\sqrt{3} - \sqrt{3} = \sqrt{3}$

16. **A** Multiply numerator and denominator by $\sqrt{10}$.

17. **B** Use the order of operations to combine to simplest terms.
$2n + 3n^2 - 5n \times 3 - 6n^2 =$
$2n + 3n^2 - 15n - 6n^2 =$
$-13n - 3n^2$

18. **C** Multiply numbers and add exponents.
$(2.4 \times 1.3) = 3.12$
$(10^8 \times 10^{-5}) = 10^3$

19. **D** Subtract $6x$ from both sides.
$11x - 5\,(-6x) = -6 + 6x\,(-6x)$
$5x - 5 = -6$
Add 5 to both sides.
$5x - 5\,(+5) = -6\,(+5)\quad 5x = -1$
Divide both sides by 5.
$5x/5 = -\frac{1}{5}\quad x = -\frac{1}{5}$

20. **C** Use formula $P = 2.2K$
$15.6/2.2 = 15.6/2.2 = K$
$7.09 = K$

21. **A** Plug in the value of x and combine terms.
$f(-1) = -4(-1)$ to the 3rd $-5(-1)$ squared $+ (-1) - 10 = +4\ -5 - 1 - 10$
$f(-1) = -12$

22. **A** $(3x - 2)\,(2x + 1) = 6x^2 - x - 2$

23. **D** Set the equation equal to zero.
$2x^2 - x - 3 = 0$
Factor out and set each equal to zero.
$2x^2 - x - 3 = 0$
$(2x - 3)\,(x + 1) = 0$
$2x - 3 = 0 \qquad x + 1 = 0$
$2x = 3 \qquad\quad x = -1$
$2x/2 = \frac{3}{2}$
$x = 1\frac{1}{2} \qquad$ Real Roots $= \{-1, 1\frac{1}{2}\}$

24. **B** Follow the steps given on page 170.

25. **D** Rent represents 60% of the monthly expenses.

26. **C** Organize the numbers in order:
0, 2, 4, 5, 6, 7, 7, 8, 10.
The item that occurs as the middle term is 6. 6 is the median of this set of data.

27. **A** How many combinations of 5 of 8 cars?

$$\frac{8!}{3!5!} = \frac{8 \cdot 7 \cdot 6 \cdot 5 \cdot 4 \cdot 3 \cdot 2 \cdot 1}{3 \cdot 2 \cdot 1 \cdot 5 \cdot 4 \cdot 3 \cdot 2 \cdot 1} = 56$$

28. **D**

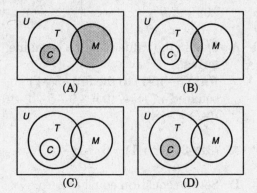

    (A) Not true.

    (B) Only those items in the shaded area fit the conditions.

    (C) Not true—no item can be a member of all sets (C, T, M).

    (D) All members of set C are also members of set T.

29. **B** This problem illustrates the distributive property.

    $a(4 + 3) = a(4) + a(3)$

30. **D** $5 \times 10^2 = 500$
         $+2 \times 100 = 2$
         $+3 \times 10\ = .3$
         $\underline{+6 \times 10 = .06}$
             502.36

31. **A** 0.63 is read 63 hundredths.

32. **C** Substitute value of x in each equation to check for a true statement.

    (A) $3(-2) - 1 \geq 6$

         $-6 - 1 \geq 6$

         $-7 \geq 6$ [not true]

    (B) $-4(-2) - (-2) = -3$

         $8 + 2 = -3$

         $10 = -3$ [not true]

    (C) $2(-2) + 1 \leq -1$

         $-4 + 1 \leq -1$

         $-3 \leq -1$ [true]

    (D $-2 - 5 \geq 1$

         $-7 = 1$ [not true]

33. **B** To find an estimated average round. $40 + 100 = 140/2 = 70$

34. **A** m $\angle Y$ = m $\angle H$ because they are alternate interior angles formed by transversal m.

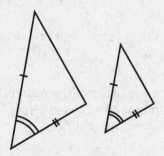

35. **C** These triangles are congruent because one triangle exactly matches the other. Triangles cannot be proven congruent if they have only equal angles.

36. **B** $\angle$A and $\angle$B are vertical angles and their measures are equal.

37. **C** Meters are a measure of length. The depth of a swimming pool would best be measured in meters.

38. **D** The commutative property of multiplication states $a \times b = b \times a$.

39. **C** Substitute the value of x in each of the equations.

i. $\frac{1}{5} - \frac{1}{2} \le 0$
$\frac{2}{10} - \frac{5}{10} \le 0$
$-\frac{3}{10} \le 0$ [true] $x = 5$ is a solution

ii. $(2x - 12)(-x + 3) = 4$
$(2(5) - 12)(-(5) + 3) = 4$
$(10 - 12)(-5 + 3) = 4$
$(-2)(-2) = 4$
$4 = 4$ [true] $x = 5$ is a solution

iii. $-3x - 4 = -12x$
$-3(5) - 4 = -12(5)$
$-15 - 4 = -60$
$-19 = -60$ [not true] $x = 5$ is not a solution.

40. **D** $\frac{1}{3}\pi r^2 h^2 = \frac{1}{3}\pi(3)^2(12) = \frac{1}{3}\pi(9)$
$(12) = \pi(3)(12) = 36\pi$

41. **B** Find the length of the diagonal $3^2 + 4^2 = x^2$ $25 = x^2$ $x = 5$ feet
Find the perimeter. $3 + 3 + 4 + 4 = 14$ feet.
Add the perimeter and the length of the diagonal. $14 + 5 = 19$ feet.

42. **D** $(x^2)^3 = x^6$ $(y^3)(y^2) = y^5$
$(x^2)^3(y^3)(y^2) = x^6 y^5$

43. **C** Divide each term by -5.

44. **C** 1 inch of snow is equal to 01.75 inches of rain $[1/1.75]$
5 inches of snow is equal to r inches of rain.
$1/.175 = 5/r$

45. **D** (A) Many points meet neither condition.
(B) y never equals $-x$.
(C) x is not always less than 4.
(D) Correctly describes the graph.

46. **D** Figure out what the mean, median, and mode are for the data shown in the graph. The mode is 2 million (Tampa, Tallahassee, and Jacksonville). The mean (the average) of the funding is 2.4 million. The median of the data is 2 million. Given this information, only choice D can be true.

47. **D** The survey's target is all seniors. Therefore, choice D is the best answer.

48. **C** The statement given can be written as p → q.
The negation of the statement can be written as p and not q.
This translates as *If I pass this test, I will not apply to law school.*

49. **A** There are 12 lollipops all together, and 4 of them are lemon.
$\frac{4}{12}$ equals probability of choosing a lemon on the first try. After taking out one lemon, there are 11 lollipops, 3 of them lemon. $\frac{3}{11} =$ probability of choosing a lemon on the second try. $\frac{4}{12} \times \frac{3}{11} =$ probability of 2 lemons.

50. **A** *If Kerry does not wear a hat, he will get sunburned.* The logically equivalent statement would be not q not p.

51. **B** p → q, not q → not p.

52. **C** If p then q is equivalent to p or not q.

53. **A** Each term is multiplied by $-\frac{1}{3}$; therefore, the next term would be $-\frac{5}{9} \times -\frac{1}{3} = \frac{5}{27}$

54. **C** Subtract 4 from the inequality.
$9 - 4 < x + 4 - 4 < 10 - 4$
$5 < x < 6$

55. **D** There is a positive relationship between the test score and the number of years in math courses.

 **PRACTICE TEST 2**

Take this test in a realistic, timed setting after you take all the Practice Test 1 subtests.

Ask a friend to proctor the test. Take this test in one sitting according to the schedule below. Allow a 10 minute break between subtests.

Essay	60 minutes
English Language Skills/Reading	80 minutes
Mathematics	90 minutes

SCORE TRACKING CHART

Use this chart to track your scores.

Essay

☐ × 2 = ☐ (A total score of 6 or more is passing.)

Rating   Total Score

English Language Skills

☐ − 5 = ☐ (A raw score of 26 to 28 or higher is usually passing.)

Number Correct   Raw Score

Reading

☐ − 5 = ☐ (A raw score of 24 to 26 or higher is usually passing.)

Number Correct   Raw Score

Mathematics

☐ − 5 = ☐ (A raw score of 33 to 35 or higher is usually passing.)

Number Correct   Raw Score

ESSAY

60 minutes

Take this practice subtest in a realistic, timed setting. Do not take this practice subtest until you have reviewed Chapter 3, English Language Skills, and Chapter 4, Essay.

The test rules allow you exactly one hour to write your essay. Write your outline below and write your essay on the following lined pages. Remember, your outline is not read and it is not graded. Do not try to copy your essay.

Write an essay on one of these two topics.

1. An event that affected the history of the world.

2. A teacher who is a positive role model.

You may write your initial thoughts below. Only the essay is scored.

_____

_____

_____

_____

_____

_____

_____

_____

_____

_____

_____

_____

_____

_____

_____

_____

_____

_____

_____

_____

_____

_____

_____

_____

_____

_____

_____

_____

_____

_____

_____

_____

(Show your completed essay to an English professor or an English teacher. Ask them to rate your essay using the rating scale and criteria on page 97.)

ENGLISH LANGUAGE SKILLS/READING

80 minutes

Answer the multiple-choice questions on the following pages.
   Use the answer sheet that follows.

ENGLISH LANGUAGE SKILLS/READING

English Language Skills

1 Ⓐ Ⓑ Ⓒ Ⓓ Ⓔ	9 Ⓐ Ⓑ Ⓒ Ⓓ Ⓔ	17 Ⓐ Ⓑ Ⓒ Ⓓ Ⓔ	25 Ⓐ Ⓑ Ⓒ Ⓓ Ⓔ	33 Ⓐ Ⓑ Ⓒ Ⓓ Ⓔ
2 Ⓐ Ⓑ Ⓒ Ⓓ Ⓔ	10 Ⓐ Ⓑ Ⓒ Ⓓ Ⓔ	18 Ⓐ Ⓑ Ⓒ Ⓓ Ⓔ	26 Ⓐ Ⓑ Ⓒ Ⓓ Ⓔ	34 Ⓐ Ⓑ Ⓒ Ⓓ Ⓔ
3 Ⓐ Ⓑ Ⓒ Ⓓ Ⓔ	11 Ⓐ Ⓑ Ⓒ Ⓓ Ⓔ	19 Ⓐ Ⓑ Ⓒ Ⓓ Ⓔ	27 Ⓐ Ⓑ Ⓒ Ⓓ Ⓔ	35 Ⓐ Ⓑ Ⓒ Ⓓ Ⓔ
4 Ⓐ Ⓑ Ⓒ Ⓓ Ⓔ	12 Ⓐ Ⓑ Ⓒ Ⓓ Ⓔ	20 Ⓐ Ⓑ Ⓒ Ⓓ Ⓔ	28 Ⓐ Ⓑ Ⓒ Ⓓ Ⓔ	36 Ⓐ Ⓑ Ⓒ Ⓓ Ⓔ
5 Ⓐ Ⓑ Ⓒ Ⓓ Ⓔ	13 Ⓐ Ⓑ Ⓒ Ⓓ Ⓔ	21 Ⓐ Ⓑ Ⓒ Ⓓ Ⓔ	29 Ⓐ Ⓑ Ⓒ Ⓓ Ⓔ	37 Ⓐ Ⓑ Ⓒ Ⓓ Ⓔ
6 Ⓐ Ⓑ Ⓒ Ⓓ Ⓔ	14 Ⓐ Ⓑ Ⓒ Ⓓ Ⓔ	22 Ⓐ Ⓑ Ⓒ Ⓓ Ⓔ	30 Ⓐ Ⓑ Ⓒ Ⓓ Ⓔ	38 Ⓐ Ⓑ Ⓒ Ⓓ Ⓔ
7 Ⓐ Ⓑ Ⓒ Ⓓ Ⓔ	15 Ⓐ Ⓑ Ⓒ Ⓓ Ⓔ	23 Ⓐ Ⓑ Ⓒ Ⓓ Ⓔ	31 Ⓐ Ⓑ Ⓒ Ⓓ Ⓔ	39 Ⓐ Ⓑ Ⓒ Ⓓ Ⓔ
8 Ⓐ Ⓑ Ⓒ Ⓓ Ⓔ	16 Ⓐ Ⓑ Ⓒ Ⓓ Ⓔ	24 Ⓐ Ⓑ Ⓒ Ⓓ Ⓔ	32 Ⓐ Ⓑ Ⓒ Ⓓ Ⓔ	40 Ⓐ Ⓑ Ⓒ Ⓓ Ⓔ

Check the answers and explanations on page 298.

Reading

1 Ⓐ Ⓑ Ⓒ Ⓓ Ⓔ	10 Ⓐ Ⓑ Ⓒ Ⓓ Ⓔ	19 Ⓐ Ⓑ Ⓒ Ⓓ Ⓔ	28 Ⓐ Ⓑ Ⓒ Ⓓ Ⓔ	37 Ⓐ Ⓑ Ⓒ Ⓓ Ⓔ
2 Ⓐ Ⓑ Ⓒ Ⓓ Ⓔ	11 Ⓐ Ⓑ Ⓒ Ⓓ Ⓔ	20 Ⓐ Ⓑ Ⓒ Ⓓ Ⓔ	29 Ⓐ Ⓑ Ⓒ Ⓓ Ⓔ	38 Ⓐ Ⓑ Ⓒ Ⓓ Ⓔ
3 Ⓐ Ⓑ Ⓒ Ⓓ Ⓔ	12 Ⓐ Ⓑ Ⓒ Ⓓ Ⓔ	21 Ⓐ Ⓑ Ⓒ Ⓓ Ⓔ	30 Ⓐ Ⓑ Ⓒ Ⓓ Ⓔ	39 Ⓐ Ⓑ Ⓒ Ⓓ Ⓔ
4 Ⓐ Ⓑ Ⓒ Ⓓ Ⓔ	13 Ⓐ Ⓑ Ⓒ Ⓓ Ⓔ	22 Ⓐ Ⓑ Ⓒ Ⓓ Ⓔ	31 Ⓐ Ⓑ Ⓒ Ⓓ Ⓔ	40 Ⓐ Ⓑ Ⓒ Ⓓ Ⓔ
5 Ⓐ Ⓑ Ⓒ Ⓓ Ⓔ	14 Ⓐ Ⓑ Ⓒ Ⓓ Ⓔ	23 Ⓐ Ⓑ Ⓒ Ⓓ Ⓔ	32 Ⓐ Ⓑ Ⓒ Ⓓ Ⓔ	41 Ⓐ Ⓑ Ⓒ Ⓓ Ⓔ
6 Ⓐ Ⓑ Ⓒ Ⓓ Ⓔ	15 Ⓐ Ⓑ Ⓒ Ⓓ Ⓔ	24 Ⓐ Ⓑ Ⓒ Ⓓ Ⓔ	33 Ⓐ Ⓑ Ⓒ Ⓓ Ⓔ	
7 Ⓐ Ⓑ Ⓒ Ⓓ Ⓔ	16 Ⓐ Ⓑ Ⓒ Ⓓ Ⓔ	25 Ⓐ Ⓑ Ⓒ Ⓓ Ⓔ	34 Ⓐ Ⓑ Ⓒ Ⓓ Ⓔ	
8 Ⓐ Ⓑ Ⓒ Ⓓ Ⓔ	17 Ⓐ Ⓑ Ⓒ Ⓓ Ⓔ	26 Ⓐ Ⓑ Ⓒ Ⓓ Ⓔ	35 Ⓐ Ⓑ Ⓒ Ⓓ Ⓔ	
9 Ⓐ Ⓑ Ⓒ Ⓓ Ⓔ	18 Ⓐ Ⓑ Ⓒ Ⓓ Ⓔ	27 Ⓐ Ⓑ Ⓒ Ⓓ Ⓔ	36 Ⓐ Ⓑ Ⓒ Ⓓ Ⓔ	

Check the answers and explanations on page 299.

Remove answer sheet by cutting on dotted line.

ENGLISH LANGUAGE SKILLS

Select the word or phrase that best fits the context of the sentence.

1. As a child she read the *Hardy Boys* books and was in _____ of the author, Franklin Dixon.

   (A) awe
   (B) respect
   (C) respectful

2. The War of 1812 is one of the least _____ wars in American history.

   (A) understand
   (B) grasped
   (C) understood

Mark the letter of the underlined text that is not needed in the passage.

3. On April 18, 1775, English General Gage
     A

   left Boston to commandeer arms at
              B

   Concord. Revere and Dawes rode out

   to alert the Minutemen. The English
    C   D

   troops first encountered Minutemen
   when they met them in Lexington.
           E

   (A) On April 18
   (B) commandeer
   (C) to alert
   (D) English
   (E) when they met them in

4. Miami, Florida, is named after Miami,
                            A

   Ohio. The two towns were both home
                       B

   to the same Native American tribe.
         C

   This tribe was forced to travel from
        D

   Ohio to Florida.
        E

   (A) Miami
   (B) both
   (C) same
   (D) tribe
   (E) Ohio to Florida

Choose the sentence with no structural errors that most clearly and effectively states the idea.

5. (A) The relationship between organisms and their habitat refers to the meaning of ecology.
   (B) Ecology refers to the relationship between organisms and their habitat.
   (C) Ecology refers to organisms and their ecosystem and the relationship between the two.

6. (A) With only the clothes on her back, the tired traveler was taken home by the taxi driver.
   (B) The tired traveler was taken home by the taxi driver with only the clothes on her back.
   (C) The taxi driver drove the tired traveler home with only the clothes on her back.

7. (A) The teacher is hardworking, helpful, and cares about her students.
   (B) The teacher is hardworking, helpful, and caring.
   (C) The teacher is a hard worker, helpful, and cares about her students.

8. (A) Run through the gym, walk down the hall, and tiptoe past the office, is the way to get into class if you're late to school.
   (B) Running through the gym, walking down the hall, and tiptoeing past the office, is the way to get into class if you're late to school.
   (C) Run through the gym, walking down the hall, and tiptoe past the office, is the way to get into class if you're late to school.

Select the option that best states the meaning of the underlined sentence.

---

9. The littlest baseball player's league doesn't look exactly like the real game. Since in their games the adults pitch the ball, the players are not allowed to pitch.

   (A) Since in their games the adults pitch the ball, the players are not allowed to pitch.
   (B) Because the players are not allowed to pitch, the adults pitch the ball.
   (C) Because adults pitched in these games, even though they were too old for the league, the players didn't get a chance to pitch.
   (D) Until the adults were permitted to pitch, the players were not allowed to pitch in the league.

10. More television buyers are becoming interested in digital television. When compared to other types of television sets, this type is more expensive, harder to find, and has better picture quality.

    (A) When compared to other types of television sets, this type is more expensive, harder to find, and has better picture quality.
    (B) Just because this type of television has better picture quality doesn't mean that it is not more expensive and harder to find.
    (C) Because this type of television has a better picture quality, it is more expensive and harder to find.
    (D) This type of television is more expensive and harder to find, but television buyers are becoming more interested because of the better picture quality.

Choose the sentence below that correctly and logically presents the comparison.

---

11. (A) Using a real oven to cook food is better than using a microwave oven.
    (B) Using a real oven to cook food is far more better than using a microwave oven.
    (C) Using a real oven to cook food is better from using a microwave oven.

12. (A) Florida is the best.
    (B) Florida is better than any other state.
    (C) Florida is better than any other.

13. (A) I found my trip to Key West to be as enjoyable, if not more enjoyable than, any I have taken.
    (B) I found my trip to Key West to be as enjoyable, if not more enjoyable, than any I have taken.
    (C) I found my trip to Key West to be as enjoyable as, if not more enjoyable than, any I have taken.

14. (A) When I compared meat quality, I found that their meat was leanest.
    (B) When I compared meat quality, I found that their meat was leaner.
    (C) When I compared food quality, I found that their meat was lean.

Choose the correct replacement for the underlined portion.

15. The dog likes to run by the lake.

    (A) ran
    (B) running
    (C) runned
    (D) no change is necessary

16. The committee was about to chose the finalists.

    (A) choose
    (B) chosen
    (C) chosed
    (D) no change is necessary

The selections that follow contain some errors, which appear in the underlined part of the test questions. Read the passage. Then answer each question by selecting the answer choice that corrects the error. Choose *No change is necessary* if there is no error. Each item contains no more than one error.

First Passage

Computer graphing programs are capable of graphing almost any equations including advanced equations from calculus the student just types in the equation and the graph appears on the computer screen. The graphing program can also show the numerical solution for any entered equation. I like having a computer program that performs the mechanical aspects of these dificult calculations. However, these programs do not teach about graphing or mathematics that is because the computer does not explain what is going on. A person could type in an equation, get an answer, and have not the slightest idea what either meant.

Relying on this mindless kind of graphing and calculation. Students will be completely unfamiliar with the meaning of the equations they write or the results they get. They will not be able to understand how to create a graph from an equation or to understands the basis for the more complicated calculations.

It may be true that a strictly mechanical approach is used by some teachers, however, there certainly is a place for students who already understand equations and graphing to have a computer program. But the teacher will never be replaced in his classroom by these computer programs. Mathematical competence assume that understanding precedes rote calculation.

17. Computer graphing programs are
    <u>capable</u> of graphing almost any
        A
    equations <u>including</u> advanced equations
              B
    from <u>calculus the</u> student just types in
         C
    the equation and the graph appears on
    the computer screen.

    (A) available
    (B) incorporating
    (C) calculus. The
    (D) No change is necessary.

18. The graphing <u>program can</u> also show the
                  A
    <u>numerical</u> solution for any <u>entered</u>
    B   C
    equation.

    (A) program, can
    (B) number
    (C) entranced
    (D) No change is necessary.

19. I like having a computer program that
    <u>performs</u> the mechanical aspects of
    A
    these <u>dificult</u> <u>calculations.</u>
          B   C

    (A) perform
    (B) difficult
    (C) calculation
    (D) No change is necessary.

20. However, these programs <u>do not</u> teach
                             A
    about graphing or <u>mathematics that</u>
                       B
    is <u>because</u> the computer does not
        C
    explain what is going on.

    (A) does not
    (B) mathematics. That
    (C) is, because
    (D) No change is necessary.

21. A person could type in an <u>equation, get</u>
                                 A
    an answer, and <u>have not</u> the
                    B
    slightest idea what <u>either</u> meant.
                         C

    (A) equation get
    (B) has not
    (C) neither
    (D) No change is necessary.

22. Relying on this mindless kind of
    graphing and <u>calculation. Students</u> will
                  A
    be completely <u>unfamiliar with</u> the
                   B
    meaning of the equations they write or
    the results they <u>get</u>.
                      C

    (A) calculation, students
    (B) unfamiliar, with
    (C) got
    (D) No change is necessary.

23. They will not be able to understand how
    to <u>create</u> a graph from an equation or to
       A
    <u>understands</u> the <u>basis</u> for the more
    B   C
    complicated calculations.

    (A) creates
    (B) understand
    (C) bias
    (D) No change is necessary.

24. It may be <u>true that</u> a strictly mechanical
              A
    approach is used by some
    <u>teachers, however,</u> there certainly is a
    B,C
    place for students who already
    understand equations and graphing to
    have a computer program.

    (A) true, that
    (B) teachers: however,
    (C) teachers; however,
    (D) No change is necessary.

25. <u>But the</u> teachers will never be replaced
    A

    in <u>his classroom</u> by <u>these</u> computer
    B C

    programs.

    (A) But, the
    (B) their classrooms
    (C) this
    (D) No change is necessary.

26. Mathematical <u>competence</u> <u>assume</u> that
    A B

    understanding <u>precedes</u> rote calculation.
    C

    (A) competense
    (B) assumes
    (C) proceeds
    (D) No change is necessary.

Second Passage

The Board of Adjustment can exempt a person from the requirements of a particular land-use ordnance. Several cases has come before the board concerning three ordinances. One ordnance states that religious and other organizations cannot build places of worship or meeting halls in residential zones. A second ordinance states "any garage must be less than 25 percent of the size of a house." A third ordinance restricts a person's right. To convert a one-family house to a two-family house. Its interesting to note how a person can be in favor of an exemption in one case but opposed to exemption in another. For example one homeowner applied to build a garage 45 percent of the size of her house, but was opposed to a neighbor converting his house from one-family to two-family. This second homeowner was opposed to a church being built in his neighborhood: however, the woman opposed to his proposal was all for the church construction project. Have decisions result from pressure on Board of Adjustment members who also live in the community? It must sometimes seem that any boards decision is the wrong one. But that is what Boards of

Adjustment are for and we can only hope that this example of America in action will best serve the community and we who live there.

27. The Board of Adjustment can <u>exempt</u> a
    A

    person from the requirements of a
    <u>particular</u> land-use <u>ordnance</u>.
    B C

    (A) exemt
    (B) perticular
    (C) ordinance
    (D) No change is necessary.

28. Several cases <u>has</u> come before the
    A

    board <u>concerning</u> three <u>ordinances</u>.
    B C

    (A) have
    (B) concern
    (C) ordinance
    (D) No change is necessary.

29. A second ordinance <u>states</u>: "<u>Any</u> garage
    A

    must be <u>less than</u> 25 percent of the
    B

    <u>size of</u> a house."
    C

    (A) states; "any
    (B) lesser of
    (C) sizes of
    (D) No change is necessary.

30. <u>Its</u> interesting to note how a person can
    A

    be <u>in favor</u> of an exemption in one case
    B

    but opposed to an <u>exemption</u> in another.
    C

    (A) It's
    (B) favored
    (C) exempted
    (D) No change is necessary.

31. For <u>example one</u> homeowner applied to
      A
 build a garage 45 percent <u>of</u> the size
                   B
 of her house, but was opposed to a
 neighbor <u>converting</u> his house from
            C
 one-family to two-family.

 (A) example, one
 (B) for
 (C) converted
 (D) No change is necessary.

32. This second homeowner was opposed to
 a church being built in his
 <u>neighborhood however, the</u> woman
       A, B
 opposed to his proposal <u>was all</u> for
               C
 the church construction project.

 (A) neigborhood; however
 (B) neighborhood; however,
 (C) is all
 (D) No change is necessary.

33. <u>Have</u> decisions result from pressure on
   A
 Board of Adjustment <u>members</u> who
               B
 also <u>live in the</u> community?
      C

 (A) Do
 (B) member
 (C) lived in
 (D) No change is necessary.

34. It must <u>sometimes seem</u> that any <u>boards</u>
          A   B
 decision is the wrong <u>one.</u>
              C

 (A) sometimes, seem
 (B) board's
 (C) ones
 (D) No change is necessary.

35. But <u>that</u> is what Boards of Adjustment
     A
 are for and we can only hope
 that this example of <u>America</u> in action
                B
 will best serve the community and
 <u>we</u> who live there.
  C

 (A) But, that
 (B) American
 (C) us
 (D) No change is necessary.

36. <u>A</u> third ordinance restricts a <u>person's</u>
  A   B
 <u>right. To</u> convert a one-family house
      C
 to a two-family house.

 (A) An
 (B) persons
 (C) right to
 (D) No change is necessary.

> Select the answer choice that corrects
> the underlined portion of the sentence.
> Choose *No change is necessary* if there
> is no error.

37. Lisa believed in being <u>happy, that is, she</u>
 believed in doing what was best for her.

 (A) happy. That is she
 (B) happy: that is, she
 (C) happy; that is, she
 (D) No change is necessary.

38. The whole day was filled with
 <u>excitement; a</u> festive lunch, the
 company of good friends, and a joyous
 ceremony.

 (A) excitement: a
 (B) excitement, a
 (C) excitement a
 (D) No change is necessary.

39. <u>Because, the soccer game was being played indoors, Chad wore sneakers instead of spikes.</u>

   (A) Because the soccer game was being played indoors, Chad wore sneakers instead of spikes.
   (B) Because the soccer game was being played indoors. Chad wore sneakers instead of spikes.
   (C) Because, the soccer game was being played indoors Chad wore sneakers instead of spikes.
   (D) No change is necessary.

40. Blaire was getting some last advice about taking the test. <u>"You'll ace it", said her brother, "Do your best", said her father, "We'll love you either way", said her mother.</u>

   (A) "You'll ace it," said her brother, "Do your best," said her father, "We'll love you either way," said her mother.
   (B) "You'll ace it," said her brother; "Do your best," said her father; "We'll love you either way," said her mother.
   (C) "You'll ace it", said her brother; "Do your best", said her father; "We'll love you either way", said her mother.
   (D) No change is necessary.

READING

> Choose the answer that best describes the relationship between the sentence parts.

1. Many senators believe that a tax increase is necessary; however, any vote for the increase might lead to their defeat in an election.

   (A) definition
   (B) contrast
   (C) time order
   (D) addition

> Read this passage and then mark the best answer for each item.

There was very little oxygen in the earth's atmosphere about 3.5 billion years ago. We know that molecules
Line (much smaller than a cell) can develop
(5) spontaneously in this type of environment. This is how life probably began on earth about 3.4 billion years ago.

Eventually these molecules linked together to form complex groupings of
(10) molecules. These earliest organisms must have been able to ingest and live on nonorganic compounds. Over a period of time, these organisms adapted and began using the sun's energy. The organ-
(15) isms began to use photosynthesis, which released oxygen into the oceans and the atmosphere. The stage was set for more advanced life forms.

The first cells were prokaryotes (bacte-
(20) ria), which created energy (respired) without oxygen (anaerobic). Next these cells developed into blue-green algae prokaryotes, which were aerobic (creating energy with oxygen) and used photo-
(25) synthesis. The advanced eukaryotes were developed from these primitive cells.

Algae developed about 750 million years ago. Even this simple cell contained an enormous amount of DNA and heredi-
(30) tary information. It took about 2.7 billion years to develop life to this primitive form. This very slow process moved somewhat faster in the millennia that followed as animal and plant forms slowly emerged.
(35) Animals developed into vertebrate (backbone) and invertebrate (no backbone) species. Mammals became the dominant vertebrate species and insects became the dominant invertebrate spe-
(40) cies. As animals developed, they adapted to their environment. The best adapted survived. This process is called natural selection. Entire species have vanished from earth.
(45) Mammals and dinosaurs coexisted for more than 100 million years. During that time, dinosaurs were the dominant species. When dinosaurs became extinct 65 million years ago, mammals survived.
(50) Freed of dinosaurian dominance, mammals evolved into the dominant creatures they are today. Despite many years of study, it is not known what caused the dinosaurs to become extinct or why
(55) mammals survived.

2. This passage suggests

   (A) that mammals were the more intelligent species
   (B) how life evolved on earth
   (C) that mammals and dinosaurs were natural enemies
   (D) the environment did not affect evolution

3. What is the relationship within the sentence beginning on line 45?

   (A) comparison
   (B) simple listing
   (C) generalization and example
   (D) addition

4. The author's purpose for writing this passage is to

   (A) entertain
   (B) narrate
   (C) persuade
   (D) inform

5. The tone of this passage is best described as

   (A) objective
   (B) depressed
   (C) angry
   (D) cheerful

6. The organizational pattern of the fifth paragraph (lines 35–44) is best described as:

   (A) comparison
   (B) summary
   (C) classification
   (D) simple listing

7. The main idea of the second paragraph (lines 8–18) is

   (A) Molecules can only ingest nonorganic compounds.
   (B) Evolution is based on adaptation.
   (C) Photosynthesis allowed organisms to exist without the need of sunlight.
   (D) Oxygen is more important to life than the sun's energy.

8. Is the last sentence in the passage primarily a statement of fact or opinion?

   (A) fact
   (B) opinion

> Some words have been deleted from this passage. Mark the letter for the word or phrase that best fills in the blank.

Current scholarship indicates that Native Americans (Indians) came to this continent about 30,000 years ago. They passed over a land bridge near what is now the Bering Strait between Siberia and Alaska. These Native Americans _____(9)_____ spread throughout all of North, Central, and South America.

__(10)___ with a glacier covering Alaska, the Aleuts had established a culture on the Aleutian islands off southern Alaska by 5000 BC. This hunting/fishing society has retained much of its ancient character.

Primitive northern woodland cultures developed in the northeastern United States about 3000 BC. These cultures included the Algonquian-speaking tribes, ___(11)___ the Shawnee and the Iroquois Federation. There is evidence that Northern Woodland Indians may have been exposed to outside contact hundreds of years before the arrival of Columbus.

9. (A) never
   (B) eventually
   (C) in spite of this
   (D) although

10. (A) Although
    (B) Nevertheless
    (C) Even
    (D) However

11. (A) nor
    (B) and
    (C) through
    (D) such as

> Read this passage and then mark the best answer for each item.

The Vietnam war stretched across the twelve years of the Kennedy and Johnson administrations and into the
Line presidency of Richard Nixon. While the
(5) war officially began with Kennedy as president, its actual beginnings stretch back many years.

Before the war, Vietnam was called French Indochina. During World War II,
(10) the United States supported Ho Chi Minh in Vietnam as he attacked Japan. After the war, the United States supported the French instead of Ho Chi Minh, as France sought to regain control
(15) of its former colony.

Fighting broke out between the French and Ho Chi Minh with support from Mao Ze-dong (Mao Tse-tung), the leader of mainland China. Even with sub-
(20) stantial material aid from the United States, France could not defeat Vietnam. In 1950 the French were defeated at Dien Bien Phu.

Subsequent negotiations in Geneva di-
(25) vided Vietnam into North and South with Ho Chi Minh in control of the North. Ngo Dinh Diem was installed by the United States as a leader in the South. Diem never gained popular support in
(30) the South. Following a harsh crackdown by Diem, the Vietcong organized to fight against him. During the Eisenhower administration, 2000 American "advisors" were sent to South Vietnam.

(35) When Kennedy came to office, he approved a CIA coup to overthrow Diem. When Johnson took office he was not interested in compromise. In 1964 Johnson started a massive buildup of
(40) forces in Vietnam until the number ultimately reached more than 500,000. The Gulf of Tonkin Resolution, passed by Congress, gave Johnson discretion in pursuing the war.

(45) Living and fighting conditions were terrible. Although American forces had many victories, neither that nor the massive bombing of North Vietnam led to victory. In 1968, the Vietcong launched the
(50) Tet Offensive. While ground gained in the offensive was ultimately recaptured, the offensive shook the confidence of military leaders.

At home, there were deep divisions.
(55) War protests sprang up all over the United States. Half a million people protested in New York during 1967, while the tension between hawks and doves increased throughout the country.

(60) Richard Nixon was elected in 1970 in the midst of this turmoil. While vigorously prosecuting the war, he and Secretary of State Henry Kissinger were holding secret negotiations with North
(65) Vietnam. In 1973 an agreement was finally drawn up to end the war. American prisoners were repatriated although

there were still many missing in action (MIA), and U.S. troops withdrew from
(70) Vietnam.

The war cost 350,000 American casualties. The $175 billion spent on the war could have been used for Johnson's Great Society programs.

12. The tone of this passage is best described as

   (A) compassionate
   (B) reverent
   (C) serious
   (D) nostalgic

13. In this passage, the author expresses bias against

   (A) the Eisenhower administration
   (B) the French people
   (C) the military
   (D) hawks

14. The organizational pattern of the fourth paragraph (lines 24–34) is primarily

   (A) definition
   (B) comparison
   (C) cause and effect
   (D) addition

15. The passage implies which of the following?

   (A) The Vietnam War was a glorious war.
   (B) Kennedy laid the foundation for this war.
   (C) The United States paid a great price for this war.
   (D) The United States people gave united support for the war effort.

16. In context the word *popular* (line 29) means

   (A) widespread
   (B) complete
   (C) major
   (D) famous

17. In this passage, the author shows a bias against

    (A) Kennedy
    (B) Ho Chi Minh
    (C) American forces
    (D) the French

18. Select the word or phrase that best describes the relationship between the parts of the sentence.

    I can't imagine two more different people, but they do share a common language.

    (A) contrast
    (B) comparison
    (C) order
    (D) classification

Read this passage and then mark the best answer for each item.

This decade finds our society beset with unprecedented problems of crime and violence, alcohol and drug abuse,
Line sex, AIDS, high drop-out rates, teenage
(5) pregnancy, and disaffected youth. Many of these problems can be traced directly to poverty. Schools are a part of society and so they too are affected by these problems.
(10) The number of serious crimes in the United States is at the highest level in memory. Students bring guns to school and large urban areas report dozens of deaths each year from violent acts in
(15) school. Murder is the leading cause of death among African American teens. More than 70 percent of those who commit serious crimes are never caught. We live in a society where crime is rampant
(20) and crime pays.

Crime in school presents a particular problem for teachers. Some estimate that 3 percent to 7 percent of all students bring a gun with them to school. Stu-
(25) dents attack teachers every day in America. While this behavior is not defensible, attention to the principles of classroom management can be effective in heading off some of these incidents.
(30) Alcohol is the most used and abused drug. Even though it is legal, there are serious short- and long-term consequences of alcohol use. Alcoholism is the most widespread drug addiction. Untreated al-
(35) coholism can lead to death.

Tobacco is the next most widely used and abused substance. Some efforts are being made to declare tobacco a drug. Irrefutable evidence shows that tobacco
(40) use is a causative factor in hundreds of thousands of deaths each year.

Other drugs, including marijuana, cocaine, heroin, and various drugs in pill form, carry with them serious health ad-
(45) dictions and emotional problems. The widespread illicit availability of these drugs creates additional problems. Many students engage in crimes to gain the money to pay for drugs. Others may
(50) commit crimes while under the influence of drugs. Still others may commit crimes by selling drugs to make money.

More than 90 percent of students have used alcohol by the time they leave high
(55) school. About 70 percent of high school graduates have used other illegal drugs. Awareness programs that focus on drug use can have some positive effect. However, most drug and alcohol abuse and
(60) addiction have other underlying causes. These causes must be addressed for any program to be effective.

19. The tone of this passage is best described as

    (A) angry
    (B) outspoken
    (C) evasive
    (D) serious

20. In this passage, the author expresses bias against

    (A) students
    (B) alcoholics
    (C) society
    (D) teachers

21. The organizational pattern of the second paragraph (lines 10–20) is primarily

    (A) classification
    (B) addition
    (C) summary
    (D) contrast

Some words have been deleted from this passage. Mark the letter for the word or phrase that best fills in the blank.

Mohammed was born in 570 AD and went __(22)____ into Mecca in 630. The Koran contains the 114 verses of Mohammed's teachings. Around 640 AD, the religious leader Omar established an Islamic empire with Damascus as the capital. The capital was ___(23)____ moved to Baghdad. The Muslims enjoyed a prosperous economy and in the late days of the empire, Omar Khayyam wrote the *Rubaiyat*.

Muslim armies conquered Spain and much of France by about 730. A series of caliphs ruled from 750 until 1250, when an army ___(24)____ led by Ghengis Kahn sacked Baghdad and killed the last caliph.

22. (A) as a result
    (B) subsequently
    (C) evidently
    (D) presently

23. (A) therefore
    (B) for this reason
    (C) eventually
    (D) originally

24. (A) originally
    (B) conversely
    (C) presently
    (D) also

Read this passage and then mark the best answer for each item.

Humans (*Homo sapiens*) are believed to have developed in Africa about 250,000 years ago. Humans formed no-
Line madic bands that spread throughout Af-
(5) rica about 30,000 years ago. The first towns were founded in the Nile River valley about 4500 BC. Sophisticated civilizations developed throughout Egypt by about 3000 BC. At this time, Egypt occu-
(10) pied a swath of land along the Nile River and extending to the Mediterranean. Pharaohs ruled with god-like powers and there was a sophisticated bureaucracy. The Egyptians had writing (hieroglyph-
(15) ics) and invented a calendar still in use today. Pyramids were built during the Old Kingdom of Egypt from 2700 to 2150 BC. Beginning around 2150 BC, a century of weak pharaohs, civil wars and fam-
(20) ines weakened and fragmented Egypt. From about 2050 BC to 1650 BC, Egypt came together in the Middle Kingdom. In 1650 BC, foreign armies invaded and conquered Egypt. In about 1550 BC, the Egyp-
(25) tians overthrew the foreign leaders and the New Kingdom (1550–1100 BC). In the beginning of the New Kingdom, Egypt stretched along the Nile and occupied the coast of the Mediterranean out of Af-
(30) rica and in Palestine and Syria. By 1250, the Egyptian Empire was in decline. Egypt ceased to be the dominant force in the area about 750 BC.

25. In this passage, the author expresses bias against

    (A) Egypt
    (B) hieroglyphics
    (C) Homo sapiens
    (D) pharaohs

26. The tone of this passage is best described as

   (A) malicious
   (B) objective
   (C) evasive
   (D) nostalgic

27. The organizational pattern of this passage is best described as

   (A) time order
   (B) comparison
   (C) contrast
   (D) generalization

> Read this passage and then mark the best answer for each item.

We use language, including gestures and sounds, to communicate. Humans first used gestures but it was spoken lan-
Line guage that opened the vistas for human
(5) communication. Language consists of two things. First we have the thoughts that language conveys and then the physical sounds, writing and structure of the language itself.
(10)   Human speech organs (mouth, tongue, lips, and the like) were not developed to make sounds, but they uniquely determined the sounds and words humans could produce. Human speech gradually
(15) came to be loosely bound together by unique rules for grammar.
   Many believe that humans developed their unique ability to speak with the development of a specialized area of the
(20) brain called Broca's area. If this is so, human speech and language probably developed in the past 100,000 years.

28. What is the main idea of this passage?

   (A) Language consists of thoughts and physical sounds.
   (B) Human communication includes gestures.
   (C) Human speech and language slowly developed through the years.
   (D) Broca's area of the brain controls speech.

29. What is the first component of language development?

   (A) gestures
   (B) thoughts
   (C) sound
   (D) writing

30. Is the author's conclusion in the last sentence valid or invalid?

   (A) valid
   (B) invalid

> Read this passage and then mark the best answer for each item.

Information can be retrieved from books, magazines, and other print sources by simply picking up the reading
Line materials and turning and flipping
(5) through the pages. The book, newspaper, or periodical remains one of the most efficient ways to access print information.
   Print materials are also found in librar-
(10) ies or other repositories on microfilm and microfiche. Microfilms are 35mm films of books, while microfiche are flat and can contain hundreds of pages of text material. Microfilm and microfiche
(15) are read with specialized readers.
   Other information can be retrieved on or through the computer. Written materials can be entered on a computer, usually with a word processor. This information
(20) can be accessed directly through the computer's hard disk. Special features of most word processors and other utilities permit the user to search electronically for words and phrases. Sound, graphics, and anima-
(25) tion may also be stored on a computer's hard disk. These sounds and images may be accessed using specialized computer programs.
   Print materials, images, sounds, and ani-
(30) mation may also be stored on CD-ROMs designed for computer use. Information on these CD-ROMs may be accessed through a CD-ROM player, which is connected to the computer. Images and
(35) sounds on videotapes, audiotapes, music

CD-ROMs, and videodisk may also be accessed through the computer.

Computers can be connected to telephone lines using a modem. Modems al-
(40) low the computer user to retrieve information from other computers and bulletin boards. Almost all periodical and newspaper information can be retrieved through these sources. For exam-
(45) ple, Lexus/Nexis, primarily designed for lawyers, has almost every newspaper and periodical article published over the past several years. Other bulletin boards and information retrieval services con-
(50) tain a full range of text, graphics, sound and animation, and ways of searching for and retrieving this information.

31. The author's purpose for writing this passage was to

(A) persuade
(B) narrate
(C) inform
(D) entertain

32. Is the sentence *Images and sounds on videotapes...* (lines 34–37) fact or opinion?

(A) fact
(B) opinion

33. In this context, the word *repositories* (line 10) means

(A) magazines
(B) storage place
(C) replacements
(D) media

34. Which of the following describes a characteristic that distinguishes a microfilm from a microfiche?

(A) A microfiche is read by a specialized reader.
(B) Microfilms use 35mm film.
(C) Microfiche stores printed material.
(D) Microfilm is found in libraries.

35. The author's statement in the last sentence of the first paragraph is

(A) valid
(B) invalid

Read this passage and then mark the best answer for each item.

The United States National Park system is extensive, although most land dedicated to the park system is in the
Line western states. This is no doubt the case
(5) because these lands are occupied by states most recently admitted to the union. I have some very happy personal memories of Yellowstone National Park, having visited there on several occa-
(10) sions. All of my visits came before the series of fires that burned much of the park's forested areas.

My most unusual recollection dates back a number of years when I was part
(15) of a group waiting for the Old Faithful geyser to erupt. A young child was standing about twenty yards away looking at something on the ground. The group gathered around where the child was
(20) standing. And while Old Faithful erupted, we all watched a small, rusty water pipe leaking onto the ground. I never understood what it was about the pipe that drew everyone's interest. It
(25) must have to do with a child's wonder.

36. What is the main idea of this passage?

(A) Yellowstone National Park has experienced many fires.
(B) The National Park system is extensive.
(C) The importance of an event does not always come from its complexity.
(D) Old Faithful is a great tourist attraction.

37. Which of the following statements from the passage is a true statement?

   (A) People were concerned about the leaky pipe.
   (B) The author has not been back to Yellowstone recently.
   (C) The child was very young.
   (D) Old Faithful did not erupt that day.

38. In this context, the word *erupted* (line 21) means

   (A) made a loud noise
   (B) gurgled
   (C) simmered
   (D) burst forth

The computers in the college dormitories are actually more sophisticated than the computers in the college computer labs, and they cost less. It seems that the person who bought the dormitory computers looked around until she found powerful computers at a low price. The person who runs the labs just got the computers offered by the regular supplier.

Line
(5)

39. The author of this passage shows bias for

   (A) the person who bought the computers for the dorms
   (B) the person who bought the computers for the labs
   (C) computer salesmen
   (D) college purchasing agents

40. If the author were orally presenting this passage, his or her tone of voice would probably be

   (A) outraged
   (B) sarcastic
   (C) defiant
   (D) indifferent

41. Is the paragraph above a statement of fact or opinion?

   (A) fact
   (B) opinion

MATHEMATICS

90 minutes

Take this practice subtest in a realistic, timed setting. Do not take this subtest until you have reviewed Chapter 5, Mathematics.

The test rules allow you exactly 90 minutes to complete this practice subtest. You have a little over one and one-half minutes to answer each question. Answer the easier questions right away and leave the more difficult questions until the end of the test.

Use the answer sheet that follows.

Mathematics

1 Ⓐ Ⓑ Ⓒ Ⓓ Ⓔ	12 Ⓐ Ⓑ Ⓒ Ⓓ Ⓔ	23 Ⓐ Ⓑ Ⓒ Ⓓ Ⓔ	34 Ⓐ Ⓑ Ⓒ Ⓓ Ⓔ	45 Ⓐ Ⓑ Ⓒ Ⓓ Ⓔ
2 Ⓐ Ⓑ Ⓒ Ⓓ Ⓔ	13 Ⓐ Ⓑ Ⓒ Ⓓ Ⓔ	24 Ⓐ Ⓑ Ⓒ Ⓓ Ⓔ	35 Ⓐ Ⓑ Ⓒ Ⓓ Ⓔ	46 Ⓐ Ⓑ Ⓒ Ⓓ Ⓔ
3 Ⓐ Ⓑ Ⓒ Ⓓ Ⓔ	14 Ⓐ Ⓑ Ⓒ Ⓓ Ⓔ	25 Ⓐ Ⓑ Ⓒ Ⓓ Ⓔ	36 Ⓐ Ⓑ Ⓒ Ⓓ Ⓔ	47 Ⓐ Ⓑ Ⓒ Ⓓ Ⓔ
4 Ⓐ Ⓑ Ⓒ Ⓓ Ⓔ	15 Ⓐ Ⓑ Ⓒ Ⓓ Ⓔ	26 Ⓐ Ⓑ Ⓒ Ⓓ Ⓔ	37 Ⓐ Ⓑ Ⓒ Ⓓ Ⓔ	48 Ⓐ Ⓑ Ⓒ Ⓓ Ⓔ
5 Ⓐ Ⓑ Ⓒ Ⓓ Ⓔ	16 Ⓐ Ⓑ Ⓒ Ⓓ Ⓔ	27 Ⓐ Ⓑ Ⓒ Ⓓ Ⓔ	38 Ⓐ Ⓑ Ⓒ Ⓓ Ⓔ	49 Ⓐ Ⓑ Ⓒ Ⓓ Ⓔ
6 Ⓐ Ⓑ Ⓒ Ⓓ Ⓔ	17 Ⓐ Ⓑ Ⓒ Ⓓ Ⓔ	28 Ⓐ Ⓑ Ⓒ Ⓓ Ⓔ	39 Ⓐ Ⓑ Ⓒ Ⓓ Ⓔ	50 Ⓐ Ⓑ Ⓒ Ⓓ Ⓔ
7 Ⓐ Ⓑ Ⓒ Ⓓ Ⓔ	18 Ⓐ Ⓑ Ⓒ Ⓓ Ⓔ	29 Ⓐ Ⓑ Ⓒ Ⓓ Ⓔ	40 Ⓐ Ⓑ Ⓒ Ⓓ Ⓔ	51 Ⓐ Ⓑ Ⓒ Ⓓ Ⓔ
8 Ⓐ Ⓑ Ⓒ Ⓓ Ⓔ	19 Ⓐ Ⓑ Ⓒ Ⓓ Ⓔ	30 Ⓐ Ⓑ Ⓒ Ⓓ Ⓔ	41 Ⓐ Ⓑ Ⓒ Ⓓ Ⓔ	52 Ⓐ Ⓑ Ⓒ Ⓓ Ⓔ
9 Ⓐ Ⓑ Ⓒ Ⓓ Ⓔ	20 Ⓐ Ⓑ Ⓒ Ⓓ Ⓔ	31 Ⓐ Ⓑ Ⓒ Ⓓ Ⓔ	42 Ⓐ Ⓑ Ⓒ Ⓓ Ⓔ	53 Ⓐ Ⓑ Ⓒ Ⓓ Ⓔ
10 Ⓐ Ⓑ Ⓒ Ⓓ Ⓔ	21 Ⓐ Ⓑ Ⓒ Ⓓ Ⓔ	32 Ⓐ Ⓑ Ⓒ Ⓓ Ⓔ	43 Ⓐ Ⓑ Ⓒ Ⓓ Ⓔ	54 Ⓐ Ⓑ Ⓒ Ⓓ Ⓔ
11 Ⓐ Ⓑ Ⓒ Ⓓ Ⓔ	22 Ⓐ Ⓑ Ⓒ Ⓓ Ⓔ	33 Ⓐ Ⓑ Ⓒ Ⓓ Ⓔ	44 Ⓐ Ⓑ Ⓒ Ⓓ Ⓔ	55 Ⓐ Ⓑ Ⓒ Ⓓ Ⓔ

Check the answers and explanations on page 300.

1. $-\frac{1}{4} - \frac{1}{6}$ equals

(A) $\frac{5}{12}$
(B) $-\frac{5}{12}$
(C) $\frac{1}{12}$
(D) $-\frac{1}{12}$

2. $(\frac{3}{4}) \times (-2\frac{1}{2})$ equals

(A) $-2\frac{3}{8}$
(B) $1\frac{7}{8}$
(C) $-1\frac{7}{8}$
(D) $2\frac{3}{8}$

3. $-3.2 + (-6.32)$ equals

(A) -9.52
(B) 9.52
(C) 3.12
(D) -3.12

4. $-0.5 + 2.5$ equals

(A) 3
(B) -3
(C) -2
(D) 2

5. How much would you have left after decreasing 40 by 25% of itself?

(A) 15
(B) 30
(C) 50
(D) 65

6. What percent of 500 is 210?

(A) 238%
(B) 210%
(C) 42%
(D) 72%

7. $(3^2)^3$ equals

(A) $(12)^2$
(B) $(9)^5$
(C) $(3)^6$
(D) $(3)^{2+3}$

8. Find the numeral for $(6 \times 10^3) + (2 \times 10) + (3 \times \frac{1}{10}) + (5 \times \frac{1}{10^3})$

(A) 6,235
(B) 6,020.305
(C) 62.35
(D) 6,002.35

9. $\frac{11}{20}$ equals

(A) 55%
(B) 11%
(C) .55%
(D) .11

10. What symbol would make this a true statement?
$$4.5\bar{3} \underline{} 4.536$$

(A) $>$
(B) $=$
(C) $\geq$
(D) $<$

11. The monthly sales for the 15 sales people at Postman Realty range from $250,000 to $850,000. What is a reasonable estimate of the average sales per person?

(A) $400,000
(B) $550,000
(C) $600,000
(D) $750,000

12. Find the pattern for the linear relationship in each ordered pair. What is the missing term?
    (5, 1.25) (4, 1) (3, 0.75) (2, 0.5) (18, __)

(A) 1.25
(B) 4.5
(C) 6
(D) 4.75

13. The campers at Spring Lake Day Camp are forming bowling teams. When the campers form teams of 2, 4, or 5, there is always one person left. What is the smallest number of campers who want to bowl?

    (A) 21
    (B) 11
    (C) 5
    (D) 41

14. Find the measure of the piece of candy to the nearest $\frac{1}{4}$ centimeter.

    (A) 10.75 cm
    (B) 11 cm
    (C) 10.5 cm
    (D) 10 cm

15. What is the total number of kilometers around the right triangle pictured?

    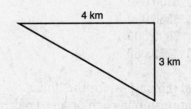

    (A) 7
    (B) 5
    (C) 12
    (D) 25

16. Find the area of a triangular garden with a base of 4 meters and a height of 6 meters.

    (A) 24 sq. m
    (B) 12 sq. m
    (C) 10 sq. m
    (D) 5 sq. m

17. Find the volume of a right circular cylinder that is 15 cm high and has a diameter of 6 cm.

    (A) 90π cubic cm
    (B) 90π sq. cm
    (C) 135π cubic cm
    (D) 135π sq. cm

    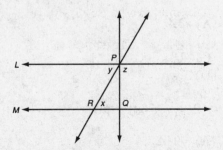

18. Study this diagram and decide which of the statements are true.

    (A) $\triangle PQR$ is an obtuse triangle
    (B) $\angle y$ and $\angle z$ are supplementary angles
    (C) $\angle x$ is congruent to $\angle y$
    (D) $\angle x$ is congruent to $\angle z$

    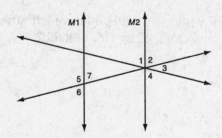

19. Line M1 is parallel to line M2. Find the pair of vertical angles.

    (A) 1 and 2
    (B) 5 and 6
    (C) 6 and 7
    (D) 1 and 3

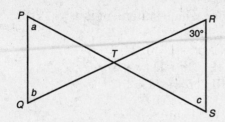

20. Find a true statement about triangle *PQT* and triangle *RST*.

    (A) ∠*a* is congruent to ∠*b*.
    (B) The measure of ∠*c* = 30 degrees.
    (C) *PQ/RS* = *PT/TS*.
    (D) The measure of ∠*PTQ* equals the measure of ∠*RTS*.

21. Which of the following units could you NOT use to estimate the amount of milk a person drinks in one year?

    (A) liters
    (B) gallons
    (C) cubic inches
    (D) square feet

22. Examine these figures. What is the measure of ∠*y*?

    (A) 45°
    (B) 105°
    (C) 135°
    (D) 180°

23. Blaire is making a rectangular 5 foot by 12 foot quilt for her bed. She wants some trim to go around the perimeter and across both diagonals of the quilt. How much trim does she need?

    (A) 24 feet
    (B) 60 feet
    (C) 66 feet
    (D) 169 feet

24. $\sqrt{20} + 3\sqrt{5}$ equals

    (A) $3\sqrt{25}$
    (B) 15
    (C) $5\sqrt{5}$
    (D) $6\sqrt{15}$

25. $\dfrac{15}{\sqrt{5}}$ equals

    (A) 3
    (B) $3\sqrt{5}$
    (C) 15
    (D) $5\sqrt{5}$

26. $15(x + 3y) - (5x - y)$ equals

    (A) $-2x + 8y$
    (B) $10x + 46y$
    (C) $-2x + 44y$
    (D) $10x + 8y$

27. $0.009 \times 549{,}000$ equals

    (A) 494.1
    (B) 61,000
    (C) 4.941×10^3
    (D) 4.941×10^2

28. If $5x - (x - 2) = 0$, then

    (A) $x = -\frac{1}{2}$
    (B) $x = \frac{1}{2}$
    (C) $x = 5$
    (D) $x = 2$

29. $5 - 9w > 4 + 3w$. Solve for *w*.

    (A) $w > \frac{1}{12}$
    (B) $w > 12$
    (C) $w < \frac{1}{12}$
    (D) $w < 6$

30. If $A = \pi r^2$, find *A* when $\pi = 3.14$ and $r = 3$.

    (A) 15.7
    (B) 9.42
    (C) 18.84
    (D) 28.26

31. If $f(x) = x^2 + 3x + 2$, find $f(5)$

    (A) 484
    (B) 42
    (C) 27
    (D) 17

32. Which is a linear factor of $6x^2 + 11x + 4$?

    (A) $(2x + 4)$
    (B) $(3x + 1)$
    (C) $(3x + 4)$
    (D) $(6x + 7)$

33. Find the solution for this quadratic equation: $2x^2 - 2x - 1 = 0$

    (A) $+ 16, - 16$

    (B) $\dfrac{1 + \sqrt{3}}{2}, \dfrac{1 - \sqrt{3}}{2}$

    (C) $2\sqrt{2}, -2\sqrt{2}$
    (D) $+4\sqrt{2}, -4\sqrt{2}$

34. Find the correct solution for this system of linear equations:

    $x - 2y = 8$
    $2y - x = 4$

    (A) $(0, 2)$
    (B) $(1, 2)$
    (C) $\{(x, y) : 3x - 3y = 12\}$
    (D) empty set

35. Find the expression that is equal to $2^3 (x^2)^3 (y^3)^3$

    (A) $5 x^5 y^6$
    (B) $8 x^6 y^9$
    (C) $8 x^5 y^6$
    (D) $2 x^8 y^6$

36. For which statement is $x = -\frac{1}{3}$ a solution?
    I. $x^2 - 1 = 0$
    II. $(3x + 1)(x + 6) = 0$
    III. $|5x + 2| < 2$

    (A) I only
    (B) II and III only
    (C) I and III only
    (D) none of the above

37. Select the answer choice that correctly expresses the conditions of the following problem.

    During a 24-hour period, 1,500 cars pass through a toll booth. Let x represent the number of cars passing through the toll booth during a one-week period of time.

    (A) $1500/1 = x/7$
    (B) $x/1500 = 1/7$
    (C) $1500/24 = x/1$
    (D) $1500/x = 2/1$

38. Which graph correctly represents the conditions: $x \geq 5$ and $-5 < y < 5$.

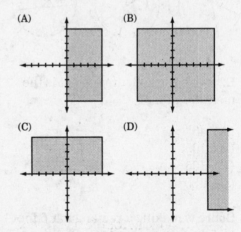

39. Find an inequality equivalent to:
    $-9 < 3p < 54$

    (A) $3 < p < 18$
    (B) $-3 < p < 18$
    (C) $-3 > p > 18$
    (D) $18 < p < -3$

40. Chad is driving nonstop to Miami. He averages 60 mph for the first 80 miles of the 120-mile trip. He has to slow down to 50 mph for the remainder of the trip. How long will it take him to get to Miami?

(A) 2 hours
(B) 2 hours, 8 minutes
(C) 1.5 hours
(D) 3 hours, 8 minutes

41. Select the answer choice that meets the following conditions: The sum of two consecutive even numbers is 38.

(A) $(n) + (n + 1) = 38$
(B) $(2n) + (2n + 2) = 38$
(C) $(2n) + (2n) = 38$
(D) $(2n + 2) + (n + 2) = 38$

42. The circle graph shows how much of her monthly salary Blaire spends on each category. What percent of her budget is spent on rent and food?

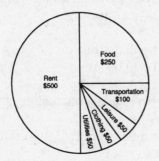

(A) 50%
(B) 75%
(C) 80%
(D) 5%

43. Select the mean for the data given: 50, 20, 42, 45, 48, 50

(A) 45
(B) 50
(C) 42.5
(D) 45.5

44. The Dorm Council is filling vacancies from the residence halls for dorm counselors. Three of the five candidates from Washington Hall will be selected. In how many different ways can the counselors be selected?

(A) 10
(B) 8
(C) 15
(D) ⅗

45. If you have a 65% chance to get into the psychology class that you want, what is the probability you will not get in the class?

(A) 65%
(B) .35
(C) not enough information given
(D) .45

46. The following plot shows students' grades compared to study time. Choose the statement that best describes the given data.

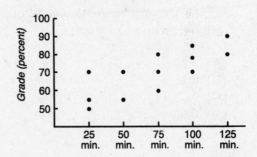

(A) There appears to be no relationship between study time and grades obtained.
(B) An increase in study time will earn a higher grade.
(C) There appears to be a positive relationship between study time and grades obtained.
(D) There appears to be a negative relationship between study time and grades obtained.

Credits	Percent
18–16	10%
15–13	58%
12–10	22%
under 10	10%

47. The table shows the distribution of credits taken by freshman students.

    What percent of the students take at least 13 credits?

    (A) 58%
    (B) 32%
    (C) 68%
    (D) not enough information given

Flavors	Diet	Regular
Cherry	10%	15%
Orange	20%	45%
Root Beer	5%	5%

48. This chart shows the types of drinks ordered at the snack bar during a recent baseball game.

    What is the probability that someone ordered an orange soda?

    (A) 0.20
    (B) 0.45
    (C) 0.35
    (D) 0.65

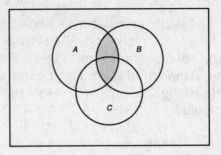

49. The Venn diagram above shows the relationship of Sets A, B, and C. If none of the regions are empty, the shaded area represents

    (A) those elements that are in A and B but not C
    (B) those elements that are in A and B and C
    (C) those elements that are in A and B
    (D) those elements that are not in B and C

50. Which logical conclusion can be drawn from these statements?

    I. If it is snowing, then I will be late.
    II. It is not snowing.

    (A) I will not be late.
    (B) I will be late.
    (C) I will be early.
    (D) No logical conclusion can be drawn.

51. Write the negation of this statement:

    If it's raining, I will get wet.

    (A) I will get wet, or it's not raining.
    (B) I will not get wet, or it's raining.
    (C) I will not get wet, and it's raining.
    (D) I will not get wet, and it's not raining.

52. From among the following true conclusions, select the one that is valid.

    (A) All whole numbers are integers. All integers are fractions, so all whole numbers are fractions.
    (B) All whole numbers are integers and no fractions are integers, so all whole numbers are fractions.
    (C) All negative numbers are not positive numbers. Some fractions are negative numbers, so all positive numbers are fractions.
    (D) Some negative numbers are not whole numbers. Some negative numbers are not fractions, so all negative numbers are fractions.

53. What valid conclusion can be drawn from the statement:

    If it snows, then you will shovel your walk. You shovel your walk.

    (A) It snowed.
    (B) It did not snow.
    (C) It did not rain.
    (D) No valid conclusion can be drawn.

54. Choose the logical equivalence that lets you transform statement I into statement II.

    I. If the bridge is not crowded, the tunnel will be crowded.
    II. If the tunnel is not crowded, then the bridge will be crowded.

    (A) p → q is equivalent to not p → not q.
    (B) p → q is equivalent to q → p.
    (C) p → q is equivalent to not q or not p.
    (D) p → q is equivalent to not q → not p.

55. Which of the following is the negation of the statement:

    Some of the voters are not happy and all of the delegates are not happy.

    (A) Some of the voters are happy and all of the delegates are happy.
    (B) The voters are not happy and the delegates are not happy.
    (C) None of the voters are happy, or all of the delegates are not happy.
    (D) All of the voters and delegates are happy.

PRACTICE TEST 2—ANSWERS AND EXPLANATIONS

English Language Skills

1. **A** The meaning of all three words is appropriate, but only the word *awe* makes sense in this statement.

2. **C** Only the word *understood* makes sense in this sentence.

3. **E** The phrase *when they met them* is not needed. The previous word, *encountered*, tells us that the English troops met the Minutemen.

4. **B** The word *both* is not needed because it repeats the information given by *two towns*.

5. **B** This choice a straightforward and clear presentation of the idea.

6. **A** This choice is clear and effective. In the other choices, we can't tell whether the driver or the passenger has only the clothes on her back.

7. **B** This choice employs a parallel structure; the others do not.

8. **B** This choice employs a parallel structure and uses verbal nouns (gerunds) as the subjects of the sentence.

9. **B** The reasonable conclusion is that the adults pitch because the children are not allowed to, not the other way around. This idea is best developed in choice B.

10. **D** Television buyers are most interested in new digital television sets because of the better picture quality. This idea is best presented in choice D.

11. **A** Choice A is very clear, while the other choices include inappropriate word choices.

12. **B** Only choice B clearly indicates the comparison to another state.

13. **C** The wording of all three choices is identical except for the correct use of *as* in choice C. The commas are incorrectly placed in choice B.

14. **A** Choice A, *leanest*, is correct when comparing more than two things. This comparison clearly implies that more than two things have been compared.

15. **D** The original choice, *run*, is correct.

16. **A** Choice A shows the infinitive form of the verb.

17. **C** The underlined portion labeled *C* shows where a new sentence should begin.

18. **D** This sentence is correct.

19. **B** The word *difficult* is misspelled in the sentence.

20. **B** The underlined portion labeled *B* shows where a new sentence should begin.

21. **D** This sentence is correct.

22. **A** A new sentence should not begin at the underlined portion labeled *A*.

23. **B** The word *understands* should be *understand*.

24. **C** The punctuation is correctly shown in choice C.

25. **B** The correct possessive is *their*, referring to the plural *teachers*.

26. **B** The correct verb for the singular subject is *assumes*.

27. **C** The word *ordinance* is incorrectly spelled in the sentence.

28. **A** The correct verb for the plural subject is *have*.

29. **D** This sentence is correct.

30. **A** The correct contraction for *it is* is *it's*.

31. **A** Place a comma after the introductory phrase *For example*.

32. **B** The correct punctuation for the portion labeled *A, B* is found in choice B.

33. **A** Change *Have* to *Do* to agree with the verb *result*.

34. **B** The correct punctuation for the possessive is found in choice B.

35. **C** The verb form *will best serve* requires the objective *us*.

36. **C** A new sentence should not begin at underlined portion C.

37. **C** The correct punctuation for the underlined portion is found in choice C.

38. **A** Use a colon to set off a list.

39. **A** When the dependent clause comes first, a comma is used to separate it from the main clause.

40. **B** Commas always go inside quotation marks, and the three independent clauses must be separated by semicolons or periods.

Reading

1. **D** Relationships Within Sentences. The second part of the sentence adds more information.

2. **B** Draw Inferences and Conclusions. The passage does not explicitly describe how life evolved but does suggest a chain of evolution. None of the other choices can be supported by the reading.

3. **A** Relationships Within Sentences. This sentence shows something that mammals and dinosaurs have in common. That is, they inhabited the planet together for over 100 million years.

4. **D** Author's Purpose. The passage states facts, clarifies, and explains. The author makes no particular attempt to persuade the reader.

5. **A** Author's Tone. The author objectively states information and displays no particular emotion.

6. **C** Organized Pattern. The author classifies the animals into different groups.

7. **B** Main Idea. The entire paragraph describes ways in which animals adapted to the environment.

8. **B** Fact or Opinion. Even though the statement is definite, some would disagree and the statement cannot be proven true or false.

9. **B** Relationships Within Sentences. The missing word shows that the spread happened over a period of time.

10. **C** Relationships Within Sentences. *Even* expresses the idea that the culture was established in spite of the presence of the glaciers.

11. **D** Relationships Within Sentences. The phrase *such as* informs the reader that the names of Algonquian-speaking tribes follows.

12. **C** Author's Tone. The writing is serious, not reminiscent, respectful, or sympathetic.

13. **A** Bias. In the last sentence of the fourth paragraph the quotes around the word "advisors" depicts sarcasm.

14. **D** Organizational Pattern. Information is being given in addition to previous information.

15. **C** Draw Inferences and Conclusions. The author summarizes his or her thoughts in the last two sentences.

16. **A** Words in Context. *Popular* means the common, everyday people.

17. **C** Bias. The author expresses a bias against American forces.

18. **B** Relationships Within Sentences. The sentence shows two things that these very different people have in common.

19. **D** Author's Tone. The author's tone reflects the seriousness of these problems.

20. **C** Bias. In the second paragraph, the author is quite outspoken against society in general.

21. **B** Organizational Pattern. The author is supporting his facts on crime by adding new material.

22. **B** Relationships Within Sentences. The word *subsequently* shows the order in which the two events occurred.

23. **C** Relationships Within Sentences. The word *eventually* shows that the move was made after a period of time.

24. **A** Relationships Within Sentences. *Originally* tells the reader that the army was not led by Ghengis Kahn when it sacked Baghdad.

25. **D** Bias. The statements *Pharaohs that ruled with god-like powers* and *a century of weak pharaohs* show a bias against Egypt's ancient royalty.

26. **B** Author's Tone. The author objectively states the facts.

27. **A** Organizational Pattern. The author starts in Africa about 250,000 years ago and ends with Egypt around 750 BC.

28. **C** Main Idea. The author gradually traces the evolution of speech and language.

29. **B** Supporting Details. The author clearly states in the first paragraph that thought precedes speech.

30. **A** Valid or Invalid. The conclusion is valid based on the assumption that the stated facts are true.

31. **C** Author's Purpose. This is not an entertaining narrative. It was written to inform.

32. **A** Fact or Opinion. It would be easy to determine the truth or falsity of this statement.

33. **B** Words in Context. A repository is a place to deposit and store particular items.

34. **B** Supporting Details. Microfilm and microfiche are similar in many ways, but only microfilm is stored on 35 mm film.

35. **B** Valid or Invalid. The statement may be true, but it is not supported by a valid argument.

36. **C** Main Idea. The author's intent is to demonstrate how things of apparently little import can overshadow seemingly important events.

37. **B** Fact or Opinion. This is the only statement that can be proved by the material in the passage.

38. **D** Words in Context. When geysers erupt, they burst forth.

39. **A** Bias. The writer favors the person who bought the dorm computers.

40. **B** Author's Tone. The tone would be sarcastic because the purchaser of the dorm computers did a better job.

41. **A** Fact or Opinion. The information in the paragraph can be verified.

Mathematics

1. **B** The signs are the same, so keep the sign.
   $-1/4 + -1/6 = -3/12 + -2/12 = -5/12$

2. **C** Multiply. The signs are different, so the answer is negative.
   $3/4 \times -5/2 = -15/8 = -1\,7/8$

3. **A** Add. The signs are both negative, so the answer is negative.

4. **D** The signs are not the same. Subtract $2.5 - 0.5 = 2$. Use the plus sign.

5. **B** $25\% = 1/4$ $1/4$ of $40 = 10$ $40 - 10 = 30$

6. **C** Write the equation: $\_\% \times 500 = 210$
   $\_\% = 210/500 = 0.42 = 42\%$

7. **C** To raise a power to another, multiply the powers.

8. **B** Write the whole numbers for the powers. There are no hundreds or hundredths.
   $6 \times 1,000 + 2 \times 10 + 3 \times 0.1 + 5 \times 1/1000$
   $= 6,020.305$

9. **A** Write 11/20 as 55/100 = $.\overline{55}$ = 55%

10. **D** The line over the 3 in .53 means there is a 3 in the hundredths place. $3 < 6$ so $4.5\overline{3} < 4.536$

11. **B** Subtract $\$850,000 - \$250,000 = \$600,000$. Divide $\$600,000$ by $2 = \$300,000$. $\$250,000 + \$300,000 = \$550,000$ the best estimate.

12. **B** Divide the first term by 4 (multiply by $1/4$) to get the second term.

13. **A** Only 21 and 41 have a remainder of 1 when divided by 2, 4, and 5. 21 is the smallest number.

14. **A** The candy bar is more than halfway between 10.5 and 11.0 cm.

15. **C** First, you must find the hypotenuse.
   $4^2 + 3^2 = 25$ $\sqrt{25} = 5$ $5 + 4 + 3 = 12$

16. **B** $A = 1/2\,bh;$ $1/2 \times 24 = 12.$

17. **C** $V = \pi r^2 h$. The diameter is 6, so the radius is 3. $3^2 = 9$
   $V = (9)(15)\pi = 135\,\pi.$

18. **C** The transversal R cuts the parallel lines so that x and y are alternate interior angles. Alternate interior angles are congruent.

19. **C** Vertical angles are formed by two intersecting lines.

20. **D** They are vertical angles, so their measures are equal. There is not enough information to decide if answer choices A, B, or C are true.

21. **D** All of the others are measures of capacity.

22. **C** The diagrams show that the two adjacent angles total 180°. The measure of $\angle y = 180° - 45° = 135°$.

23. **B** The perimeter is 34 feet. Each diagonal is a hypotenuse $25 + 144 = 169\sqrt{169} = 13$
$13 + 13 + 34 = 60$

24. **C** Simplify $\sqrt{20} = 2\sqrt{5}$ Add
$2\sqrt{5} + 3\sqrt{5} = 5\sqrt{5}$

25. **B** Multiply numerator and denominator by $\sqrt{5}$.
$$\frac{15}{\sqrt{5}} \times \frac{\sqrt{5}}{\sqrt{5}} = \frac{15\sqrt{5}}{5} = 3\sqrt{5}$$

26. **B** Use the distributive property.
$15(x + 3y) - 5(x-y) = 15x + 45y - 5x + 1$
$= 10x + 46y.$

27. **C** $0.009 \times 549{,}000 = 4941 = 4.941 \times 10^3$

28. **A** Substitute the different values for x to find that the answer is $-\frac{1}{2}$.

29. **C** $5 - 9w > 4 + 3w$
$\underline{\quad +9w \qquad + 9w \quad}$
$\quad 5 \quad > 4 + 12w$
$\underline{-4 \qquad -4 \quad}$
$\quad 1 \quad > \quad 12w \qquad w < 1/12$

30. **D** $3.14 \times 3 \times 3 = 28.26$

31. **B** Substitute 5 for x. $25 + 15 + 2 = 42$

32. **C** Follow the steps described in the book.

33. **B** Follow the steps described in the book.

34. **D** There is no solution. These lines are parallel.

35. **B** Multiply the exponents to simplify.
$2^3 (x^2)^3 = 8 x^6 y^9$

36. **B** Substitute $-\frac{1}{3}$ for x in each statement to find the answer.

37. **A** Use a proportion.
$$\frac{\text{cars in 24 hours}}{1 \text{ day}} = \frac{\text{cars in a week}}{7 \text{ days}}$$
$$\frac{1500}{1} = \frac{x}{7}$$

38. **D** The vertical axis includes 5 to –5. The horizontal axis includes 5 and greater.

39. **B** Divide each term by 3.

40. **B** $\frac{80}{60} = 1\frac{1}{3}$ $\frac{40}{50} = \frac{4}{5}$
$1\frac{1}{3} + \frac{4}{5} = 1\frac{5}{15} + \frac{12}{15} = 2\frac{2}{15} = 2\frac{8}{60} = 2$ hours, 8 minues.

41. **B** Even numbers are represented as $2n$. Find the next even number by adding 2.

42. **B** $\frac{750}{1{,}000} = \frac{75}{100} = 0.75 = 75\%$

43. **C** Add the numbers and divide by 6.

44. **A** There are 10 ways of selecting candidates from Washington Hall.
$$\frac{5!}{2!3!} = \frac{5 \cdot \overset{2}{\cancel{4}} \cdot \cancel{3} \cdot \cancel{2} \cdot \cancel{1}}{\cancel{2} \cdot \cancel{1} \cdot \cancel{3} \cdot \cancel{2} \cdot \cancel{1}} = 10$$

45. **B** $1 - 0.65 = 0.35$

46. **C** The data points are clustered about a line from lower left to upper right.

47. **C** At least 13 means 13 and above.
$58\% + 10\% = 68\%$

48. **D** Include both diet and regular soda.
$45\% + 20\% = 65\% = 0.65$

49. **C** The elements are all in Set A and Set B.

50. **D** None of the choices follow a rule which allows you to draw a logical conclusion.

51. **C** p implies q is equivalent to p and not q.

52. **A** Draw the set diagrams to see that A is the only valid conclusion.

53. **D** No conclusion can be drawn. p implies q is NOT equivalent to q implies p.

54. **D** The review section lists the logical equivalents of statements.

55. **C** Refer to the review section for the rules for forming negations.

8 COMPUTER-ADAPTIVE CLAST (CAT-CLAST)

INTRODUCTION
What Is the CAT-CLAST?

The CAT-CLAST is a computer-adaptive form of the CLAST administered and scored on a computer. Only the multiple-choice subtests of English Language Skills, Reading, and Mathematics are available, but there is no CAT-CLAST ESSAY. Your score on this form of the test is given immediately after you take the test. Official score reports are mailed within three weeks.

A survey of Florida colleges reveals that most students prefer to retake the CLAST in this computer-adaptive form. It is strongly recommended that you retake any failed multiple-choice subtests on the CAT-CLAST.

Where Is the CAT-CLAST Given?

The CAT-CLAST is offered at these colleges. Additional sites may be added.

> Broward Community College—North
> Central Florida Community College
> Florida Gulf Coast College
> Florida State University
> Miami-Dade Community College—North, Kendall, and Wolfson
> Okaloosa-Walton Community College
> Pensacola Junior College
> Palm Beach Community College
> Santa Fe Community College
> University of Central Florida
> University of Florida
> University of Miami
> University of North Florida
> University of South Florida

When Is the CAT-CLAST Given?

The CAT-CLAST is given frequently throughout the year. Contact the test center at the college at which you expect to take the test. Advanced registration is normally required.

How Often May I Take the CAT-CLAST?

You must wait at least thirty days before you may retake the same CAT-CLAST subtest. If you take the test more frequently than allowed, the computer system will immediately figure it out and your score will not count.

How Long Do I Have to Complete Each Subtest?

You have twice as long for each subtest as you did on the original administration.

English Language Skills	2 hours 40 minutes
Reading	2 hours 40 minutes
Mathematics	3 hours

The CAT-CLAST

The CAT-CLAST is based on the same set of objectives as the paper-and-pencil CLAST. The question types are exactly the same. The scaled scores and the approximate percentage of questions you need to answer correctly are all the same.

However there are four important differences: (1) questions are based on previous responses; (2) there are fewer questions; (3) more difficult questions are worth more points; and (4) you can't skip questions.

Questions Are Based on Previous Responses

The computer-adaptive CLAST is unique because questions are generated based on your previous responses. If you miss an easy question, the computer will give you another easy question. If you get the easy question correct, the computer will give you a more difficult question. Miss a difficult question and the computer will give you one less difficult.

Fewer Questions

Another difference is the number of items on the test. The following chart shows the average number of items for each of the subtests. Your test may have somewhat more or somewhat fewer items.

Average Number of Items on CAT-CLAST

English Language Skills	20 items
Reading	20 items
Mathematics	30 items

More Difficult Questions Are Worth More

What so few questions, the final score is influenced by the difficulty of the items you answer. Answering more difficult questions earns you more points.

You Can't Skip Questions

When you see a question on the CAT-CLAST, you can't skip it and come back later. You must answer it. If you skip it, the computer will mark it wrong.

Wait! Isn't This More Difficult?

No. It is actually easier. This is the test to take.

STRATEGIES FOR PASSING THE CAT-CLAST

What Is the Most Important Strategy for Passing the CAT-CLAST?

Take your time! The experts all agree that if you take your time you will do much better on the CAT-CLAST. When you see a question, take your time. Come up with your best answer.

Let's compare the time you have for each question taking the paper-and-pencil retake or the CAT-CLAST retake. You have twice the initial administration time for each test.

CLAST Re-Take Comparison

Subtest	Time	Paper-Pencil	CAT-CLAST
English Language Skills	160 minutes	40 items	20 items
		4 minutes each	8 minutes each
Reading	160 minutes	41 items	20 items
		4 minutes each	8 minutes each
Mathematics	180 minutes	55 items	30 items
		3 minutes each	6 minutes each

And you have twice as long for each question on the CAT-CLAST. This extra time improves your chances of getting a better score.

Any Other Strategies?

Yes, a few.

1. Remember, you can't skip questions and come back later. Answer each question as it appears.

2. Don't try to figure out which questions are easier and which questions are more difficult. Just do your best on each question.

3. On the English Language Skills and Reading subtests you will see reading passages on the screen. You will have to read them on the computer screen. Use the up-down arrows on the computer to view the entire passage. If the passage is used for more than one question, it will stay on the screen until you have answered all of the questions.

4. Five broad areas of mathematics are tested on the CLAST. You can expect questions from each of these areas to appear on the CAT-CLAST.

5. The proctor will give you scrap paper to use with the Mathematics test.

ADDITIONAL ANSWER SHEET

English Language Skills

1 Ⓐ Ⓑ Ⓒ Ⓓ Ⓔ	9 Ⓐ Ⓑ Ⓒ Ⓓ Ⓔ	17 Ⓐ Ⓑ Ⓒ Ⓓ Ⓔ	25 Ⓐ Ⓑ Ⓒ Ⓓ Ⓔ	33 Ⓐ Ⓑ Ⓒ Ⓓ Ⓔ
2 Ⓐ Ⓑ Ⓒ Ⓓ Ⓔ	10 Ⓐ Ⓑ Ⓒ Ⓓ Ⓔ	18 Ⓐ Ⓑ Ⓒ Ⓓ Ⓔ	26 Ⓐ Ⓑ Ⓒ Ⓓ Ⓔ	34 Ⓐ Ⓑ Ⓒ Ⓓ Ⓔ
3 Ⓐ Ⓑ Ⓒ Ⓓ Ⓔ	11 Ⓐ Ⓑ Ⓒ Ⓓ Ⓔ	19 Ⓐ Ⓑ Ⓒ Ⓓ Ⓔ	27 Ⓐ Ⓑ Ⓒ Ⓓ Ⓔ	35 Ⓐ Ⓑ Ⓒ Ⓓ Ⓔ
4 Ⓐ Ⓑ Ⓒ Ⓓ Ⓔ	12 Ⓐ Ⓑ Ⓒ Ⓓ Ⓔ	20 Ⓐ Ⓑ Ⓒ Ⓓ Ⓔ	28 Ⓐ Ⓑ Ⓒ Ⓓ Ⓔ	36 Ⓐ Ⓑ Ⓒ Ⓓ Ⓔ
5 Ⓐ Ⓑ Ⓒ Ⓓ Ⓔ	13 Ⓐ Ⓑ Ⓒ Ⓓ Ⓔ	21 Ⓐ Ⓑ Ⓒ Ⓓ Ⓔ	29 Ⓐ Ⓑ Ⓒ Ⓓ Ⓔ	37 Ⓐ Ⓑ Ⓒ Ⓓ Ⓔ
6 Ⓐ Ⓑ Ⓒ Ⓓ Ⓔ	14 Ⓐ Ⓑ Ⓒ Ⓓ Ⓔ	22 Ⓐ Ⓑ Ⓒ Ⓓ Ⓔ	30 Ⓐ Ⓑ Ⓒ Ⓓ Ⓔ	38 Ⓐ Ⓑ Ⓒ Ⓓ Ⓔ
7 Ⓐ Ⓑ Ⓒ Ⓓ Ⓔ	15 Ⓐ Ⓑ Ⓒ Ⓓ Ⓔ	23 Ⓐ Ⓑ Ⓒ Ⓓ Ⓔ	31 Ⓐ Ⓑ Ⓒ Ⓓ Ⓔ	39 Ⓐ Ⓑ Ⓒ Ⓓ Ⓔ
8 Ⓐ Ⓑ Ⓒ Ⓓ Ⓔ	16 Ⓐ Ⓑ Ⓒ Ⓓ Ⓔ	24 Ⓐ Ⓑ Ⓒ Ⓓ Ⓔ	32 Ⓐ Ⓑ Ⓒ Ⓓ Ⓔ	40 Ⓐ Ⓑ Ⓒ Ⓓ Ⓔ

Reading

1 Ⓐ Ⓑ Ⓒ Ⓓ Ⓔ	10 Ⓐ Ⓑ Ⓒ Ⓓ Ⓔ	19 Ⓐ Ⓑ Ⓒ Ⓓ Ⓔ	28 Ⓐ Ⓑ Ⓒ Ⓓ Ⓔ	37 Ⓐ Ⓑ Ⓒ Ⓓ Ⓔ
2 Ⓐ Ⓑ Ⓒ Ⓓ Ⓔ	11 Ⓐ Ⓑ Ⓒ Ⓓ Ⓔ	20 Ⓐ Ⓑ Ⓒ Ⓓ Ⓔ	29 Ⓐ Ⓑ Ⓒ Ⓓ Ⓔ	38 Ⓐ Ⓑ Ⓒ Ⓓ Ⓔ
3 Ⓐ Ⓑ Ⓒ Ⓓ Ⓔ	12 Ⓐ Ⓑ Ⓒ Ⓓ Ⓔ	21 Ⓐ Ⓑ Ⓒ Ⓓ Ⓔ	30 Ⓐ Ⓑ Ⓒ Ⓓ Ⓔ	39 Ⓐ Ⓑ Ⓒ Ⓓ Ⓔ
4 Ⓐ Ⓑ Ⓒ Ⓓ Ⓔ	13 Ⓐ Ⓑ Ⓒ Ⓓ Ⓔ	22 Ⓐ Ⓑ Ⓒ Ⓓ Ⓔ	31 Ⓐ Ⓑ Ⓒ Ⓓ Ⓔ	40 Ⓐ Ⓑ Ⓒ Ⓓ Ⓔ
5 Ⓐ Ⓑ Ⓒ Ⓓ Ⓔ	14 Ⓐ Ⓑ Ⓒ Ⓓ Ⓔ	23 Ⓐ Ⓑ Ⓒ Ⓓ Ⓔ	32 Ⓐ Ⓑ Ⓒ Ⓓ Ⓔ	41 Ⓐ Ⓑ Ⓒ Ⓓ Ⓔ
6 Ⓐ Ⓑ Ⓒ Ⓓ Ⓔ	15 Ⓐ Ⓑ Ⓒ Ⓓ Ⓔ	24 Ⓐ Ⓑ Ⓒ Ⓓ Ⓔ	33 Ⓐ Ⓑ Ⓒ Ⓓ Ⓔ	
7 Ⓐ Ⓑ Ⓒ Ⓓ Ⓔ	16 Ⓐ Ⓑ Ⓒ Ⓓ Ⓔ	25 Ⓐ Ⓑ Ⓒ Ⓓ Ⓔ	34 Ⓐ Ⓑ Ⓒ Ⓓ Ⓔ	
8 Ⓐ Ⓑ Ⓒ Ⓓ Ⓔ	17 Ⓐ Ⓑ Ⓒ Ⓓ Ⓔ	26 Ⓐ Ⓑ Ⓒ Ⓓ Ⓔ	35 Ⓐ Ⓑ Ⓒ Ⓓ Ⓔ	
9 Ⓐ Ⓑ Ⓒ Ⓓ Ⓔ	18 Ⓐ Ⓑ Ⓒ Ⓓ Ⓔ	27 Ⓐ Ⓑ Ⓒ Ⓓ Ⓔ	36 Ⓐ Ⓑ Ⓒ Ⓓ Ⓔ	

Mathematics

1 Ⓐ Ⓑ Ⓒ Ⓓ Ⓔ	12 Ⓐ Ⓑ Ⓒ Ⓓ Ⓔ	23 Ⓐ Ⓑ Ⓒ Ⓓ Ⓔ	34 Ⓐ Ⓑ Ⓒ Ⓓ Ⓔ	45 Ⓐ Ⓑ Ⓒ Ⓓ Ⓔ
2 Ⓐ Ⓑ Ⓒ Ⓓ Ⓔ	13 Ⓐ Ⓑ Ⓒ Ⓓ Ⓔ	24 Ⓐ Ⓑ Ⓒ Ⓓ Ⓔ	35 Ⓐ Ⓑ Ⓒ Ⓓ Ⓔ	46 Ⓐ Ⓑ Ⓒ Ⓓ Ⓔ
3 Ⓐ Ⓑ Ⓒ Ⓓ Ⓔ	14 Ⓐ Ⓑ Ⓒ Ⓓ Ⓔ	25 Ⓐ Ⓑ Ⓒ Ⓓ Ⓔ	36 Ⓐ Ⓑ Ⓒ Ⓓ Ⓔ	47 Ⓐ Ⓑ Ⓒ Ⓓ Ⓔ
4 Ⓐ Ⓑ Ⓒ Ⓓ Ⓔ	15 Ⓐ Ⓑ Ⓒ Ⓓ Ⓔ	26 Ⓐ Ⓑ Ⓒ Ⓓ Ⓔ	37 Ⓐ Ⓑ Ⓒ Ⓓ Ⓔ	48 Ⓐ Ⓑ Ⓒ Ⓓ Ⓔ
5 Ⓐ Ⓑ Ⓒ Ⓓ Ⓔ	16 Ⓐ Ⓑ Ⓒ Ⓓ Ⓔ	27 Ⓐ Ⓑ Ⓒ Ⓓ Ⓔ	38 Ⓐ Ⓑ Ⓒ Ⓓ Ⓔ	49 Ⓐ Ⓑ Ⓒ Ⓓ Ⓔ
6 Ⓐ Ⓑ Ⓒ Ⓓ Ⓔ	17 Ⓐ Ⓑ Ⓒ Ⓓ Ⓔ	28 Ⓐ Ⓑ Ⓒ Ⓓ Ⓔ	39 Ⓐ Ⓑ Ⓒ Ⓓ Ⓔ	50 Ⓐ Ⓑ Ⓒ Ⓓ Ⓔ
7 Ⓐ Ⓑ Ⓒ Ⓓ Ⓔ	18 Ⓐ Ⓑ Ⓒ Ⓓ Ⓔ	29 Ⓐ Ⓑ Ⓒ Ⓓ Ⓔ	40 Ⓐ Ⓑ Ⓒ Ⓓ Ⓔ	51 Ⓐ Ⓑ Ⓒ Ⓓ Ⓔ
8 Ⓐ Ⓑ Ⓒ Ⓓ Ⓔ	19 Ⓐ Ⓑ Ⓒ Ⓓ Ⓔ	30 Ⓐ Ⓑ Ⓒ Ⓓ Ⓔ	41 Ⓐ Ⓑ Ⓒ Ⓓ Ⓔ	52 Ⓐ Ⓑ Ⓒ Ⓓ Ⓔ
9 Ⓐ Ⓑ Ⓒ Ⓓ Ⓔ	20 Ⓐ Ⓑ Ⓒ Ⓓ Ⓔ	31 Ⓐ Ⓑ Ⓒ Ⓓ Ⓔ	42 Ⓐ Ⓑ Ⓒ Ⓓ Ⓔ	53 Ⓐ Ⓑ Ⓒ Ⓓ Ⓔ
10 Ⓐ Ⓑ Ⓒ Ⓓ Ⓔ	21 Ⓐ Ⓑ Ⓒ Ⓓ Ⓔ	32 Ⓐ Ⓑ Ⓒ Ⓓ Ⓔ	43 Ⓐ Ⓑ Ⓒ Ⓓ Ⓔ	54 Ⓐ Ⓑ Ⓒ Ⓓ Ⓔ
11 Ⓐ Ⓑ Ⓒ Ⓓ Ⓔ	22 Ⓐ Ⓑ Ⓒ Ⓓ Ⓔ	33 Ⓐ Ⓑ Ⓒ Ⓓ Ⓔ	44 Ⓐ Ⓑ Ⓒ Ⓓ Ⓔ	55 Ⓐ Ⓑ Ⓒ Ⓓ Ⓔ

Remove answer sheet by cutting on dotted line.

ADDITIONAL ANSWER SHEET

English Language Skills

1 Ⓐ Ⓑ Ⓒ Ⓓ Ⓔ	9 Ⓐ Ⓑ Ⓒ Ⓓ Ⓔ	17 Ⓐ Ⓑ Ⓒ Ⓓ Ⓔ	25 Ⓐ Ⓑ Ⓒ Ⓓ Ⓔ	33 Ⓐ Ⓑ Ⓒ Ⓓ Ⓔ
2 Ⓐ Ⓑ Ⓒ Ⓓ Ⓔ	10 Ⓐ Ⓑ Ⓒ Ⓓ Ⓔ	18 Ⓐ Ⓑ Ⓒ Ⓓ Ⓔ	26 Ⓐ Ⓑ Ⓒ Ⓓ Ⓔ	34 Ⓐ Ⓑ Ⓒ Ⓓ Ⓔ
3 Ⓐ Ⓑ Ⓒ Ⓓ Ⓔ	11 Ⓐ Ⓑ Ⓒ Ⓓ Ⓔ	19 Ⓐ Ⓑ Ⓒ Ⓓ Ⓔ	27 Ⓐ Ⓑ Ⓒ Ⓓ Ⓔ	35 Ⓐ Ⓑ Ⓒ Ⓓ Ⓔ
4 Ⓐ Ⓑ Ⓒ Ⓓ Ⓔ	12 Ⓐ Ⓑ Ⓒ Ⓓ Ⓔ	20 Ⓐ Ⓑ Ⓒ Ⓓ Ⓔ	28 Ⓐ Ⓑ Ⓒ Ⓓ Ⓔ	36 Ⓐ Ⓑ Ⓒ Ⓓ Ⓔ
5 Ⓐ Ⓑ Ⓒ Ⓓ Ⓔ	13 Ⓐ Ⓑ Ⓒ Ⓓ Ⓔ	21 Ⓐ Ⓑ Ⓒ Ⓓ Ⓔ	29 Ⓐ Ⓑ Ⓒ Ⓓ Ⓔ	37 Ⓐ Ⓑ Ⓒ Ⓓ Ⓔ
6 Ⓐ Ⓑ Ⓒ Ⓓ Ⓔ	14 Ⓐ Ⓑ Ⓒ Ⓓ Ⓔ	22 Ⓐ Ⓑ Ⓒ Ⓓ Ⓔ	30 Ⓐ Ⓑ Ⓒ Ⓓ Ⓔ	38 Ⓐ Ⓑ Ⓒ Ⓓ Ⓔ
7 Ⓐ Ⓑ Ⓒ Ⓓ Ⓔ	15 Ⓐ Ⓑ Ⓒ Ⓓ Ⓔ	23 Ⓐ Ⓑ Ⓒ Ⓓ Ⓔ	31 Ⓐ Ⓑ Ⓒ Ⓓ Ⓔ	39 Ⓐ Ⓑ Ⓒ Ⓓ Ⓔ
8 Ⓐ Ⓑ Ⓒ Ⓓ Ⓔ	16 Ⓐ Ⓑ Ⓒ Ⓓ Ⓔ	24 Ⓐ Ⓑ Ⓒ Ⓓ Ⓔ	32 Ⓐ Ⓑ Ⓒ Ⓓ Ⓔ	40 Ⓐ Ⓑ Ⓒ Ⓓ Ⓔ

Reading

1 Ⓐ Ⓑ Ⓒ Ⓓ Ⓔ	10 Ⓐ Ⓑ Ⓒ Ⓓ Ⓔ	19 Ⓐ Ⓑ Ⓒ Ⓓ Ⓔ	28 Ⓐ Ⓑ Ⓒ Ⓓ Ⓔ	37 Ⓐ Ⓑ Ⓒ Ⓓ Ⓔ
2 Ⓐ Ⓑ Ⓒ Ⓓ Ⓔ	11 Ⓐ Ⓑ Ⓒ Ⓓ Ⓔ	20 Ⓐ Ⓑ Ⓒ Ⓓ Ⓔ	29 Ⓐ Ⓑ Ⓒ Ⓓ Ⓔ	38 Ⓐ Ⓑ Ⓒ Ⓓ Ⓔ
3 Ⓐ Ⓑ Ⓒ Ⓓ Ⓔ	12 Ⓐ Ⓑ Ⓒ Ⓓ Ⓔ	21 Ⓐ Ⓑ Ⓒ Ⓓ Ⓔ	30 Ⓐ Ⓑ Ⓒ Ⓓ Ⓔ	39 Ⓐ Ⓑ Ⓒ Ⓓ Ⓔ
4 Ⓐ Ⓑ Ⓒ Ⓓ Ⓔ	13 Ⓐ Ⓑ Ⓒ Ⓓ Ⓔ	22 Ⓐ Ⓑ Ⓒ Ⓓ Ⓔ	31 Ⓐ Ⓑ Ⓒ Ⓓ Ⓔ	40 Ⓐ Ⓑ Ⓒ Ⓓ Ⓔ
5 Ⓐ Ⓑ Ⓒ Ⓓ Ⓔ	14 Ⓐ Ⓑ Ⓒ Ⓓ Ⓔ	23 Ⓐ Ⓑ Ⓒ Ⓓ Ⓔ	32 Ⓐ Ⓑ Ⓒ Ⓓ Ⓔ	41 Ⓐ Ⓑ Ⓒ Ⓓ Ⓔ
6 Ⓐ Ⓑ Ⓒ Ⓓ Ⓔ	15 Ⓐ Ⓑ Ⓒ Ⓓ Ⓔ	24 Ⓐ Ⓑ Ⓒ Ⓓ Ⓔ	33 Ⓐ Ⓑ Ⓒ Ⓓ Ⓔ	
7 Ⓐ Ⓑ Ⓒ Ⓓ Ⓔ	16 Ⓐ Ⓑ Ⓒ Ⓓ Ⓔ	25 Ⓐ Ⓑ Ⓒ Ⓓ Ⓔ	34 Ⓐ Ⓑ Ⓒ Ⓓ Ⓔ	
8 Ⓐ Ⓑ Ⓒ Ⓓ Ⓔ	17 Ⓐ Ⓑ Ⓒ Ⓓ Ⓔ	26 Ⓐ Ⓑ Ⓒ Ⓓ Ⓔ	35 Ⓐ Ⓑ Ⓒ Ⓓ Ⓔ	
9 Ⓐ Ⓑ Ⓒ Ⓓ Ⓔ	18 Ⓐ Ⓑ Ⓒ Ⓓ Ⓔ	27 Ⓐ Ⓑ Ⓒ Ⓓ Ⓔ	36 Ⓐ Ⓑ Ⓒ Ⓓ Ⓔ	

Mathematics

1 Ⓐ Ⓑ Ⓒ Ⓓ Ⓔ	12 Ⓐ Ⓑ Ⓒ Ⓓ Ⓔ	23 Ⓐ Ⓑ Ⓒ Ⓓ Ⓔ	34 Ⓐ Ⓑ Ⓒ Ⓓ Ⓔ	45 Ⓐ Ⓑ Ⓒ Ⓓ Ⓔ
2 Ⓐ Ⓑ Ⓒ Ⓓ Ⓔ	13 Ⓐ Ⓑ Ⓒ Ⓓ Ⓔ	24 Ⓐ Ⓑ Ⓒ Ⓓ Ⓔ	35 Ⓐ Ⓑ Ⓒ Ⓓ Ⓔ	46 Ⓐ Ⓑ Ⓒ Ⓓ Ⓔ
3 Ⓐ Ⓑ Ⓒ Ⓓ Ⓔ	14 Ⓐ Ⓑ Ⓒ Ⓓ Ⓔ	25 Ⓐ Ⓑ Ⓒ Ⓓ Ⓔ	36 Ⓐ Ⓑ Ⓒ Ⓓ Ⓔ	47 Ⓐ Ⓑ Ⓒ Ⓓ Ⓔ
4 Ⓐ Ⓑ Ⓒ Ⓓ Ⓔ	15 Ⓐ Ⓑ Ⓒ Ⓓ Ⓔ	26 Ⓐ Ⓑ Ⓒ Ⓓ Ⓔ	37 Ⓐ Ⓑ Ⓒ Ⓓ Ⓔ	48 Ⓐ Ⓑ Ⓒ Ⓓ Ⓔ
5 Ⓐ Ⓑ Ⓒ Ⓓ Ⓔ	16 Ⓐ Ⓑ Ⓒ Ⓓ Ⓔ	27 Ⓐ Ⓑ Ⓒ Ⓓ Ⓔ	38 Ⓐ Ⓑ Ⓒ Ⓓ Ⓔ	49 Ⓐ Ⓑ Ⓒ Ⓓ Ⓔ
6 Ⓐ Ⓑ Ⓒ Ⓓ Ⓔ	17 Ⓐ Ⓑ Ⓒ Ⓓ Ⓔ	28 Ⓐ Ⓑ Ⓒ Ⓓ Ⓔ	39 Ⓐ Ⓑ Ⓒ Ⓓ Ⓔ	50 Ⓐ Ⓑ Ⓒ Ⓓ Ⓔ
7 Ⓐ Ⓑ Ⓒ Ⓓ Ⓔ	18 Ⓐ Ⓑ Ⓒ Ⓓ Ⓔ	29 Ⓐ Ⓑ Ⓒ Ⓓ Ⓔ	40 Ⓐ Ⓑ Ⓒ Ⓓ Ⓔ	51 Ⓐ Ⓑ Ⓒ Ⓓ Ⓔ
8 Ⓐ Ⓑ Ⓒ Ⓓ Ⓔ	19 Ⓐ Ⓑ Ⓒ Ⓓ Ⓔ	30 Ⓐ Ⓑ Ⓒ Ⓓ Ⓔ	41 Ⓐ Ⓑ Ⓒ Ⓓ Ⓔ	52 Ⓐ Ⓑ Ⓒ Ⓓ Ⓔ
9 Ⓐ Ⓑ Ⓒ Ⓓ Ⓔ	20 Ⓐ Ⓑ Ⓒ Ⓓ Ⓔ	31 Ⓐ Ⓑ Ⓒ Ⓓ Ⓔ	42 Ⓐ Ⓑ Ⓒ Ⓓ Ⓔ	53 Ⓐ Ⓑ Ⓒ Ⓓ Ⓔ
10 Ⓐ Ⓑ Ⓒ Ⓓ Ⓔ	21 Ⓐ Ⓑ Ⓒ Ⓓ Ⓔ	32 Ⓐ Ⓑ Ⓒ Ⓓ Ⓔ	43 Ⓐ Ⓑ Ⓒ Ⓓ Ⓔ	54 Ⓐ Ⓑ Ⓒ Ⓓ Ⓔ
11 Ⓐ Ⓑ Ⓒ Ⓓ Ⓔ	22 Ⓐ Ⓑ Ⓒ Ⓓ Ⓔ	33 Ⓐ Ⓑ Ⓒ Ⓓ Ⓔ	44 Ⓐ Ⓑ Ⓒ Ⓓ Ⓔ	55 Ⓐ Ⓑ Ⓒ Ⓓ Ⓔ

Remove answer sheet by cutting on dotted line.

ADDITIONAL ANSWER SHEET

English Language Skills

1 Ⓐ Ⓑ Ⓒ Ⓓ Ⓔ	9 Ⓐ Ⓑ Ⓒ Ⓓ Ⓔ	17 Ⓐ Ⓑ Ⓒ Ⓓ Ⓔ	25 Ⓐ Ⓑ Ⓒ Ⓓ Ⓔ	33 Ⓐ Ⓑ Ⓒ Ⓓ Ⓔ
2 Ⓐ Ⓑ Ⓒ Ⓓ Ⓔ	10 Ⓐ Ⓑ Ⓒ Ⓓ Ⓔ	18 Ⓐ Ⓑ Ⓒ Ⓓ Ⓔ	26 Ⓐ Ⓑ Ⓒ Ⓓ Ⓔ	34 Ⓐ Ⓑ Ⓒ Ⓓ Ⓔ
3 Ⓐ Ⓑ Ⓒ Ⓓ Ⓔ	11 Ⓐ Ⓑ Ⓒ Ⓓ Ⓔ	19 Ⓐ Ⓑ Ⓒ Ⓓ Ⓔ	27 Ⓐ Ⓑ Ⓒ Ⓓ Ⓔ	35 Ⓐ Ⓑ Ⓒ Ⓓ Ⓔ
4 Ⓐ Ⓑ Ⓒ Ⓓ Ⓔ	12 Ⓐ Ⓑ Ⓒ Ⓓ Ⓔ	20 Ⓐ Ⓑ Ⓒ Ⓓ Ⓔ	28 Ⓐ Ⓑ Ⓒ Ⓓ Ⓔ	36 Ⓐ Ⓑ Ⓒ Ⓓ Ⓔ
5 Ⓐ Ⓑ Ⓒ Ⓓ Ⓔ	13 Ⓐ Ⓑ Ⓒ Ⓓ Ⓔ	21 Ⓐ Ⓑ Ⓒ Ⓓ Ⓔ	29 Ⓐ Ⓑ Ⓒ Ⓓ Ⓔ	37 Ⓐ Ⓑ Ⓒ Ⓓ Ⓔ
6 Ⓐ Ⓑ Ⓒ Ⓓ Ⓔ	14 Ⓐ Ⓑ Ⓒ Ⓓ Ⓔ	22 Ⓐ Ⓑ Ⓒ Ⓓ Ⓔ	30 Ⓐ Ⓑ Ⓒ Ⓓ Ⓔ	38 Ⓐ Ⓑ Ⓒ Ⓓ Ⓔ
7 Ⓐ Ⓑ Ⓒ Ⓓ Ⓔ	15 Ⓐ Ⓑ Ⓒ Ⓓ Ⓔ	23 Ⓐ Ⓑ Ⓒ Ⓓ Ⓔ	31 Ⓐ Ⓑ Ⓒ Ⓓ Ⓔ	39 Ⓐ Ⓑ Ⓒ Ⓓ Ⓔ
8 Ⓐ Ⓑ Ⓒ Ⓓ Ⓔ	16 Ⓐ Ⓑ Ⓒ Ⓓ Ⓔ	24 Ⓐ Ⓑ Ⓒ Ⓓ Ⓔ	32 Ⓐ Ⓑ Ⓒ Ⓓ Ⓔ	40 Ⓐ Ⓑ Ⓒ Ⓓ Ⓔ

Reading

1 Ⓐ Ⓑ Ⓒ Ⓓ Ⓔ	10 Ⓐ Ⓑ Ⓒ Ⓓ Ⓔ	19 Ⓐ Ⓑ Ⓒ Ⓓ Ⓔ	28 Ⓐ Ⓑ Ⓒ Ⓓ Ⓔ	37 Ⓐ Ⓑ Ⓒ Ⓓ Ⓔ
2 Ⓐ Ⓑ Ⓒ Ⓓ Ⓔ	11 Ⓐ Ⓑ Ⓒ Ⓓ Ⓔ	20 Ⓐ Ⓑ Ⓒ Ⓓ Ⓔ	29 Ⓐ Ⓑ Ⓒ Ⓓ Ⓔ	38 Ⓐ Ⓑ Ⓒ Ⓓ Ⓔ
3 Ⓐ Ⓑ Ⓒ Ⓓ Ⓔ	12 Ⓐ Ⓑ Ⓒ Ⓓ Ⓔ	21 Ⓐ Ⓑ Ⓒ Ⓓ Ⓔ	30 Ⓐ Ⓑ Ⓒ Ⓓ Ⓔ	39 Ⓐ Ⓑ Ⓒ Ⓓ Ⓔ
4 Ⓐ Ⓑ Ⓒ Ⓓ Ⓔ	13 Ⓐ Ⓑ Ⓒ Ⓓ Ⓔ	22 Ⓐ Ⓑ Ⓒ Ⓓ Ⓔ	31 Ⓐ Ⓑ Ⓒ Ⓓ Ⓔ	40 Ⓐ Ⓑ Ⓒ Ⓓ Ⓔ
5 Ⓐ Ⓑ Ⓒ Ⓓ Ⓔ	14 Ⓐ Ⓑ Ⓒ Ⓓ Ⓔ	23 Ⓐ Ⓑ Ⓒ Ⓓ Ⓔ	32 Ⓐ Ⓑ Ⓒ Ⓓ Ⓔ	41 Ⓐ Ⓑ Ⓒ Ⓓ Ⓔ
6 Ⓐ Ⓑ Ⓒ Ⓓ Ⓔ	15 Ⓐ Ⓑ Ⓒ Ⓓ Ⓔ	24 Ⓐ Ⓑ Ⓒ Ⓓ Ⓔ	33 Ⓐ Ⓑ Ⓒ Ⓓ Ⓔ	
7 Ⓐ Ⓑ Ⓒ Ⓓ Ⓔ	16 Ⓐ Ⓑ Ⓒ Ⓓ Ⓔ	25 Ⓐ Ⓑ Ⓒ Ⓓ Ⓔ	34 Ⓐ Ⓑ Ⓒ Ⓓ Ⓔ	
8 Ⓐ Ⓑ Ⓒ Ⓓ Ⓔ	17 Ⓐ Ⓑ Ⓒ Ⓓ Ⓔ	26 Ⓐ Ⓑ Ⓒ Ⓓ Ⓔ	35 Ⓐ Ⓑ Ⓒ Ⓓ Ⓔ	
9 Ⓐ Ⓑ Ⓒ Ⓓ Ⓔ	18 Ⓐ Ⓑ Ⓒ Ⓓ Ⓔ	27 Ⓐ Ⓑ Ⓒ Ⓓ Ⓔ	36 Ⓐ Ⓑ Ⓒ Ⓓ Ⓔ	

Mathematics

1 Ⓐ Ⓑ Ⓒ Ⓓ Ⓔ	12 Ⓐ Ⓑ Ⓒ Ⓓ Ⓔ	23 Ⓐ Ⓑ Ⓒ Ⓓ Ⓔ	34 Ⓐ Ⓑ Ⓒ Ⓓ Ⓔ	45 Ⓐ Ⓑ Ⓒ Ⓓ Ⓔ
2 Ⓐ Ⓑ Ⓒ Ⓓ Ⓔ	13 Ⓐ Ⓑ Ⓒ Ⓓ Ⓔ	24 Ⓐ Ⓑ Ⓒ Ⓓ Ⓔ	35 Ⓐ Ⓑ Ⓒ Ⓓ Ⓔ	46 Ⓐ Ⓑ Ⓒ Ⓓ Ⓔ
3 Ⓐ Ⓑ Ⓒ Ⓓ Ⓔ	14 Ⓐ Ⓑ Ⓒ Ⓓ Ⓔ	25 Ⓐ Ⓑ Ⓒ Ⓓ Ⓔ	36 Ⓐ Ⓑ Ⓒ Ⓓ Ⓔ	47 Ⓐ Ⓑ Ⓒ Ⓓ Ⓔ
4 Ⓐ Ⓑ Ⓒ Ⓓ Ⓔ	15 Ⓐ Ⓑ Ⓒ Ⓓ Ⓔ	26 Ⓐ Ⓑ Ⓒ Ⓓ Ⓔ	37 Ⓐ Ⓑ Ⓒ Ⓓ Ⓔ	48 Ⓐ Ⓑ Ⓒ Ⓓ Ⓔ
5 Ⓐ Ⓑ Ⓒ Ⓓ Ⓔ	16 Ⓐ Ⓑ Ⓒ Ⓓ Ⓔ	27 Ⓐ Ⓑ Ⓒ Ⓓ Ⓔ	38 Ⓐ Ⓑ Ⓒ Ⓓ Ⓔ	49 Ⓐ Ⓑ Ⓒ Ⓓ Ⓔ
6 Ⓐ Ⓑ Ⓒ Ⓓ Ⓔ	17 Ⓐ Ⓑ Ⓒ Ⓓ Ⓔ	28 Ⓐ Ⓑ Ⓒ Ⓓ Ⓔ	39 Ⓐ Ⓑ Ⓒ Ⓓ Ⓔ	50 Ⓐ Ⓑ Ⓒ Ⓓ Ⓔ
7 Ⓐ Ⓑ Ⓒ Ⓓ Ⓔ	18 Ⓐ Ⓑ Ⓒ Ⓓ Ⓔ	29 Ⓐ Ⓑ Ⓒ Ⓓ Ⓔ	40 Ⓐ Ⓑ Ⓒ Ⓓ Ⓔ	51 Ⓐ Ⓑ Ⓒ Ⓓ Ⓔ
8 Ⓐ Ⓑ Ⓒ Ⓓ Ⓔ	19 Ⓐ Ⓑ Ⓒ Ⓓ Ⓔ	30 Ⓐ Ⓑ Ⓒ Ⓓ Ⓔ	41 Ⓐ Ⓑ Ⓒ Ⓓ Ⓔ	52 Ⓐ Ⓑ Ⓒ Ⓓ Ⓔ
9 Ⓐ Ⓑ Ⓒ Ⓓ Ⓔ	20 Ⓐ Ⓑ Ⓒ Ⓓ Ⓔ	31 Ⓐ Ⓑ Ⓒ Ⓓ Ⓔ	42 Ⓐ Ⓑ Ⓒ Ⓓ Ⓔ	53 Ⓐ Ⓑ Ⓒ Ⓓ Ⓔ
10 Ⓐ Ⓑ Ⓒ Ⓓ Ⓔ	21 Ⓐ Ⓑ Ⓒ Ⓓ Ⓔ	32 Ⓐ Ⓑ Ⓒ Ⓓ Ⓔ	43 Ⓐ Ⓑ Ⓒ Ⓓ Ⓔ	54 Ⓐ Ⓑ Ⓒ Ⓓ Ⓔ
11 Ⓐ Ⓑ Ⓒ Ⓓ Ⓔ	22 Ⓐ Ⓑ Ⓒ Ⓓ Ⓔ	33 Ⓐ Ⓑ Ⓒ Ⓓ Ⓔ	44 Ⓐ Ⓑ Ⓒ Ⓓ Ⓔ	55 Ⓐ Ⓑ Ⓒ Ⓓ Ⓔ

Remove answer sheet by cutting on dotted line.

ADDITIONAL ANSWER SHEET

English Language Skills

1 Ⓐ Ⓑ Ⓒ Ⓓ Ⓔ	9 Ⓐ Ⓑ Ⓒ Ⓓ Ⓔ	17 Ⓐ Ⓑ Ⓒ Ⓓ Ⓔ	25 Ⓐ Ⓑ Ⓒ Ⓓ Ⓔ	33 Ⓐ Ⓑ Ⓒ Ⓓ Ⓔ
2 Ⓐ Ⓑ Ⓒ Ⓓ Ⓔ	10 Ⓐ Ⓑ Ⓒ Ⓓ Ⓔ	18 Ⓐ Ⓑ Ⓒ Ⓓ Ⓔ	26 Ⓐ Ⓑ Ⓒ Ⓓ Ⓔ	34 Ⓐ Ⓑ Ⓒ Ⓓ Ⓔ
3 Ⓐ Ⓑ Ⓒ Ⓓ Ⓔ	11 Ⓐ Ⓑ Ⓒ Ⓓ Ⓔ	19 Ⓐ Ⓑ Ⓒ Ⓓ Ⓔ	27 Ⓐ Ⓑ Ⓒ Ⓓ Ⓔ	35 Ⓐ Ⓑ Ⓒ Ⓓ Ⓔ
4 Ⓐ Ⓑ Ⓒ Ⓓ Ⓔ	12 Ⓐ Ⓑ Ⓒ Ⓓ Ⓔ	20 Ⓐ Ⓑ Ⓒ Ⓓ Ⓔ	28 Ⓐ Ⓑ Ⓒ Ⓓ Ⓔ	36 Ⓐ Ⓑ Ⓒ Ⓓ Ⓔ
5 Ⓐ Ⓑ Ⓒ Ⓓ Ⓔ	13 Ⓐ Ⓑ Ⓒ Ⓓ Ⓔ	21 Ⓐ Ⓑ Ⓒ Ⓓ Ⓔ	29 Ⓐ Ⓑ Ⓒ Ⓓ Ⓔ	37 Ⓐ Ⓑ Ⓒ Ⓓ Ⓔ
6 Ⓐ Ⓑ Ⓒ Ⓓ Ⓔ	14 Ⓐ Ⓑ Ⓒ Ⓓ Ⓔ	22 Ⓐ Ⓑ Ⓒ Ⓓ Ⓔ	30 Ⓐ Ⓑ Ⓒ Ⓓ Ⓔ	38 Ⓐ Ⓑ Ⓒ Ⓓ Ⓔ
7 Ⓐ Ⓑ Ⓒ Ⓓ Ⓔ	15 Ⓐ Ⓑ Ⓒ Ⓓ Ⓔ	23 Ⓐ Ⓑ Ⓒ Ⓓ Ⓔ	31 Ⓐ Ⓑ Ⓒ Ⓓ Ⓔ	39 Ⓐ Ⓑ Ⓒ Ⓓ Ⓔ
8 Ⓐ Ⓑ Ⓒ Ⓓ Ⓔ	16 Ⓐ Ⓑ Ⓒ Ⓓ Ⓔ	24 Ⓐ Ⓑ Ⓒ Ⓓ Ⓔ	32 Ⓐ Ⓑ Ⓒ Ⓓ Ⓔ	40 Ⓐ Ⓑ Ⓒ Ⓓ Ⓔ

Reading

1 Ⓐ Ⓑ Ⓒ Ⓓ Ⓔ	10 Ⓐ Ⓑ Ⓒ Ⓓ Ⓔ	19 Ⓐ Ⓑ Ⓒ Ⓓ Ⓔ	28 Ⓐ Ⓑ Ⓒ Ⓓ Ⓔ	37 Ⓐ Ⓑ Ⓒ Ⓓ Ⓔ
2 Ⓐ Ⓑ Ⓒ Ⓓ Ⓔ	11 Ⓐ Ⓑ Ⓒ Ⓓ Ⓔ	20 Ⓐ Ⓑ Ⓒ Ⓓ Ⓔ	29 Ⓐ Ⓑ Ⓒ Ⓓ Ⓔ	38 Ⓐ Ⓑ Ⓒ Ⓓ Ⓔ
3 Ⓐ Ⓑ Ⓒ Ⓓ Ⓔ	12 Ⓐ Ⓑ Ⓒ Ⓓ Ⓔ	21 Ⓐ Ⓑ Ⓒ Ⓓ Ⓔ	30 Ⓐ Ⓑ Ⓒ Ⓓ Ⓔ	39 Ⓐ Ⓑ Ⓒ Ⓓ Ⓔ
4 Ⓐ Ⓑ Ⓒ Ⓓ Ⓔ	13 Ⓐ Ⓑ Ⓒ Ⓓ Ⓔ	22 Ⓐ Ⓑ Ⓒ Ⓓ Ⓔ	31 Ⓐ Ⓑ Ⓒ Ⓓ Ⓔ	40 Ⓐ Ⓑ Ⓒ Ⓓ Ⓔ
5 Ⓐ Ⓑ Ⓒ Ⓓ Ⓔ	14 Ⓐ Ⓑ Ⓒ Ⓓ Ⓔ	23 Ⓐ Ⓑ Ⓒ Ⓓ Ⓔ	32 Ⓐ Ⓑ Ⓒ Ⓓ Ⓔ	41 Ⓐ Ⓑ Ⓒ Ⓓ Ⓔ
6 Ⓐ Ⓑ Ⓒ Ⓓ Ⓔ	15 Ⓐ Ⓑ Ⓒ Ⓓ Ⓔ	24 Ⓐ Ⓑ Ⓒ Ⓓ Ⓔ	33 Ⓐ Ⓑ Ⓒ Ⓓ Ⓔ	
7 Ⓐ Ⓑ Ⓒ Ⓓ Ⓔ	16 Ⓐ Ⓑ Ⓒ Ⓓ Ⓔ	25 Ⓐ Ⓑ Ⓒ Ⓓ Ⓔ	34 Ⓐ Ⓑ Ⓒ Ⓓ Ⓔ	
8 Ⓐ Ⓑ Ⓒ Ⓓ Ⓔ	17 Ⓐ Ⓑ Ⓒ Ⓓ Ⓔ	26 Ⓐ Ⓑ Ⓒ Ⓓ Ⓔ	35 Ⓐ Ⓑ Ⓒ Ⓓ Ⓔ	
9 Ⓐ Ⓑ Ⓒ Ⓓ Ⓔ	18 Ⓐ Ⓑ Ⓒ Ⓓ Ⓔ	27 Ⓐ Ⓑ Ⓒ Ⓓ Ⓔ	36 Ⓐ Ⓑ Ⓒ Ⓓ Ⓔ	

Mathematics

1 Ⓐ Ⓑ Ⓒ Ⓓ Ⓔ	12 Ⓐ Ⓑ Ⓒ Ⓓ Ⓔ	23 Ⓐ Ⓑ Ⓒ Ⓓ Ⓔ	34 Ⓐ Ⓑ Ⓒ Ⓓ Ⓔ	45 Ⓐ Ⓑ Ⓒ Ⓓ Ⓔ
2 Ⓐ Ⓑ Ⓒ Ⓓ Ⓔ	13 Ⓐ Ⓑ Ⓒ Ⓓ Ⓔ	24 Ⓐ Ⓑ Ⓒ Ⓓ Ⓔ	35 Ⓐ Ⓑ Ⓒ Ⓓ Ⓔ	46 Ⓐ Ⓑ Ⓒ Ⓓ Ⓔ
3 Ⓐ Ⓑ Ⓒ Ⓓ Ⓔ	14 Ⓐ Ⓑ Ⓒ Ⓓ Ⓔ	25 Ⓐ Ⓑ Ⓒ Ⓓ Ⓔ	36 Ⓐ Ⓑ Ⓒ Ⓓ Ⓔ	47 Ⓐ Ⓑ Ⓒ Ⓓ Ⓔ
4 Ⓐ Ⓑ Ⓒ Ⓓ Ⓔ	15 Ⓐ Ⓑ Ⓒ Ⓓ Ⓔ	26 Ⓐ Ⓑ Ⓒ Ⓓ Ⓔ	37 Ⓐ Ⓑ Ⓒ Ⓓ Ⓔ	48 Ⓐ Ⓑ Ⓒ Ⓓ Ⓔ
5 Ⓐ Ⓑ Ⓒ Ⓓ Ⓔ	16 Ⓐ Ⓑ Ⓒ Ⓓ Ⓔ	27 Ⓐ Ⓑ Ⓒ Ⓓ Ⓔ	38 Ⓐ Ⓑ Ⓒ Ⓓ Ⓔ	49 Ⓐ Ⓑ Ⓒ Ⓓ Ⓔ
6 Ⓐ Ⓑ Ⓒ Ⓓ Ⓔ	17 Ⓐ Ⓑ Ⓒ Ⓓ Ⓔ	28 Ⓐ Ⓑ Ⓒ Ⓓ Ⓔ	39 Ⓐ Ⓑ Ⓒ Ⓓ Ⓔ	50 Ⓐ Ⓑ Ⓒ Ⓓ Ⓔ
7 Ⓐ Ⓑ Ⓒ Ⓓ Ⓔ	18 Ⓐ Ⓑ Ⓒ Ⓓ Ⓔ	29 Ⓐ Ⓑ Ⓒ Ⓓ Ⓔ	40 Ⓐ Ⓑ Ⓒ Ⓓ Ⓔ	51 Ⓐ Ⓑ Ⓒ Ⓓ Ⓔ
8 Ⓐ Ⓑ Ⓒ Ⓓ Ⓔ	19 Ⓐ Ⓑ Ⓒ Ⓓ Ⓔ	30 Ⓐ Ⓑ Ⓒ Ⓓ Ⓔ	41 Ⓐ Ⓑ Ⓒ Ⓓ Ⓔ	52 Ⓐ Ⓑ Ⓒ Ⓓ Ⓔ
9 Ⓐ Ⓑ Ⓒ Ⓓ Ⓔ	20 Ⓐ Ⓑ Ⓒ Ⓓ Ⓔ	31 Ⓐ Ⓑ Ⓒ Ⓓ Ⓔ	42 Ⓐ Ⓑ Ⓒ Ⓓ Ⓔ	53 Ⓐ Ⓑ Ⓒ Ⓓ Ⓔ
10 Ⓐ Ⓑ Ⓒ Ⓓ Ⓔ	21 Ⓐ Ⓑ Ⓒ Ⓓ Ⓔ	32 Ⓐ Ⓑ Ⓒ Ⓓ Ⓔ	43 Ⓐ Ⓑ Ⓒ Ⓓ Ⓔ	54 Ⓐ Ⓑ Ⓒ Ⓓ Ⓔ
11 Ⓐ Ⓑ Ⓒ Ⓓ Ⓔ	22 Ⓐ Ⓑ Ⓒ Ⓓ Ⓔ	33 Ⓐ Ⓑ Ⓒ Ⓓ Ⓔ	44 Ⓐ Ⓑ Ⓒ Ⓓ Ⓔ	55 Ⓐ Ⓑ Ⓒ Ⓓ Ⓔ

Remove answer sheet by cutting on dotted line.